Negative Natural Theology

OXFORD STUDIES IN PHILOSOPHICAL THEOLOGY

Series Editors: Judith Wolfe and Cyril O'Regan

This series widens the horizons of philosophical theology by drawing on the resources of continental philosophy to enable constructive new theological work. It focuses on conceptually central questions and on theologically constructive work.

Negative Natural Theology

God and the Limits of Reason

CHRISTOPHER J. INSOLE

Great Clarendon Street, Oxford, OX2 6DP,
United Kingdom

Oxford University Press is a department of the University of Oxford.
It furthers the University's objective of excellence in research, scholarship,
and education by publishing worldwide. Oxford is a registered trade mark of
Oxford University Press in the UK and in certain other countries

© Christopher J. Insole 2024

The moral rights of the author have been asserted

All rights reserved. No part of this publication may be reproduced, stored in a retrieval system, transmitted, used for text and data mining, or used for training artificial intelligence, in any form or by any means, without the prior permission in writing of Oxford University Press, or as expressly permitted by law, by licence or under terms agreed with the appropriate reprographics rights organization. Enquiries concerning reproduction outside the scope of the above should be sent to the Rights Department, Oxford University Press, at the address above.

You must not circulate this work in any other form
and you must impose this same condition on any acquirer

Published in the United States of America by Oxford University Press
198 Madison Avenue, New York, NY 10016, United States of America

British Library Cataloguing in Publication Data

Data available

Library of Congress Control Number: 2024945899

ISBN 9780198932970

DOI: 10.1093/9780198933007.001.0001

Printed and bound by
CPI Group (UK) Ltd, Croydon, CR0 4YY

The manufacturer's authorised representative in the EU for product safety
is Oxford University Press España S.A. of el Parque Empresarial San
Fernando de Henares, Avenida de Castilla,
2 – 28830 Madrid (www.oup.es/en).

Acknowledgements

The book came out of a research project, called 'Negative Natural Theology: Freedom and the Limits of Reason', which was funded by the Templeton Religion Trust, as part of the overarching project, 'Widening Horizons in Philosophical Theology'. The 'Negative Natural Theology' project was oriented around two workshops, where nine of us—theologians, literary scholars and philosophers, atheists and believers, and somewhere in between—have met, and enjoyed serious, sensitive, non-posturing, and honest conversations. These participants were Akeel Bilgrami, Clare Carlisle, Benjamin DeSpain, David Dwan, Lexi Eikelboom, Philip Goff, Jennifer Herdt, Karen Kilby, Simon Oliver, and Mark Wynn. I have also benefitted from conversations on the topic with Ed Epsen, Joshua Furnal, Lewis Ayres, Robert Song, Gerard Loughlin, Paul Murray, Mike Higton, Stephen Plant, Nathaniel Warne, Sarah Coakley, Frankie Ward, Brad Myers, Andrew Chiltern, and Jerry Hooker. For her leadership and inspiration in overseeing the Widening Horizons project, and for her friendship, advice, and encouragement in the process of writing of this book, I would like to thank Judith Wolfe.

I have also enjoyed and benefitted from conversations with leaders of other Widening Horizons projects, including Agata Bielik-Robson, Amber Bowen, Philip Gonzales, Philip Goodchild, and Darren Sarisky, and with King Ho-Leung.

I would like to thank Faber & Faber and Random House, USA, for permission to quote from some poems by Wallace Stevens: 'A Discovery of Thought', 'The Snow Man', 'Two Illustrations that the World is What You Make of It', and 'Nuances of a Theme by Williams'.

This book is dedicated to Lisa and Rory, who, together, are very good at pointing out what I don't know, but supporting me—with kindness, lively conversation, and intellectual stimulation—in projects where I try to articulate what might be interesting about not knowing things.

Contents

Prologue   1

1. The Cosmic Question: Thomas Nagel and Perspectives on Life   11

2. The Existence of the Word God: Reference and Mystery   35

3. Absurd and Holy Mystery: Karl Rahner and Albert Camus   57

4. Humanism Not Mysterious: The Happy Human   82

5. William James' Radical Empiricism and Modern Paganism   113

6. Absolute Idealism and Derek Parfit on What Really Matters   139

7. Becoming Divine: Kant and Jung   158

Epilogue: The Varieties of Philosophical Experience   178

Bibliography   181
Index   187

Prologue

Negative Natural Theology

Our lives are, more or less and to different degrees, beset by limits, tensions, conflicts, fragmentation, and disintegration. When there is a desire for a type of wholeness, or, at least, a partial integration, this can bring about a range of affects and reactions, including conflict, tension, anxiety, yearning, and despair.

When we bring these tensions and desires to conscious expression and reflection, we can be said to engage in thinking. Whenever this happens, we become 'thinkers', even if we are not professionally 'qualified' or employed as such. Some thinkers, when engaging with such limits and tensions, lean into the concept of God, or the divine, and others do not.

At other times, I have found, thinkers orient themselves around a conceptual space that has some divine features, although the concept of the divine is not explicitly employed, or, even, is explicitly rejected.

In this context, what might be at stake in employing—explicitly or implicitly—the concept of the divine, or not doing so?

Furthermore, what are the hidden and lost textures and possibilities for thinking and speaking about God and the divine?

My intention is to probe 'what is at stake' in the choice (if it is that) to talk about God/the divine, and different conceptions of the divine, or not to do so. By 'what is at stake', I mean: what moves us, or persuades us, or blocks us, or enables us, to want to speak about God, or not, in different ways? We can embrace a wide and deep curiosity about what this might include: reasons, evidence, and arguments, certainly, but also more intuitive and affective dimensions, including imagination and emotion. Also relevant are unconscious drives and factors. Concepts can convince, or fail to convince, but, also, they can attract and repel.

'Negative natural theology' engages with these questions. This book is an exercise in negative natural theology.[1]

It is sometimes said that believing in God, or not, comes down to something that is 'just temperament'. But, what is 'just temperament'? Is this already a philosophically saturated—or, an insufficiently curious and probing—way of framing

---

[1] There will be two further books: Christopher Insole, *Unhinged: The God Question* (forthcoming), and a multi-authored work, *The Varieties of Philosophical Experience: Negative Natural Theology* (forthcoming).

Negative Natural Theology. Christopher J. Insole, Oxford University Press. © Christopher J. Insole 2024.
DOI: 10.1093/9780198933007.003.0001

the issue? Our 'spade is turned'. But what is it about the spade/the ground that makes it turn *there*? Can we say something a bit more textured and informative about 'temperament'? We might also reflect on the ways in which 'what is at stake' can only be fully drawn out using a range of types of thinking, drawing on a range of disciplines. This might include psychology, anthropology, literature, and psychodynamic approaches, which explore the preconscious and unconscious. At points in this book I do lean, lightly, but with a measure of trust, into some of these disciplines.

I have found that some thinkers, such as Thomas Nagel, who I engage with throughout the book, are at great pains to distance their approaches from the divine, or God. Reference to the divine is denigrated variously as being from the 'middle-ages', or the 'dark ages', as being 'superstitious', 'pre-scientific', involving 'medieval superstition',[2] 'rampant Platonism',[3] or an 'injection of the supernatural', and a recourse to pre-enlightenment animism or 'meta-persons'. Consider, for example, Nagel's admission: not only does he not believe in a God, but he, admits, 'I hope there is not a God!':

I don't want there to be a God; I don't want the universe to be like that.[4]

At the same time, there is, in some cases, an acknowledged unease about this quick dismissal of the category of divinity. Nagel, for example, admits to sharing in a culturally widespread 'fear of religion', which fear he himself is 'strongly subject to'.[5] Nonetheless, Nagel considers that this same fear has 'large and often pernicious consequences for modern intellectual life', buttressing up with ideology rather than evidence, or reflection, a reductionist and materialist conception of nature.[6]

In a book such as this, there is a constant temptation to slide into demarcation disputes, about the limits of philosophy and theology, or the concept of religion, or the secular. I decline the invitation to engage in this sort of throat clearing, and will offer no opening definitions of philosophy, theology, or religion. Such definitions never hold, and rarely help, and frequently irritate. It is, in any case, the point of the project to place into question the notion that there are strong and clear divisions here. Even the most aggressively 'atheist' or 'secular' of philosophers can have a strong theological or religious watermark running through their biography, psychology, and work (consider Nietzsche and Lutheranism). Furthermore, thinking about the divine occurs in many areas that would not regard themselves as either philosophy or theology, including poetry, literature, and anthropology. It is unwise to tie our hands at the start of an exploration. We are interested in honest

---

[2] John McDowell, *Mind and World* (Cambridge, MA: Harvard University Press, 1996), 109.
[3] Ibid., 85.
[4] Thomas Nagel, 'Evolutionary Naturalism and the Fear of Religion', in *The Last Word* (New York and Oxford: Oxford University Press, 1997), 127–143, 130.
[5] Ibid.
[6] Ibid.

PROLOGUE 3

thinking about God, in the light of limits, tensions and fragmentations, wherever that thinking comes from. That's it.

And, as I affirmed above: everyone and anyone is a thinker, when and if they think. Vocational and professional theologians and philosophers are supposed to bring a particular focus, perspective, and learning to this basic human activity, although, perhaps, this very focus and learning can, at times, be a temptation away from the beating heart of the original vocation, and what philosophy and theology should be in service to.

Given this wariness of demarcation disputes, there might be a question mark placed over my decision to call the whole project 'negative natural theology', a term inspired by the work of Rowan Williams.[7] Are we not back into demarcation disputes—'natural theology', 'negative theology', 'theology'? The combination of these words generates, I find, a pleasing dissonance, which provocatively helps to undercut confident demarcation rulings. It brings about a bit of creative chaos. This is due to the pairing of the adjectives 'negative' and 'natural'. 'Natural theology' involves speaking about God without reference to revelation, tradition, or sources of authority, using the resources of 'reason alone'.[8] 'Negative theology' is concerned with the ways in which some types of reasoning, thinking, and speaking might run out, without this necessarily being an ending.[9] The term, 'Negative Natural

---

[7] Rowan Williams, *The Edge of Words: God and the Habits of Language* (London: Bloomsbury, 2014). There are two elements to Rowan Williams' 'renewed natural theology', which we might separate out into the 'formal' and the 'substantive'. The 'formal' dimension is Williams' recommendation that natural theology be viewed as a set of practices, where we run to the edge of reason/words/philosophy, in relation to whatever it is we are talking about. Williams gives, as examples, Aquinas on causation (pp. 6–7), and Kant's reflections on morality (11–14), which, for Kant, tip over into divinity, although Williams finds that Kant's God is stranded in an 'ontological no-man's land' (13). The substantive dimension of Williams' natural theology is the decision to treat communication itself, or intersubjectivity in language, as the object that is thought about (and, of course, employed in the very thinking about it). For drawing my attention to the importance of separating out these dimensions, I am indebted to a conversation with Sarah Coakley. I am concerned, here, more with the formal aspect of Williams' call, and take up the invitation to renew the conception of the practice of natural theology in relation to other areas of concern, in this case, in particular, Nagel's 'cosmic question', introduced in the next chapter. In responding to Williams' work Graham Ward asks: 'how do we respond appropriately (weigh the word) to such a meditation?', that is to say, to Williams' *Edge of Words*, which is a 'saying and a doing', an 'argument and a performance', 'Metaphor in Bone', *Modern Theology* 31/4 (2015), 618–624, 619. Ward replies: 'I suggest by prolonging it and adding to its "difficulty". That is, entering into the longing it articulates and extending, supplementing, protracting it into other directions. My directions. Your directions. We will each prolong it differently. Difference is a gift; it makes the *difficult* more *difficult*' (620). This is precisely what I attempt to do in this book.

[8] Recent texts on natural theology tend not to engage with negative theology, or with the notion of the limits of reason and argument: indeed, they are rather fascinated by, and invested in, a confidence in a type of reason. One might cite here two collections of essays: *The Oxford Handbook of Natural Theology*, ed. by Russell Re Manning (Oxford: Oxford University Press, 2013), and *The Blackwell Companion to Natural Theology*, ed. by William Lane Craig and J.P. Moreland (London: Wiley-Blackwell, 2009). Each book covers a multitude of perspectives, including science, philosophy, and theology, with a range of arguments from morality, from religious experience, and from consciousness. In neither collection is there a consideration of negative theology, or a preoccupation with the limits of a particular type of argumentation.

[9] Works that engage with theology at the edge of reason, and in liminal spaces, include the following: David Tracey, *Fragments: The Existential Situation of Our Time: Selected Essays* (Chicago:

4 NEGATIVE NATURAL THEOLOGY

Theology', can be held to with a lightness and critical distance. It serves as an ice-breaker, a provocation, setting up a sort of dissonance within which discussion can occur.

The term 'negative natural theology', to describe the project outlined above, has increasingly grown on me, although at points, I have had my doubts about it. Perhaps this is appropriate: there ought, really, to be nothing dogmatic or certain about negative natural theology. Even 'natural theology' is a pleasingly fraught term, itself continually contested, which means it is plastic and ripe for various appropriations. In some circles it is even somewhat contaminated. Perhaps, it is a branch of philosophy that attempts to engage with the question of God without recourse to revelation, authority, or faith. Perhaps, it is not really proper philosophy, or proper theology. Whatever else it is, it involves *thinking* about God, and consequent activities such as speaking, communicating, and inquiring. Its dubious entitlement to citizenship in a number of different jurisdictions—theology and philosophy—makes it attractive to me, with its mercurial and potentially disreputable connotations. It is a creature of the borderlands, with little confidence in the different authorities who announce at junctures the shifting of official categories and borderlands. This is even more so for its shadowy twin, *negative* natural theology, who will sit at any hearth that might receive it, at least for a while, and even if only on the edge of things.

Whatever else it is, 'negative natural theology', involves thinking about God, in the light of, and under the shadow of, limits, tensions, and fragmentations in our lives, with the question of what is at stake never far from the surface. Anyone can do it, if and when they want to. It does not replace traditional systematic or philosophical theology, and the same people might do both at different times. 'Negative natural theology' is not a 'school of thought', with shared assumptions and premises. Rather, it involves a willingness to have a particular type of conversation, at least sometimes. In this, it resembles the recent 'scriptural reasoning' movement more than influential substantive movements such as 'radical orthodoxy' or 'the Yale school'. To engage in some scriptural reasoning involves a willingness to enter a space where believers from different faith traditions engage with the same scriptural texts. Negative natural theology engages with fundamental commitments, in the shadow of limits, asking what lies beyond a certain type of abstract argumentative reasoning.

University of Chicago Press, 2019), Denys Turner, *God, Mystery, and Mystification* (Notre Dame, Indiana: University of Notre Dame Press, 2019), and Karen Kilby, *God, Evil and the Limits of Theology* (London: Bloomsbury, 2020). There has also been an engagement with negative theology through an interest in Wittgensteinian approaches and grammatical approaches to Thomas Aquinas: see Simon Hewitt, *Negative Theology and Philosophical Analysis* (London: Palgrave, 2020), and Stephen Mulhall, *The Great Riddle: Wittgenstein, Nonsense, Theology and Philosophy* (Oxford: Oxford University Press, 2018).

As such, this book is intentionally not a piece of (positive) theology, where we work from within a tradition to arrive at direct claims about the being, nature, existence, and action of God, or about created things in relation to God. This does not mean, therefore, that I am *against* these intellectual projects. I may engage in them again, as I have done before. In the Epilogue of this book, I lean slightly into positive theology, for just a moment, sketching briefly why one might have high theological grounds for being sympathetic to some of the material presented in the chapters of this book. This is a promissory note, a gesture, a hand wave, and far from being a rigorous defence.

With any intellectual project, it is interesting to explore the underlying motivation for carrying it out: this, indeed, is part of the whole point of negative natural theology. Often what gives the motivation a little spice is a degree of frustration, or a sense that something is lacking in the conversation, or in the conduct of a discipline. My desire to carry out negative natural theology has four underlying motivations that I am able to identify at the moment, which I will set out under four headings: a shared predicament; the divine trace; the impoverishment of philosophy; and the impoverishment of theology.

A shared predicament

Frequently, secular thought and modern theology have a shared predicament, oriented around a common understanding of limits, fragmentations, and tensions. For modern theology, God can provide some sort of response to this predicament. There are two different ways in which the concept of God might offer such a response. It might be that belief in God is not motivated by the desire to engage with a tension, limit, or fragmentation; but, that once a belief in God is already in place, if such a tension comes into view, believing in God might help. Or, it might be that belief in God is explicitly motivated by a desire to engage with the tension, or limit.

It may be, of course, that the emergence of this common predicament only arises in the form it does, because belief in God has become optional, problematic, questionable.[10] As such, the predicament is a distinctively *modern* one, generated in the wake of Kantian and post-Kantian concerns. This seems to be quite likely. This relativizes the problem, of course, to a particular time and place. But, for those in that time and place, knowing that the framework is relative and contingent, does not offer an easy escape route back to the pre-modern or the re-enchanted.

---

[10] See Charles Taylor, in *The Secular Age* (Cambridge, MA: Harvard University Press, 2007). Taylor regards belief in God becoming optional and problematic as one of the key characteristics of the modern secular age.

The divine trace

Sometimes, when secular or atheistic thinking engages with the same predicament as modern theology, the answers reached for have something of a divine trace to them. That is to say, they contain within them fragments of a God concept. A theologian looking at these responses might say that these fragments are truncations of an original whole, but, nonetheless, the trace of divinity is there – certainly, in movements such as absolute idealism (treated in Chapter 6), in some types of moral realism (Derek Parfit, also discussed in Chapter 6) and maybe, even, in some strands of humanism (see Chapter 4).

Part of the problem here is that we have become used to truncated and impoverished understandings of the concept of God, where the idea of God is denigrated as being little more than a wish fulfilment, a fantasy, or an anthropomorphic projection. So little of the stretch of the concept of God is known about, such that when thinkers touch upon part of this stretch, there can be little recognition of it. In part, it can feel as if God used to be adduced as a solution, but no longer plausibly can be; but, it is more that a great deal has been forgotten about what the concept of God might be, or mean. Perhaps thinkers would be more comfortable leaning into the concept of God, if they enjoyed less impoverished conceptions of God, and appreciated that some proposed solutions do have a divine trace.

Sometimes, there is a loss of belief in God, but the godless universe still has something of the shape it had, originally, because of God. I will suggest that this is the case with some strands of humanism (Chapter 4). Sometimes, maybe, the thing that is lost is not belief, or not entirely, but an understanding of the word 'God', and all that it might mean.

The impoverishment of philosophy

When philosophy neglects ways in which philosophers have believed in God and the divine, that same philosophy is in danger of losing vitality and life: of losing aspects of its memory, culture, and traditions. Furthermore, such philosophy is in danger of losing contact with the people who it might serve, challenge, and console.

Recent social attitude surveys in the UK show that around 25% of the population self-identify as atheist. This is up from a figure of 10% in 1998. In recent surveys, the percentage of people who have no affiliation to any traditional religion stands at around 52%.[11] The rise in the number of self-identified atheists may justify

---

[11] See https://www.theguardian.com/world/2019/jul/11/uk-secularism-on-rise-as-more-than-half-say-they-have-no-religion. *The Guardian* accessed these results from the British Social Attitudes Survey: https://natcen.ac.uk. Accessed 10 November 2023.

The Guardian's summary headline, 'Secularism on the Rise'. We might still note, though, that this leaves around a quarter of the population neither traditionally religious, nor self-identifying as atheist. Notably, a survey of professional academics in philosophy departments in the UK threw up the percentage of philosophers self-identifying as atheists at 58.4%, over twice the average in the general population.[12] A large study conducted across Australasia, the UK, Europe, the US and Canada, came up with the remarkable find that 72.8% of professional philosophers self-identify as atheists, and only 14.6% theist, and 12.6% as 'other'.[13] The percentage of atheists in the general populations of each of these territories varies, of course, but in all of the cases, the discrepancy between the professional philosophers and the general population was vast. For example, in the USA the percentage of people in the general population self-identifying as atheists has remained at a steady 3–4% over the last 80 years.[14] Atheism seems to be over-represented in philosophy departments.

In the mid to late twentieth century, the atmosphere in anglophone universities was hostile in relation to theology. The sense was that there was a crisis in 'God talk', where it may not even be meaningful to talk about God, given that there were no reliable ways of verifying or falsifying such claims. This shifted towards the end of the century, with a sense that if philosophy was permitted to make such difficulties for belief in God, the same 'weedkiller' would wipe out so much more also: common sense beliefs about the world that we seem to perceive, as well any significant sense of freedom, ethics, value, and beauty. Metaphysics (or something like it) was back, it seemed. As a result, Christian academic theology found a new *jouissance* and confidence, painting confident visions of a God infused and re-enchanted universe (radical orthodoxy, for example), and celebrating rich traditioned ecclesial communities drawing upon scripture (the Yale school). Philosophy itself became more confident about exploring ambitious metaphysical accounts of the world, or types of moral realism. But, philosophy did not pick up again in relation to *God*: this was passed over, speedily parcelled off, to departments with the words Theology, Religion and Divinity in their title. It is even possible that more has been said about God, the divine, the sacred, and belief, in departments of English Literature, Anthropology and Geography than it has in many departments of Philosophy.

The result of all this is a general impoverishment of the wider culture, an all or nothing menu: full traditioned belief in one of the 'big faiths', or, nothing much.

---

[12] See Helen De Cruz, 'Religious Disagreement: An Empirical Study among Academic Philosophers', *Episteme* 14/1, 2017, 71–87.

[13] David Bourget and David J. Chalmers, 'What do Philosophers Believe?', *Philosophical Studies* 170/3 (2014), 465–500.

[14] See Byron R. Johnson and Jeff Levin, 'Religion Is Dying? Don't Believe It', *Wall Street Journal* (27 July 2022).

What about, though, philosophical traditions of belief in God, at the limits of knowledge and reason, which do not draw upon revelation, tradition, or authority?

There are, of course, other possible interpretations of what I have called the over-representation of atheism in philosophy departments, in relation to the wider population. You only have to scratch about a little online to find these interpretations. The psychologist Rostam Ferdowsi, trained at California State University, after reporting that 'we have atheism/other at 85.3%', offers the following account:

> My understanding for such a difference is because of (a) high education (e.g., philosophy, theology, religious history, science and so forth) and (b) the lack of need to evoke the supernatural (e.g., good healthcare system, supportive environments, healthy mind and body, safe environments and so forth).
>
> When life is a humanistic model the need for religion or the supernatural is unneeded.[15]

On this account, atheism is not *over*-represented. Philosophers are in the vanguard, properly ahead of a general population, with their less healthy minds and bodies, and with less safe environments. Ferdowsi is only saying what many public intellectuals who style themselves as humanists (see Chapter 4) would agree with.

I do not accept that a good education, and an adequate healthcare system, will ensure that 85 out of every 100 professional philosophers come out as atheists.

The impoverishment of theology

A committed Christian theologian might even think that this sort of impoverishment of philosophy is a good thing: who needs 'pagan' philosophy pronouncing about, or reaching out to God?

I take a different view. I think it is likely to help Christian theology and Christian philosophy, if a range of philosophers become interested in the concept of God on their own terms. I will illustrate this conviction with four examples.

First of all, we might consider Augustine's *Confessions*. One way of reading this is as an account of Augustine's conversion from paganism to Christianity. It is, of course, this. But, also, and more richly understood, it is an account of a series of conversions: first of all, from Stoicism to Manicheanism, then from Manicheanism to Platonism, and only then, from Platonism to Christianity. Augustine himself tells us that on quite a number of points, Platonism brought him very close to Christianity. He even writes that in the 'books of the Platonists' he found:

---

[15] https://www.quora.com/Why-are-most-philosophers-atheists-or-agnostics. Accessed 11 November 2023.

PROLOGUE   9

[T]hat *in the beginning was the Word and the Word was with God and the Word was God: the same was in the beginning with God; all things were made by Him and without Him was nothing that was made; in Him was life and the life was the light of men, and the light shines in darkness and the darkness did not comprehend it.* And I found in those same writings that the soul of man, though *it gives testimony of the light, yet is not itself the light;* but the Word, God Himself, is *the true light which enlightens every man that comes into this world; and that He was in the world and the world was made by Him, and the world knew Him not.*

What Augustine 'did not read in those books' was:

[T]hat *the Word became flesh* ... these books did not tell me that *He emptied Himself, taking the form of a servant, being made in the likeness of men, and in habit found as a man; or that He humbled Himself becoming obedient unto death, even to the death of the cross.*[16]

Augustine seems to think that these pre-conversions to Christianity were vital steps on the way. It can be quite difficult to go from atheistic materialism to a rich faith. Sometimes when this leap is made suddenly, the faith that someone leaps into might have impoverished and problematic elements: a thin and projected anthropomorphic conception of God, for example, who emits moral laws like a tyrant.

A second example: in the third and fourth centuries, Christian philosophy, itself richly infused by strands of Platonism, was surrounded by pagan platonic philosophies, with figures such as Clement of Alexandria talking of Christianity as the 'true philosophy'. Seen from any distance, it seems clear that Christianity benefitted from, and gained life from, swimming in this sea.

A third example: when Thomas Aquinas engages with Aristotle, who he calls 'the philosopher', he frequently considers what Aristotle says about God and the divine. Aquinas' five ways draw explicitly upon Aristotelian language, ending each of the five reflections with the words, 'and that everyone calls God', meaning to refer successfully to the God that Christians believe in. Aquinas' work is sharpened and enriched by this engagement.

A fourth example: the great twentieth century theologian Karl Barth had a portrait of Kant at the bottom of the staircase that led up to his study. He would tell people that anyone who wanted to understand his work, must begin on this step. Whatever Barth meant by this, he did not mean that Christian thinking could neglect philosophy that thinks about God, even if the point of engaging with such philosophy is to sharpen the distinctive contribution of theology.

---

[16] Augustine, *Confessions,* trans. F.J. Sheed (London: Sheed and Ward, 1944), Bk. 7.9.

Exposure to philosophy that leans into a divine space may help to sharpen up some theological thinking.

There can be a pattern of thinking amongst theologians which goes a bit like this:

> To give an adequate account of human life—its meaning, our yearnings, and aspirations—you need to be able to speak about realities such as goodness, beauty, freedom, hope, a sense of transcendence.
>
> Religious philosophies are able to give such an account.
>
> Atheistic philosophies have poor resources to draw on: they focus on matter in motion, the laws of science and mathematics, and human desires, which are understood as sheer impulses.
>
> If it is difficult to *know* whether or not there is a God, what we are thrown back on is the importance of offering an adequate account of our lives. Religious philosophy is able to address important dimensions of existence that atheistic philosophy does not.
>
> Therefore, given that we don't have proof in this area, religious philosophy is proved to be superior.

The problem with this line of argument, it seems to me, is that it offers a parody of the best atheist philosophy.

It is a principle of fairness that you match like for like: the best atheist philosophy with the best religious philosophy, not the best religious philosophy with the worst atheist philosophy. The worst atheist philosophy is, appropriately enough, produced by figures who have no formal training in philosophy at all, such as Richard Dawkins. It is annoying for theologians that such *ersatz* philosophy is so influential, but, at the same time, it can make things seem easier than they really are for theologians: if *this* is the main challenge to faith, they have not much to worry about it, in intellectual terms.

If we really want to think about atheism, and the levels of humanity and self-transcendence that atheist philosophy can be capable of, we need to look for the best philosophy.

If it is true that philosophers such as Nagel and Parfit lean into a divine space, this can cut two ways. On the one hand, theologians might say, 'and that we call God'. But, these same philosophers might retort: 'that we used to call God, but do not need to anymore, with the nuance and freedom given to us by some philosophical tools and insights'. This is the sort of challenge that Christian theologians should be more gripped by, rather than being preoccupied with the misconstruals of theology offered up by some aggressive new atheists.

1

The Cosmic Question

Thomas Nagel and Perspectives on Life

Is there a way to live in harmony with the universe, and not just in it?[1]

This is the question posed by the contemporary North American philosopher Thomas Nagel. Nagel is, in principle, not religious. Indeed, he has stated not only that he does not believe in a God, but that he profoundly hopes that there is not a God.[2] Nonetheless, Nagel expresses a desire to frame some sort of 'secular answer', to what he calls the 'cosmic question', which is the question of whether we can somehow 'live not merely the life of the creature one is, but in some sense . . . participate through it in the life of the universe as a whole'. 'Without God', Nagel comments, 'it is unclear what we should aspire to harmony with'.

Nonetheless, Nagel finds that 'the aspiration to answer the cosmic question remains':

> Having, amazingly, burst into existence, one is a representative of existence itself—of the whole of it—not just because one is part of it but because it is present to one's consciousness. In each of us, the universe has come to consciousness and therefore our existence is not merely our own.[3]

Nagel calls his question the 'cosmic question'. The cosmic question is related to the perennial philosophical enquiry, as set out by Socrates: 'how should one live?'. Socrates was posing this question in the framework of an understanding of the universe within which we live. Both Nagel and Socrates are concerned with the ancient and enduring philosophical question, which is also a preoccupation of religion, of how to live, with our many desires and needs, and our finitude, within the universe within which we find ourselves thrown. In this way, we engage with the notion of philosophy as a 'way of life', as identified by Pierre Hadot,[4] taken forward

---

[1] Thomas Nagel, 'Secular Philosophy and the Religious Temperament', in *Secular Philosophy and the Religious Temperament: Essays 2002–2008* (Oxford: Oxford University Press, 2009), 3–17, 5.
[2] Nagel, *The Last Word*, 130.
[3] Nagel, 'Secular Philosophy and the Religious Temperament', 5.
[4] Pierre Hadot, *Philosophy as a Way of Life: Spiritual Exercises from Socrates to Foucault* (Oxford: Blackwell, 1995).

Negative Natural Theology. Christopher J. Insole, Oxford University Press. © Christopher J. Insole 2024.
DOI: 10.1093/9780198933007.003.0002

12 NEGATIVE NATURAL THEOLOGY

in post-Kantian continental philosophy,[5] but also, as Nagel and others demonstrate,[6] in more analytical traditions also.

In relation to this 'cosmic/Socratic question', we might envisage five types of 'increasingly committed' answer, which I now set out here in summary form[7]:

I The 'cosmic question' looks like a real question, but it is badly formed. There is no real question here.

II The question is well-formed, but it has no answer: this may lead us to a sort of counterfactual theism (if there were a God, the question would have an answer), or to despair, or to a sense of the absurdity of life.

III The question has an 'inside-out' answer: perhaps, for example, meaning is to be found from human nature.

IV The question has an 'outside-in' answer, in terms of our place in a wider reality or purpose, although we do not need to go beyond a sufficiently rich understanding of immanent reality, of the world.[8]

V The question has an 'outside-in' answer that appeals to a dimension beyond the world, a transcendent realm or reality.

I will not concern myself much with stage I. It is the sort of thing that Wittgensteinians can be heard to say, if they take the view, as Nagel ventriloquizes it, that 'to take the quest for sense outside the boundaries of those human purposes and aims relative to which all judgments of sense or senselessness must be made is an ... error of a philosophically familiar type', whereby we 'attempt to extend a concept beyond the conditions that give it meaning'.[9] Once you have answered the question as to why each particular thing is 'here' (insofar as one can), there would be no meaningful *massive* question about why everything is here, or why there is something rather than nothing, or how to live in harmony with that everything. I do not say very much about this reaction, not because I am contemptuous of it. Indeed, there is something majestic and austere about stopping at stage I. We might find such austerity in Nietzsche's comment that:

---

[5] See Simon Critchley, *Continental Philosophy: A Very Short Introduction* (Oxford: Oxford University Press, 2001).

[6] For a thoughtful account of Analytic Theology as a way of life, see William Wood, 'Analytic Theology as a Way of Life', *Journal of Analytic Theology*, 2 (2014), 43–60.

[7] Although he does not set it out in this way, Nagel goes through options that correspond to stages I–IV. It is not clear from Nagel's essay itself that a discrete stage V is marked out.

[8] I am, here, deliberately avoiding the category of 'naturalism', for reasons that I set out towards the end of this chapter. For excellent accounts of ambiguities in the term 'naturalism' see Fiona Ellis, *God, Value, and Nature* (Oxford: Oxford University Press, 2016), chs. 2–3; and 'Is Liberal Naturalism Possible', in *Naturalism and Normativity*, ed. Mario De Caro and David Macarthur (New York: Columbia University Press, 2010), 69–88.

[9] Nagel himself associates this view with Hume's 'serene naturalism' in 'Secular Philosophy and the Religious Temperament', 7. This would involve reading Hume in a highly Wittgensteinian way. Therefore, it seems less controversial exegetically to ascribe this response to the Wittgensteinian.

Once upon a time there was a star in a corner of the universe, and a planet circling that star, and on it some clever creatures who invented knowledge; and then they died, and the star went out, and it was as though nothing had happened.[10]

But, however majestic and courageous, I find, in my own case, that such answers do not survive sleepless and starry nights. And, I think it is safe to say, I am not entirely alone here, in a way that would immediately suggest perversity or irrationality.

If we turn, then, to stage II, we allow the question to stand as well-formed, but we find no answer to it. The 'no answer' response can come in three varieties, which I regard as increasingly interesting. The least interesting variety is a sort of counterfactual theism: if there were a God, this would give us the meaning required, but there is not, and, so, our life in the universe is 'meaningless'. A more interesting version of the 'there is no answer' response, is despair. Despair is not counterfactual theism, but it does, at least, offer a sort of *hommage* to God, a requiem mass for the death of God, as Nietzsche's Zarathustra put it. The prominent atheist, philosopher, and public intellectual Bertrand Russell made himself tiresome to his friends, by what has been described as his 'self-pitying' and 'self-glorifying rhetoric' as he 'went on about the … tininess of the earth, the vast and pitiless expanses of the universe and so on'.[11] Exasperated by Russell's moaning, the philosopher, and mutual friend of both Russell and Wittgenstein, Frank Ramsey, said that he was 'much less impressed than some of his friends were by the size of the universe, perhaps because he weighed 240 pounds' (that is, 109 kilos).[12]

Ramsey's quip can, in truth, lead us into a deeper level of the 'there is no answer' response: beyond despair, into a sense of absurdity. Imagine that the universe was not relatively vast. Perhaps you take up precisely one quarter of it. Does that feel better? Now, a half: better again? Or, even, you take up the entire universe. Does that feel, somehow, 'less absurd'? The notion that I take up the entire universe, or, that I am the only thing that exists, has a name: it is called solipsism. Solipsism has had its admirers, including the woman who allegedly wrote to Bertrand Russell, saying that she found it so persuasive that she did not know why everyone did not believe it. But nobody has, I think, ever been tempted to praise solipsism as a salve for a sense of *absurdity*. That is not, at least, the first or decisive temptation towards solipsism.

As Nagel comments, once the question of absurdity has been posed and felt as forceful, it is hard to stop an infinite regress.[13] If all the usual local and immanent

---

[10] Friedrich Nietzsche, 'On Truth and Lies in a Nonmoral Sense', in *Philosophy and Truth: Selections from Nietzsche's Notebooks of the Early 1870s,* trans. and ed. Daniel Breazale (Brighton: Harvester Press, 1979), opening paragraph.

[11] Bernard Williams, 'The Human Prejudice' in *Philosophy as a Humanistic Discipline* (Princeton and Oxford: Princeton University Press, 2006), 135–152, 137.

[12] Ibid., 137.

[13] For my reflections on the 'absurd' in this paragraph, I am indebted to Nagel, 'The Absurd', in *Mortal Questions* (Cambridge: Cambridge University Press, 2012), 11–23.

14 NEGATIVE NATURAL THEOLOGY

ends are felt to be insufficient resting places for a sense of purpose, then it is hard to see what is added by being all alone, or being huge, or occupying a tiny universe. In fact, intuitively, some of these possibilities feel even more laughable, more comic, more immediately 'pointless'. Here, I think Nagel is exactly right.

What gives us the sense of the absurd, Nagel suggests, is not really size or scale, but the possibility we all have, as self-conscious, of regarding ourselves both from an internal and an external point of view. Or, to be more precise, the impossibility of not so regarding ourselves.

The subjective and objective perspectives upon ourselves

This brings us to a prominent philosophical strand of reflection about our human predicament. This tradition reads many of our problems as arising from the tension between the internal and external perspectives upon our lives. I will explain what this means below. I have become persuaded that vital though this distinction is, its significance is often misconstrued; by which, I mean, I have, in the past, found myself misconstruing it.

Narratives can be helpful in philosophy: showing how one idea comes under pressure, dissolves and reconfigures, and becomes more expansive and accommodating. Accordingly, I offer here an intellectual narrative of why we might move from thinking that the tension between the subjective and objective perspectives is the heart of the matter, to relativizing its significance, with the possibility of returning to a transformed notion of why it is still central, but not quite in the way it was originally conceived.

First of all, I will unfurl what is meant by the 'subjective and objective perspectives' upon ourselves.

The subjective perspective invokes the sense we have of our own significance and agency. We exert effort and strain, to feed and clothe ourselves, to maintain our health and appearance, to engage in meaningful life projects, and to be, for example, an adequate mother/father, wife/husband, daughter/son, sister/brother, friend and colleague. We strive, and persevere, sometimes flourishing, and, at other times, suffering.

At the same time, we are able, indeed, we are unable to avoid, seeing ourselves, the whole sorry struggle, from an objective point of view, as if we were not ourselves. This perspective is 'at once sobering and comical'.[14] As Nagel puts it, we live with ourselves 24 hours a day.[15] What alternative do we have? We fuss, and stress, and are exhausting for others, and for ourselves. If we try entirely to live for others, we only make matters worse, suggests Nagel, putting us in mind, perhaps, of C.S.

[14] Nagel, 'The Absurd', 15.
[15] Ibid.

THE COSMIC QUESTION   15

Lewis' observation that one can always identify those who live entirely for others, by the haunted look on the faces of those they are with.

As Nagel puts it:

> Humans have the special capacity to step back and survey themselves, and the lives to which they are committed, with that detached amazement which comes from watching an ant struggle up a heap of sand.[16]

The same problem can be variously formulated: as the tension between the subjective and objective, or the external and internal, or the agential and observer perspectives. Another philosopher, Akeel Bilgrami approaches the tension in perspectives from a different angle.[17] One can draw attention to the impossibility of both intending to do something, and predicting that one will do it.[18] That is to say, when we *predict* that we will do something, rather than *intend* to do it, one steps outside 'of oneself and looks at oneself as the object of behavioural and causal and motivational tendencies'.[19] Or, one can distinguish a first-person and third-person point of view on oneself. When I ask 'what should I do?', or the Socratic question, 'how should I live?', I regard myself as an 'agent', and not as 'an observer of oneself', as 'a subject rather than an object'.[20] As Bilgrami comments, the grammatical categories, of the first and third-person pronoun, do not coincide with the philosophical categories, as one sees in a usage such as 'I predict that I will do x', where, in the first case, the 'I' is agentive, but, in the second case the 'I' refers 'to oneself as an object of detached study of observation'.[21] To avoid confusion, we can speak instead of 'the agent's point of view', or the 'engaged point of view', on the one hand, and of the 'observer's', or the 'detached' point of view on the other.[22] Bilgrami comments that one cannot have 'both these point of view on oneself *at the same time*'[23]—a claim I will come back to—although one can, of course, occupy these perspectives sequentially, at different times and in different respects. Similarly, and drawing on Nagel's observations, one can occupy these perspectives in rapid oscillating succession, as can be the case with some comedy. Where below I talk about the subjective/objective tension, I intend the full range of associated distinctions to be triggered: not only subjective/objective, but also internal/external, agent/observer, engaged/detached, and first-person and third-person. In

---

[16] Ibid.

[17] Bilgrami, 'The Wider Significance of Naturalism: A Genealogical Essay', in *Naturalism and Normativity*, 23–54.

[18] Ibid., 24.

[19] Ibid., 25.

[20] Ibid.

[21] Ibid.

[22] Ibid.

[23] Ibid.

16 NEGATIVE NATURAL THEOLOGY

turn, this tension can be experienced as a type of alienation, or a lack of 'harmony' with the world, or universe.

Writing about the subjective and objective perspectives, Thomas Nagel affirms that although 'the two standpoints cannot be satisfactorily integrated', the 'correct course' is 'not to assign victory to either standpoint but to hold the opposition clearly in one's mind without suppressing either element':

> [I]t is best to be aware of the ways in which life and thought are spilt, if that is how things are.[24]

The subjective/objective tension pervades human life, Nagel continues, and is therefore 'particularly prominent in the generation of philosophical problems'.[25] Nagel's work has concentrated on four topics—'the metaphysics of mind, the theory of knowledge, free will, and ethics')—but, he comments that 'there is probably no area of philosophy in which it doesn't play a significant role'.[26] My suggestion is not that religion needs to be added to the list, but, rather, that religion, or belief in God, can be—sometimes—what happens when, like Nagel, we attempt to find some sort of integration or tessellation between the subjective and objective perspectives, or to overcome the sense of alienation between them.

I want to lead us into this suggestion by asking an improper question. God, on a classical conception, could be, and perhaps once was (conceptually or temporally), absolutely alone. God is certainly, in a sense 'huge'. Could we imagine God having a sense of the absurd, thinking 'what's the point of all this?', 'what am I doing all this for?', 'why bother?'. And, then, could we conceive of God regarding the eternal activity of creation, fall and redemption, and thinking it all looks 'kind of funny?'. God saw what He had done, and saw, not that it was good, but hilarious, or quirky, or pointless. Would God strike upon the only consolation, to paraphrase Camus, that 'not to be defeated by pointlessness is what gives our being its point'? Would God, figuratively speaking, be reduced to shaking a fist, and 'continuing to live in spite of' the pointlessness'? The answer is clear to every theologian and believer: no, absolutely not. Anything that could regard its existence, or activity, as pointless and comical in this way, could not be God, whatever else it might be. And, perhaps, anything that is not God, ought to be able to look at itself as pointless and comical, some of the time, in any case, as an expression of the deep contingency and gratuity of their participation in the many-petalled flower of 'being here'. Indeed, there is something irreverent, something inappropriate, about the thought experiment offered here. But this, in itself, is revealing. Because it throws light upon an immoveable grammatical instinct about

---

[24] Nagel, *The View from Nowhere*, 6.
[25] Ibid., 6.
[26] Ibid.

the divine ('grammatical' in the sense of being a rule for the use of this concept). The impossibility of absurd comedy in relation to the divine, is interesting, and tells us something about the distinctive grammar of the notion of divinity, and the divine.

What it may tell us, I think, is this: when the notion of divinity, and the divine, is employed, we are marking a commitment to the end of absurdity, the limits of absurdity. Somehow, when we name something as divine, we are gesturing to the claim, or the hope, that a subjective and objective perspective harmonize, tessellate, and correspond, or that the seeming tension and alienation is somehow overcome. Insofar as we are divine, or participate in the divine, we are no longer funny, or laughable, or embarrassing. There will be laughter, but it will be joy, not satire.

Rethinking the subjective and objective perspectives upon ourselves

In philosophical traditions coming after Kant, this tension, or confrontation, between the subjective perspective upon our lives, and the objective perspective, is indeed taken to be generative for thinking. The possibility arises, though, that the tension need not always present itself so starkly. Also, it seems plausible to suggest that the tension might be a particularly *modern* problem. Does the tension mainly arise for worldviews that have already given over too much to the secular, the disenchanted, the mechanistic, even if the 'solution' presented does involve God in some form?

This brings us, as promised, to some of the difficulties that arise when we focus exclusively on the tension between the subjective and objective perspectives upon ourselves, as set out above.

First of all, we might bring to attention here a concern about the way in which the tension between the subjective and objective perspectives can sometimes be framed. Consider the way in which philosophers such as Nagel and Bilgrami reflect that we cannot 'at the same time' occupy the subjective and objective perspectives upon ourselves. In a way, this seems correct, but in another way, some more nuance is needed. In order to be able to occupy the subjective perspective at all, I need to be able to differentiate myself from the rest of the world. I need to be able to navigate a causally reliable pathway through the world which relies on me being able to distinguish 'me' from 'not me'. In other words, in order to be able to inhabit the subjective perspective, and to know it as such, I have to be able to see myself from the objective perspective. Then consider the 'objective perspective' upon myself. This is not a 'neutral' observation of me by me, operating as a sort of video camera, but is a perspective I am able to take upon myself, from within my self-consciousness. In order to be able to take the objective perspective upon myself, I have to be able to have a subjective perspective upon myself. The picture that emerges of the 'tension' between the subjective and objective perspectives is more of a Yin and Yang than a straight division: each perspective is a condition of possibility of the other, although one has to 'primarily' occupy one or the other perspective at any moment, and one perspective cannot be layered comprehensibly on the other.[27]

Secondly, let us grant, with Nagel, that it is not possible to inhabit both perspectives 'at the same time', or, let us say, in the light of my comments above, that one has to be dominant. But, so what? Why is this, in itself, a problem? I cannot, at the same time, both be awake, and asleep. That I cannot be both awake and asleep at the same time is not *in itself* a problem. I have to first of all notice that the two perspectives cannot be fully occupied at the same time, and then I have to *care*: there has to be something troubling, upsetting, worrying about the two perspectives, that causes me anxiety, a sense of conflict, or of yearning.

Regarding the subjective and objective perspectives upon ourselves, it seems plausible that this will only seem problematic where we have particular conceptions of what both involve. It seems, perhaps, in particular, to suit Cartesian conceptions of the self-world relationship: where the subjective perspective upon ourselves reveals a conscious, thinking immaterial soul, and the objective perspective displays sheer deterministic mechanism. This is not exactly Kant's perspective, but the preoccupation with the mechanistic nature of the objective perspective upon ourselves is certainly there in the Kantian picture also.

We might consider here Kant's much-cited reference to the 'starry heavens' in a passage from the *Groundwork,* inscribed on Kant's gravestone. The passage has a rather romantic atmosphere to it:

> Two things fill the mind with ever new and increasing admiration and reverence, the more often and more steadily one reflects on them: *the starry heavens above me and the moral law within me.*

But, in truth, when one reads the sentences around this famous passage, one finds that there is nothing romantic or heartening about the starry heavens. These heavens constitute 'an unbounded magnitude with worlds upon worlds and systems of systems', such that:

> The view of a countless multitude of worlds annihilates, as it were, my importance as an *animal creature,* which after it has been for a short time provided with vital force (one knows not how) must give back to the planet (a mere speck in the universe) the matter from which it came. (*CPrR*, 5: 162)[28]

---

[27] For impressing upon me this nuance, and its significance, I am indebted to a conversation with David Dwan.

[28] For details of Kant referencing and abbreviations, see Chapter 7, footnote 4.

The starry heavens are like a great machine, teeming with forces, moving with iron patterns of causal determinism. We have here a deeply problematic 'objective perspective' upon ourselves, which threatens to 'annihilate' our subjective sense of our significance.

We might envisage accounts of the subjective and objective perspectives that do not generate such anxiety. Attending to the objective perspective, perhaps I have an enchanted or enhanced conception of the universe within which I find myself, such that I do not find myself so isolated or alone. This might be because I am a convinced panpsychist, and so consider that, in some sense, consciousness or experience goes all the way down into all matter. Or, I might be drawn to conceptions of nature, such as we find in modern paganism (discussed in Chapter 5), which are suffused with creative imagination and value, giving the modern pagan a sense of being at home in the world. If I become convinced of absolute idealism, discussed in Chapter 6, I find that the subjective and objective begin to blend into one another. Alternatively, or, perhaps, at the same time, I might have a deflated conception of the 'subjective perspective': in a Neo-Stoic or Spinozistic fashion, perhaps I am determined to understand myself in a chastening and bracing way, which renders the 'subjective perspective' seamless and consonant with how I understand everything else. If I succeed in doing this, the 'tension' between the subjective and objective perspectives may not arise, or may be constantly queried and undercut.

What this further opens the door to is a critique of the way in which Nagel tends to explain the tension between the subjective and objective perspectives. He seems to assume that the subjective perspective upon ourselves is always a positive one, where we find ourselves significant and potent, and the objective perspective one where this sense of perspective is queried. But this is not always the case. Plenty of people do not occupy a subjective perspective—or not always—where they seem to themselves to be significant and potent. Arguably, there may be questions of gender, power, and privilege in this neighbourhood. If one's sense of potency is only queried by the vastness of the starry heavens, this may suggest that there are not too many other obstacles closer to planet Earth.

We can also reach for further layers of difficulty with conceiving the problem solely in terms of the tension between subjective and objective perspectives. Sometimes, the tensions, conflicts, and fragmentations that we experience occur not *between* these perspectives, but within them. At times, my subjective conception of myself does involve a sense of significance and vitality, but, at other times, perhaps, I feel annihilated or ashamed. One might be afflicted, to some degree, with trauma, childhood or otherwise, in a way that fractures and harms a proper perspective upon oneself.

Shame and guilt are certainly subjective perspectives upon ourselves, if anything is, and they may clash with a sense of exhilaration and vitality I also feel whilst engaging, perhaps, in the same projects or activities. Similarly, perhaps

20 NEGATIVE NATURAL THEOLOGY

I am 'religious', and a convinced Thomist, and can look at myself from an 'objective' perspective within this framework; but, also, I live in the twenty-first century, and cannot help also being able to see myself from more annihilating and deterministic perspectives. I do both. I cannot help it. Yet, there is certainly a tension between these different objectives perspectives upon myself. Other tensions and conflicts might arise also, and be pressing for me, which are not because of a tension between the subjective and objective perspectives. I might be preoccupied by questions of mortality and immortality, or by the tension between my own good and the demands of justice, or the relationship between the absolute and the relative, or the physical and the non-physical, where we are and know ourselves as both.[29]

Thinking in terms of the subjective/objective perspectives maps well onto a distinction between the first and third person perspectives. Indeed, as set out above, talking of the first and third person perspectives can be another way of pointing to the same conceptual distinction that is picked out when we refer to the subjective and objective perspectives. What can be omitted and occluded, because of such a focus, is the significance of the second-person perspective. Dislocations and fragmentations in a sense of the self often arise because of the variety of second-person perspectives upon ourselves: myself as I am known to my mother or father, in tension with myself as known by a partner, or friend. Or, the tension can occur between a second-person, first-person, and third-person perspective: myself as seen at a crucial time by my mother, interacting problematically with my own sense of myself. Psychodynamic and analytical therapies, engaged with in Chapter 7, are centrally concerned with these issues.

Clare Carlisle writes about the philosophical importance of 'the intimate relationships we have with our partners, our parents, and our children':

> Almost everyone is parented in early life (whether well or inadequately, whether by biological parents or by other caregivers) and the majority of adults live some portion of their lives in intimate partnerships; a smaller majority will have children ... Yet philosophers throughout the western tradition (with the obvious exception of Carl Jung) have been curiously reluctant to regard human beings as metaphysically and ethically situated in sexual and family relationships. I imagine this is the consequence of two closely-linked factors: a male-dominated intellectual tradition, and highly gendered conceptions of the good life which traditionally locate masculine success in public, professional achievements and feminine success in the private, domestic sphere.[30]

---

[29] For these examples of other types of tension, and persuading me of their significance, I am indebted to a response from Judith Wolfe, to a previous version of this work.

[30] Clare Carlisle, 'Spinoza and Autonomy', *Theology and Autonomy*, ed. Benjamin DeSpain and Christopher J. Insole (forthcoming).

We are interested, then, in all manner of tensions, fragmentations, compartmental-izations that lead to a sense of yearning, a desire for wholeness and integration, or, at least, a desire to somehow hold things 'together'.

God might be a concept that promises hope that we can hold together, live with, these tensions and fragmentations. The English poet and essayist Jeremy Hooker is not himself traditionally 'religious'. 'Agnostic', 'pantheist', 'animist', 'sceptical' are words he has used to describe himself. Nonetheless, Hooker reflects that the word 'God' might stand for a 'need that makes an idea possible', which is 'the need to think that, though we cannot fully know ourselves, there is a perspective in which we are fully known'.[31] Hooker is naming the fragmented perspectives that make up our lives, in-cluding but not exclusively the subjective and objective perspectives, where 'complete self-knowledge and complete knowledge of another person are equal impossibilities':

> With our mixed motives, with the knot of contradictions that we are, and with the relationships that make us, as beings subject to change, who live in time, there is no position from which we can gain complete self-knowledge. We are always on the inside of our own faces, and in life, so that ideas of the self tend to be waxwork ideas, perceptions of ourselves as effigies.[32]

The idea of God, for Hooker, circles around, as he puts it, 'a need that makes the idea possible': the need for all possible perspectives being seen at once, in a way that tessellates, harmonizes, integrates, and, revealing all, forgives all.

The contemporary philosophical theologian Judith Wolfe writes about a similar idea, from a more committed theological perspective. Wolfe acknowledges the im-portance of 'telling our story', the narrative of our lives, but reflects:

> [T]he more we insist on our individual stories, the less aware we often are how conventional the roles we take are, how influenced by the narrative models ped-dled by the latest films, books, or influencers. What feels like authenticity is often mere cliché.[33]

When lost in cliché (the perfect lover, mother, father, brother, man, woman), we can become 'rigid', in a way that forces 'other people into roles within our narrative, selecting and matching their actions to a pattern that makes sense within the plot unfolding in *our* mind':

> We are always the *protagonists* of our own lives, and cast others in roles vis-à-vis ourselves with which they (almost by definition) cannot themselves fully

---

[31] Jeremy Hooker, *Diary of a Stroke* (London: Shearsman Books, 2016), 163.
[32] Ibid.
[33] Judith Wolfe, *The Theological Imagination: Perception and Interpretation in Life, Art, and Faith* (Cambridge: Cambridge University Press, 2024), 39.

22 NEGATIVE NATURAL THEOLOGY

identify: supporting roles, or antagonistic ones. Of course we acknowledge, at least in theory, that others, too, are protagonists to themselves; but it is something of which we need continually to remind ourselves. Conversely, what role we play in one another's consciousness is very little under our control.

This can lead, Wolfe suggests, to 'profound loneliness and disorientation'.[34] We become 'to each other not real persons in a shared space, whose relative movements *affect* one another, but apparitions slotted into plays or stories that are increasingly of one's solitary imagining':

> The more we insist on the role of protagonist and cast others into supporting or antagonistic roles, the more we manoeuvre ourselves into competition or worse, find ourselves the only players among non-player characters in a cosmos without coordinates.[35]

If this is the problem—the split and fragmented roles we play, in our own lives and the lives of others—in what sense is God the answer?

Wolfe unfurls the following response:

> To some extent, the simple answer is that theology believes that we are not the ultimate tellers of the stories of our lives; that our lives are, indeed, part of a larger story, in which we do not have to be perfect protagonists, but are, as sinners loved by God, forgiven and restored to a story in which love places *all* at the centre and *all* at the service of others.[36]

Wolfe draws on the story of Orual from C.S. Lewis' *Till we Have Faces*. The story Orual 'tells about herself crumbles in her hands and runs through her fingers':

> [I]t is only when she hears her own story narrated by a god that she, too, can be Psyche—*soul, neshamah* (that great Hebrew term of endearment)—that her story turns out to be intertwined, redemptively, with the stories of whose she loves but has wounded and lost.

Wolfe reflects, 'this may well be the form that the last judgement will take: this retelling of our stories that integrates them into a larger story of love':

> It is our fervent hope that this will be so.[37]

---

[34] Ibid., 39–40.
[35] Ibid., 40.
[36] Ibid., 41.
[37] Ibid.

Only sometimes, then, is the tension between the subjective and objective perspectives upon ourselves the explicit object and theme of our thinking. 'Only sometimes', I say, albeit, sometimes, this is quite a lot of the time. Certainly, in this book, this tension is frequently our explicit object. It is so in Chapter 3, where I discuss Rahner and Camus, and in Chapter 4, when I turn my attention to contemporary humanism. In truth, it remains a central concern, amongst others, running through Chapters 5 and 6. William James is keen to show how his radical empiricism overcomes the distinction between the subjective and objective perspectives, and the absolute idealist Josiah Royce declares to pull off the same trick, using a different method. But, to overcome a tension is to acknowledge its power. It is to engage with it.

In another way, though, perhaps the tension between the objective and subjective perspectives *always remains key*. In a sense, talking of the subjective/objective perspectives might be regarded as a way of talking about the possibility of reflexive self-consciousness. To be self-conscious, I have to be able to regard myself as different from the world that is not-me, which involves being able to occupy the objective and subjective perspectives upon myself. Such reflective self-consciousness is a condition of possibility of feeling all the diverse forms of fragmentation and anxiety set out above. Perhaps, then, the tension between the subjective and objective perspectives is a condition of possibility lying behind all other fragmentations, even if it is not always itself the explicit object or theme.

The role of the concept of the divine

In relation to these diverse and fluid fractures, we can broaden out the same intuition that I set out above: that God might help to overcome the seeming tension and alienation between the subjective and objective perspectives. We might enquire whether there is a sense in which the concept of God, or the divine, can arise when one attempts to reach towards an optimal attitude towards *whatever* the limits, tensions, conflicts, fragmentations, and disintegrations are that we experience. Is the role of the God concept to offer consolation, hope, peace, courage, humility, obedience, or promise? Each of these offerings are quite different of course: peace can be achieved without hope, and consolation might not involve promise. This range of different settlements or accommodations is intended, and, in many ways is a central theme of reflection in the book.

Certainly, many thinkers do reach for the concept of God when gesturing to some such resolution or overcoming of tensions and fissures in thought. Einstein frequently makes reference to the mysterious nature of the laws of nature. He writes 'I am a deeply religious man', and that he is 'religious' insofar as he is 'imbued with the consciousness of the insufficiency of the human mind to understand deeply the harmony of the Universe which we try to formulate as "laws of nature" '. 'I believe in Spinoza's God', Einstein writes, 'who reveals himself in the orderly harmony of what exists'.[38] William James, who advocates a pluralistic pantheism, as discussed in Chapter 5, regards a reference to the divine as invoking a 'harmonious relation' with the 'higher universe', where such a relation is our 'true end'.[39] The 'absolute idealist' J.M.E. McTaggart asserts that belief in God expresses a 'conviction of a Harmony between ourselves and the universe at large'; we find the same ambition in another absolute idealist, Josiah Royce, who we discuss in Chapter 6.[40] In his own way, Nagel also confirms—in the course of resisting—the way in which the concept of God is suited to this conceptual space. In relation to his cosmic question ('how to live in harmony with the universe, and not just in it?'), Nagel comments that 'without God it is unclear what we should aspire to harmony with', although 'the aspiration to answer the cosmic question remains'.[41] Nagel admits that some of his panpsychist speculations about the need to enlarge the category of naturalism have a 'quasi-religious ring' to them, 'something vaguely Spinozistic', such that it is 'difficult to avoid the suspicion' that the enlarged naturalism will be 'religious'.[42]

The atheist philosopher Sartre provides one of the clearest accounts of the role played by the concept of God in 'reconciling' and 'harmonizing' the subjective and objective perspectives, where this tension is the explicit object of reflection.[43] Sartre's category of the 'for-itself' maps onto the subjective perspective, and the 'in-itself' onto the objective perspective. Sartre reflects that consciousness desires the ideal (and impossible) union of these, the 'in-itself-for-itself': 'to this idea', Sartre writes, 'we can give the name "God"', where the fundamental human 'project is to be God'.[44] Sartre finds, of course, that such a 'God' is an impossibility, but commentators have noted that Sartre may be drawing out a consequence of the traditional Christian formulation of divine simplicity, where, as Aquinas puts it, 'whatever is in God (the *ens causa sui*)' is 'the divine essence': 'God's act of understanding, therefore, is His essence, it is the divine being, God Himself'.[45]

---

[38] All Einstein quotes are taken from Max Jammer, *Einstein and Religion* (Princeton, New Jersey: Princeton University Press, 1999), 73, 121–122, 49.

[39] William James, *Varieties of Religious Experience, Writings 1902–1910* (New York: The Library of America, 1987), 1–478, 435.

[40] J.M.E. McTaggert, *Some Dogmas of Religion* (London: Edward Arnold Press, 1916), section 11.

[41] Nagel, 'Secular Philosophy and the Religious Temperament', 5.

[42] Nagel, 'Evolutionary Naturalism and the Fear of Religion', 130–132.

[43] For this insight, and for the references to Sartre, I am indebted to a conversation with, and an article by, King-Ho Leung, 'Hart and Sartre on God and Consciousness', *International Journal of Philosophy and Theology*, 82/1 (2021), 34–50.

[44] Jean-Paul Sartre, *Being and Nothingness: An Essay in Phenomenological Ontology*, trans. S. Richmond (London: Routledge, 2020), 735.

[45] Thomas Aquinas, *Summa Contra Gentiles*, ed. and trans. Vernon Bourke (Notre Dame, IN: University of Notre Dame Press, 1975), I.45.

This book is interested in sites in thinking about life—mostly recent or contemporary—where the concept of the divine beckons, but might also repel.

The structure and scope of the book

In broad terms, the chapters in this book move progressively from responses II to V. In Chapter 2, interacting with Janet Soskice and Martha Nussbaum, amongst others, I reflect on what we might say about the role of the concept of God in 'natural language'. I move on in Chapter 3 to regard the 'despairing' and 'absurd' responses, attending to Karl Rahner and Albert Camus, and Karen Kilby. In Chapter 4 I consider a specific type of humanism, as discussed by the anthropologist Mathew Engelke.

Under the same bracket (immanent reference to the divine), I turn (in Chapter 5) to William James' radical empiricism, which he uses to underpin his support for pluralistic pantheism. I suggest that such pluralistic pantheism may have healthy contemporary manifestations in some forms of modern paganism, as described and appreciated by Ronald Hutton and Tanya Luhrmann. In Chapter 6, I look at a dominant movement—now widely neglected—in late nineteenth- and early twentieth-century philosophy: absolute idealism. I explore why Josiah Royce regards the All, the Absolute, as divine, whereas another absolute idealist, who also speaks of the Absolute, F.H. Bradley, does not regard the All as divine: this provides a test case for asking 'what is at stake?'. I also explore whether absolute idealism might provide a perspective upon the normative non-naturalism of a recent thinker such as Derek Parfit. By 'normative non-naturalism', I mean the view that things only really *matter,* only have a normative claim on us, if, in some sense, materialistic naturalism does not offer a complete account of everything that there is. In Chapter 7, I attend to the concept of the proper, or whole self, as it features in the work of Immanuel Kant and Carl Jung. In Chapter 8, I offer some reflections on what both traditioned Christian theology, and a sceptical atheism, might make of some of the positions explored across the book, and what sort of discussion, if any, would be possible between representative of these two positions.

I have chosen to drill down on particular figures and movements, whilst being fully aware that entirely different thinkers, figures, and movements could have been chosen. My loose criteria for selecting these interlocutors include something like the following set of reflections, where, in most cases, at least three out of the four these conditions are met:

(i)   They exemplify an area of interest, in relation to thinking about limits, tensions, conflicts, fragmentation, and the divine.
(ii) They are relatively unexplored in the extant literature, or (as with Kant and James) the perspective I take upon them is relatively unexplored.

(iii) In each case, I have chosen topics, figures, or philosophical movements that represent live spiritual options, or forms of life—at the very least, but not exclusively, intellectual life—in response to the Socratic question of 'how should I live?'. My intention is not to 'invent' a new version of natural theology—or to suggest a novel, or ingenious, or speculative way of talking about divinity—which I then discuss. My intention is to engage with stuff that it 'out there' in some sense, even if, in some cases, it is quite *niche,* involving quite small numbers of followers or advocates. In some cases—for example with humanism and modern paganism—I explore the possible relationship between a current practice, movement, or form of life, and a wider genealogy, looking for latent influences, underexplored conceptual possibilities, intellectual frameworks and defences, and illuminating affinities. In this way, the book undertakes a sort of grammatical investigation into the use of different concepts of the divine, rather than attempting to say something directly about 'the divine'. There is, perhaps, an appropriate humility here. I develop this theme further below.

(iv) Many of the figures I consider are not 'standardly' regarded as being bound to a particular faith tradition (although they are influenced and shaped by such traditions), but are, to a degree 'off-piste', neither secular atheists nor traditioned Christian theologians. This is not true, of course, for Rahner, who I consider so as to provide an illuminating contrast with Camus.

There is lots that one can find to worry about in these criteria. Of especial concern, perhaps, will be (iv), which seems to involve an assumption about the limits and boundaries of a 'faith tradition'. Whilst acknowledging the difficulty, I am, nonetheless, going to leave it there, as, in my experience, it does not really help matters to attempt to anticipate and fend off these anxieties and objections, either before or after the event. I have a sense that most people, really, sort of know what I mean by this category, and I hope that the concrete treatment I deliver in the chapters, as they unfurl, goes some way towards justifying my choices. Karl Barth and Thomas Aquinas are everywhere regarded as traditioned Christian theologians; Josiah Royce and Thomas Nagel are not. Even if there is a grey area, this does not mean that everything is grey, even if, as paint colour charts tell us, black and white come in numerous varieties also.

Five themes

Through these engagements with thinkers and movements, I have found that five themes or insights repeatedly surface. I will set out a summary here of these five insights, under the following headings: distinctions, borderlands, flags, humility, freedom.

Distinctions

I have learned to mistrust some frequently employed binary distinctions, which can hinder us from seeing things properly. Often, the problem arises because it is assumed that we have a clear understanding of one side of the distinction (*x*), against which 'opposite' term (*y*) is more vaguely understood ('*y* is whatever is not *x* in this broad domain'). Here are some examples:

- Naturalism/non-naturalism
- Matter/mind
- Immanence/transcendence
- Personal/impersonal (especially when characterizing alternative conceptions of divinity)

In each case, the assumption is that the first of the terms in each distinction is more clearly understood, with the second term having a vaguer meaning, which is more or less parasitic on the supposedly more transparent first term. So, for example, the non-naturalistic goes 'beyond' the naturalistic, where, it is assumed, we know what 'naturalism' involves. We know what 'matter' is, but consciousness/mind is far more mysterious. Transcendence is 'whatever it is' that we lean into when we go beyond the immanent conception of the world. Impersonal conceptions of the divine are involved when we do not think of God as a 'person', where, broadly, we know what we mean by this.

In each case, though, I find myself puzzled. In truth, I do not know what the first term in each distinction *really* amounts to. Once this difficulty is appreciated, our already shaky grasp of the second term in the distinction becomes further loosened.

Consider, first of all, 'naturalism'. Typically the 'naturalistic' is regarded as co-extensive with the categories of natural science. But, what are/might be/will be the categories and limits of 'natural science'? Do we mean, science as it stands right now, or science as it may one day become? If the former, how can science ever progress? If the latter, who knows what this might involve?

In the literature on naturalism, we are presented with a decision as to whether we frame the category in what we might call an *a posteriori* or *a priori* way.[46] One has an *a posteriori* account if one says something along the lines of the following:

> Naturalism provides an account of the world within the categories and concepts of natural science, or, natural science as it may one day become.

---

[46] For my account of this debate I am indebted to Philip Goff, 'What is Physicalism?', in *Consciousness and Fundamental Reality* (Oxford: Oxford University Press, 2017), 23–40.

28 NEGATIVE NATURAL THEOLOGY

On this view, we have no *a priori* commitments as to what might, one day and eventually, be considered as naturalistic. Stated in such a sheer form, this keeps it entirely open what might one day be regarded as 'naturalistic'. Imagine that science begins to move, as some philosophers think is inevitable, in a panpsychist dimension: well then, 'naturalism' will include a commitment to consciousness running throughout the universe. This is hardly what naturalism means today. On this construal, naturalism does not rule out *anything*, and so fails to provide content in a meaningful distinction.

In order to block this consequence, some philosophers who want to adopt an *a posteriori* conception are willing to put in blocking clauses, such as, 'excluding the following categories and concepts', which can include: supernatural entities, God, minds, or consciousness. But this seems arbitrary, and in some cases highly controversial, such as, for example, where references to consciousness are ruled as being 'non-naturalistic'. To say that naturalism permits any categories that we may need, except for those that we rule to be *super*-natural, already implies some *a priori* rules about what the 'natural' consists in. We cannot know what is supernatural, unless we already have a firm grip on the natural.

The alternative, then, is to use an *a priori* conception more openly and explicitly, and to say something like the following:

> Naturalism is the view that reality can be fully captured in the terms of contemporary physics, where physical science restricts itself providing information about the behaviour of the things it talks about—particles, fields, spacetime.

But such a conception is also arbitrary and lacking in curiosity, in a way that limits the growth of scientific theories and exploration. It cannot be wise to index naturalism to what we currently understand of the category of nature. On either approach, *a posteriori* and *a priori,* we have difficulties.

We can move on to consider the next binary: matter and mind. A materialist thinker will say that consciousness is nothing 'over and above' matter, properly understood. Very well: but consider how our understanding of experiential self-consciousness relates to our understanding of matter. Matter now looks rather unknown and mysterious. Furthermore, is 'mind' (self-consciousness) really the puzzling part of the distinction? Especially when you consider that you have an experience of self-consciousness right now (you, right now, here, the living and breathing reader, reading this) that is far more direct and total than any definition of matter you might attempt to give.

When we speak of 'immanent' accounts of reality, we are saying something like, 'accounts of the world, sufficiently understood, that do not go beyond the world'. But, what does this mean? What is the 'world', and what constitutes a 'sufficient understanding' of it? And, at what point does a 'sufficient understanding' involve such a departure from common sense and perception that we consider the understanding so transformed as to bring us to a more 'transcendent' account?

The concept of being 'personal' is also difficult to pin down? By 'person', do we mean a self-conscious agent with a will and freedom? Some accounts that are commonly described as having an 'impersonal' conception of God (Spinozism) do not even believe that *we* are persons in this sense? So, what work is being done, in this thought-world, by the claim that God is 'impersonal', when we, also, are 'impersonal'? Some pantheistic accounts, as well as absolute idealism, ascribe thought and experience to the divine, but are described as 'impersonal': but, again, what is a 'person'? How could the carrier of thoughts and experience (even, of all thoughts and experience) not be in some sense 'personal', if the more limited fragments of this totality are considered 'persons'? Also, outside of risibly anthropomorphic reductions of the concept of God, to what extent is the God of classical Christianity—simple and triune—'personal', in the sense given when this term is contrasted with 'impersonality'?

Some of these issues are addressed at more length throughout the book. In some cases, I find the distinctions so problematic, I retire them entirely (as with naturalism/non-naturalism), except when putting forward the views of those who do employ the categories. In other cases (as with immanence and transcendence), I continue to employ the distinction, but thematize areas and times when I am not sure where the boundary lies.

Borderlands

A second theme that emerges throughout the book is the idea of borderlands. With some borderland areas, the inhabitants, landscape, habits, manners, customs, values, food, fauna, accents, and dialect for some area around the line on the map share many common features. As one moves away from the border differences—in landscape, food and fauna—appear in increasingly dense pockets, until one is clearly in a different country or region.

I could take an example close to my own geographical context: the borderland between Northumberland in England, and the Lowlands of Scotland. Some towns, such as Berwick-upon-Tweed, have oscillated over time, sometimes being considered as Scottish, at other times, as English. Such borders, of course, are far more numerous on the mainland of the European continent. I have found something analogous to this borderland between (recent) thinkers who do not use the concept of the divine, and others who do: when one moves beyond a fixation with the line on the map, many of the habits, landscape, customs, and values are shared. Although national identities may be different, the ways in which people move

30 NEGATIVE NATURAL THEOLOGY

around in their intellectual, ethical, and everyday life, display recognizable affinities and similarities.

There is another feature of borderlands, which is that the inhabitants of the borderland have far more in common with each other, than they do with fellow citizens of ostensibly the same 'nation', who may live hundreds of miles away, with a very different set of habits, manners, food, and landscape. The ('English') Northumberland farmer is far more similar to the Lowland Scottish farmer, than she or he is similar to an 'English' hedge fund manager in the City of London. Just so, some 'atheist' philosophers are far more like committed philosophical theologians, in their habits, accents and dialects, than they are like other 'atheist' philosophers. Equally, some committed theologians are far more similar to atheist thinkers, than they are to other theologians, or other types of advocate for religious commitment. I have been intrigued and moved by some of the borderland encounters that I have come across.

Flags

All that said, there is still a border. It is on the map. Often there is a sign that you pass on the road ('Welcome to Scotland'). There are also flags, with a potential for a strong identification with the flag and what it stands for, possible on either side of a border, regardless of the shared food, accents, or fauna. The flags might especially come out in (more-or-less) enjoyable, or harmless, sporting tournaments and competitions, the Six-Nations Rugby, in the case of Scotland and England, for example. Or, more darkly, they come out in situations of conflict and tension, up to and including hot warfare. If you travel from the Republic of Ireland into Northern Ireland, one has both shared borderlands, and flags: with further borders drawn within each town, city and village, the unionist area marked by red, white, and blue painted pavements, and the nationalist community marked by Irish tricolours. In this way, borders exist inside people, as well as on the map, and are vital in constituting a sense of belonging and membership.

The parallel here is well-exemplified by Nagel. Many of his habits and movements, and the landscape he looks over, seem, as Nagel admits, quite 'religious', in a Spinozistic sort of way. But, he flies the atheist flag, sometimes with a half-apology, but there it is, nonetheless: 'not only do I not believe in God, but I profoundly hope that God does not exist'.[47] On the other side, it might be thought, some theologians are so keen to stress what they do not know, their apophaticism and negativity, and the impossibility of determining what our language about God means, that it can be difficult to understand the self-identification with

---

[47] Nagel, The Last Word, 130.

a religious tradition, rather than, say, with a thoughtful agnosticism or atheism. On both 'sides' of the border there can be fear, misunderstanding, and caricature. Atheist thinkers often only consider one rather limited type of belief in God: an anthropomorphic and voluntaristic divine commander, a type of Metatron figure with dubious moral attributes. Equally, more theologically committed thinkers can give a flattened and impoverished account of what is available to philosophy that does not speak about the divine: 'if you do not believe in God', the move can be, 'one cannot give an account of value, enchantment, beauty, goodness, or consciousness'. These claims, in my experience, rarely (if ever) withstand any serious scrutiny. Although perhaps a less fraught border, there is also misunderstanding and caricature between different traditions that are prepared to speak of God: between pantheists and theists, for example, one finds some egregious characterizations of one by the other, in spite of the common borderland that is, in truth, occupied. Theists often characterize pantheists as little more than sentimental materialists; and pantheists give an account of theism that is full of pernicious dualisms—between the world and God, and between us and the non-human world—responsible for all manner of harm. Neither the pantheist nor theist would find a recognizable account of their own motives or beliefs in many of these characterizations.

Flags, of course, can also be positive: affirming a sense of belonging, of gratitude, of collegiality, festivity, and familiar bonds. The role of tradition here is an interesting one. One can belong to a tradition with gratitude, and because of humility: it is difficult to stand as a rugged and heroic epistemic individual. The thought here is that it is better to acknowledge our indebtedness to a more or less coherent body of beliefs, practices, and habits that is passed down to us, acknowledging that everyone is in a similar situation, and that we do well to work within embodied traditions. This is a universalist sort of argument for being embedded within a particular tradition, arising from our humility. But this very same set of instincts can end up in a sort of collective hubris: a certainty and inflexibility in relation to a particular tradition to which I am bound and indebted.

Humility

The book is concerned with 'what is at stake' in the choice (or desire) to use the concept of divinity, or not. To an extent, this can be unfurled in terms of explicit reasons and arguments, but this reaches a limit. I am interested in this limit, and what lies beyond and behind it. Concepts can convince, or fail to convince, but, also, attract and repel, and the deep sources of such attraction or repulsion can lie in biographical, intuitive, affective, cultural, and unconscious drives and factors.

32 NEGATIVE NATURAL THEOLOGY

We might question whether 'what is at stake' can be fully drawn out, or accessed, by different types of thinking? Here, we might consider two types of approach. First of all, anthropological studies that attend not only to the explicit arguments and justifications of groups of people, but also to the forms of life, habits, values, rituals, and sentiments. In two cases, I draw on anthropological work, attending, in Chapter 4, to Mathew Engelke's field work on the British Humanist Association (as it was then called), and, in Chapter 5, to Tanya Luhrmann's study of witchcraft and ritual magic in England in the 1980s. Secondly, we might begin to pay attention to the significance of unconscious and preconscious psychological dimensions that influence whether or not someone employs particular concepts of the divine. Some attention is paid to this into in Chapters 5 and 6, where we find William James offering an account of how different personality types gravitate towards alternative fundamental metaphysical pictures. A more resolute step is taken in this direction in Chapter 7, which looks at the ways in which Carl Jung can be understood as a faithful Kantian, developing some unfinished psychodynamic insights in Kant's work.

Freedom

When it comes to the question of whether or not to employ the category of the divine, it is difficult to resist the view that there is simply an element of freedom here, precisely because of the lack of coercive and compelling reasons or arguments, as described above. The humility leads to a type of non-posturing freedom. 'Freedom' is multi-faceted, and does not only mean 'freedom of choice', an heroic and libertarian jumping of the will, although, some 'leaps of faith' might have this quality. Freedom can also mean the growth, vitality, movement and volition of the whole person, incorporating desire and affect.

One way of understanding the link between humility and freedom, in this area, is in terms of a distinction drawn by Gabriel Marcel between a problem and a mystery. A 'problem', Marcel insists, 'can be publicly formulated, using concepts that are "objective", and its solution can be discovered by anyone'. A 'mystery' on the other hand:

> [B]elongs to a realm of human experience that cannot be formulated publicly using objective categories, and its solution must be personal and individual.[48]

---

[48] This is a quotation from Clare Mac Cumhaill and Rachael Wiseman, *Metaphysical Animals: How Four Women Brought Philosophy Back to Life* (London: Penguin, 2023), 136. For this account of Marcel, I am indebted to this work. Mac Cumhaill and Wisemann acknowledge a debt to Brendan Sweetman, 'Introduction', *A Gabriel Marcel Reader* (South Bend, Indiana: St Augustine's Press, 2011), 5.

Marcel considers that 'love, hope and faith', are mysteries and not problems. This would seem correct, especially when the concept of God arises (or is resisted) in relation to a perceived tension between subjective and objective perspectives upon our lives. Where the concept of God bridges and holds together these different perspectives, it cannot be 'resolved' either by inner observation of the subjective, the phenomenological, nor by external observation of objects, or of ourselves regarded as objects. The God concept is not a problem that can be solved. It is a mystery. And the proper attitude to mystery is humility, and the proper response, one made in freedom.

The idea here is to augment our freedom of thought, through bringing to the surface what may have been obscured, forgotten, or repressed. When one thinks of a tradition, one tends to think of what is remembered, of what is carried over and preserved. Benjamin DeSpain draws attention to the way in which 'forgetting is also a necessary function of a tradition's transmission'.[49] DeSpain cites Joseph Mueller's reflection that 'memory cannot function correctly unless it engages in some forgetting'.[50] Amplifying Mueller's reflections, Philipp Rosemann writes:

[A]s a tradition decides what it needs for its present tasks, it relegates to the deeper recesses of memory aspects of the past that it judges to be irrelevant. Such aspects are then confined to unread manuscripts, unopened books, dusty archives, and rarely visited storerooms.[51]

The negative natural theology project takes up the invitation to explore 'the possibility of renaissances',[52] such that 'these forgotten pieces of the collective memory' can be 'recovered, to varying degrees' as 'different situations' demand different 'responses'.[53]

It should be clear that the project of renewing negative natural theology can be more or less infinitely open-ended in relation to the topics, thinkers, periods, and preoccupations that might be of interest, and the methods that can be employed. If the project succeeds, it will be because it helps to open up a space that is more free, curious, undogmatic (in a literal and colloquial sense), empathic, and compassionate, helping us to become more aware in our thinking. A renewed negative natural theology can be open, free, aware, curious, and attentive to a range of

---

[49] Benjamin DeSpain, 'All Too Human', in *The Varieties of Philosophical Experience: Negative Natural Theology* (forthcoming). DeSpain is himself drawing upon Joseph G. Mueller, 'Forgetting as a Principle of Continuity in Tradition', *Theological Studies*, 70 (2009), 751–781.

[50] Mueller, 'Forgetting as Principle', 767–768.

[51] Philipp W. Rosemann, *Charred Root of Meaning: Continuity, Transgression, and the Other in Christian Tradition* (Grand Rapids, Michigan: William B. Eerdman's Publishing Company, 2017), 134.

[52] Rosemann, *Charred Root*, 2.

[53] DeSpain, 'All Too Human'.

resources and disciplines, from science (as with panpsychism), to literature, art, anthropology and psychology. Where it attends to the past, it will be in order to open up new roads into the future.

I turn in the next chapter to a consideration of the existence and 'meaning' of the word God.

2

The Existence of the Word God

Reference and Mystery

Karl Rahner reflects on the significance of the mere existence of the word God:

> We do not have an experience of God as we have of a tree, another person and other external realities which, although they are perhaps never there before us absolutely nameless, yet they evoke their name by themselves because they simply appear within the realm of our experience at a definite point in time and space, and so by themselves they press immediately for a name. We can say, therefore, that what is most simple and most inescapable for human beings with regard to the question of God is the fact that the word 'God' exists in his intellectual and spiritual existence.
>
> The mere fact that this word exists is worth thinking about.[1]

The issue that Rahner raises here can be framed as a question in the philosophy of language, and can be meaningfully raised, whatever formal commitment one has to religious belief, or to atheism. The question can be put in the following terms: what sort of contribution does the concept of 'divinity', or 'the divine', or 'God', make to natural language?

Any adequate account of what sort of contribution the concept of the 'God' and 'the divine' makes will have to be able to account for a range of evident phenomena: that the concept of the divine is a part of natural language, that people from an early age are initiated into the rules of using the concept, and can continue to use it, albeit shifting their commitments and usage, whilst considering this to be a continuity in an ongoing practice, rather than a change of topic. Speakers using the concept can be understood by other speakers, and they can be meaningfully corrected about their usage, with agreements and disagreements occurring in ways that are (sometimes) amenable to negotiation, and types of evidence, including reason, authority, and experience. Something counts, in various contexts, as a correct or incorrect use of the term. As well as disagreement within communities of usage, speakers often consider there to be an overlap in usage across different communities, practices, and traditions, sufficient to generate meaningful

---

[1] Karl Rahner, *Foundations of Christian Faith: An Introduction to the Idea of Christianity*, trans. William V. Dych (New York: Crossroad, 2016), 45.

Negative Natural Theology. Christopher J. Insole, Oxford University Press. © Christopher J. Insole 2024.
DOI: 10.1093/9780198933007.003.0003

36   NEGATIVE NATURAL THEOLOGY

discourse about agreement and disagreement, including 'interfaith' discussions. Furthermore, some speakers find considerable salience, consolation, hope, promise, and meaning in the use of the concept; for some, it is one of the most central aspects of their identity, providing a sense of purpose, and of hope in their lives.

My intention is to honour these contours of 'natural language' in relation to language about God, divinity, and the divine, and not to erect a formal, revised, or 'improved' account, which puts into question, or renders tenuous, natural features of language use. As Rahner puts it, the word 'God' exists, and it is worth thinking about. We might not be sure if God exists, but the word does; it is out there, doing work, and this work is the object of our study and reflection. As I set out in the previous chapter, the intention of the book is to pay attention to uses of the concept of God that are, in some sense, 'out there', and not to invent or refine a new type of natural theology.

After dismissing a straightforward construal of 'God' as either a proper name, or a title, I begin by considering Janet Martin Soskice's suggestion, made in *Metaphor and Religious Language*,[2] that 'God' might function like a 'natural kind' term (such as 'water', 'gold', or 'tiger'). I discuss problems both with Soskice's approach, and with its deeper underpinnings in Saul Kripke's work *Naming and Necessity*.[3] I attempt to summarize some recent insights from philosophy of language, arising since Kripke's influential lectures, concerning better ways to conceive of the role of natural kind terms.

I suggest a way in which this improved conception of natural kind terms might assist our various investigations into a range of uses of the notion of the divine. Specifically, what it promises is a way beyond sheer equivocation between different uses of the word God, or, even, beyond the loosest and most minimal family-resemblance concept. By finding something 'common' across different uses of the word 'God', it is possible that something becomes visible to us: a common aspiration across peoples and times, between different self-identified faith traditions, and alternative spiritualities, including Spinozism, Stoicism, modern paganism, and pantheism. We may also render visible generative grey areas, and some interesting philosophical attraction towards, and reticence about, speaking about the divine.

In the Prologue and Chapter 1, I came at the question of God, or not God, from the perspective of thinking about a widely shared human predicament: fragmentation and tension, and a yearning. In this chapter, the approach is rather different. Here, I think about natural language, and how different types of word refer, and have content, even where complete and true descriptions may evade us.[4] I understand the two approaches as dovetailing, or mirroring one another: given the

---

[2] Martin Soskice, *Metaphor and Religious Language* (Oxford: Oxford University Press, 1985).
[3] Saul Kripke, *Naming and Necessity* (Oxford: Blackwell Publishing, 1972).
[4] For bringing to light this distinction between different types of approach—one focussing on the human condition, the other on how words refer—and pushing me on their relationship, I am indebted to a response to a previous version of this chapter from Judith Wolfe.

human condition, the shared predicament, how might we understand the way in which the word God aspires to refer in natural language? As a name, a title, a description, or something else?

Proper names and titles

In the course of offering a rather unsympathetic dismissal of 'naturalistic pantheism', the Christian philosopher of religion Brian Leftow offers some reflections on what he calls the 'God-Role', commenting that:

> We determine the God-role, even if we do not determine what fills it.[5]

Leftow finds that:

> To be God, something must be the sole item to play this role. The bare syntax of 'God' makes this clear. Either 'God' is a proper name, or 'God' is a title (like 'Pope') only one thing at a time can correctly bear.[6]

This might seem a natural enough starting point, when taking up Rahner's invitation to reflect on the word God. It is not clear, though, that 'God' does function like a proper name or a title. Both titles and proper names would seem to be too contingently related to their objects. The paradigmatic use of names is along the following lines:

> This individual is called Richard.

And a typical ascription of a title would be along these lines:

> Richard is the King/Pope.

In both cases, Richard might have gone by a different name, or not have been King/Pope (and one day will not be). We could not say similarly of an 'item' (as Leftow puts it):

> This individual is called God.
> Or
> This individual has the title of God.

---

[5] Brian Leftow, 'Naturalistic Pantheism', in *Alternative Concepts of God: Essays on the Metaphysics of the Divine*, ed. Andrew A. Buckareff and Yujin Nagasawa (Oxford: Oxford University Press, 2016), 64–90, 67.
[6] Ibid.

38 NEGATIVE NATURAL THEOLOGY

This identification is too contingent and dependent upon a type of baptism/dubbing. To be *God,* within classical monotheism (to stick close to Leftow's paradigm) needs a more intrinsic connection between God and what makes God, God. A child might legitimately wonder why she or he had not been born into the title and role of being the Prince of Wales: there is something arbitrary about not being so born. But, if a child had a similar puzzlement about not being 'God', this would reveal a confusion about the type of concept that 'God' is. As children grow into the language, they would find out that this is not a correct use of the concept. Believers may use titles to evoke various properties of God, and what is owed to God ('King' and 'Lord'), but it does not seem that the concept 'God' is a title. Although 'God' does not seem to function quite like a proper name, the question of how proper names refer, when they do, is itself an interesting one, which takes us to category of 'natural kinds'.

Natural kinds and rigid designation

To an unusual extent in philosophy, the work of the philosopher of language Saul Kripke led to a significant consensus around one particular negative claim: that, however it is that proper names ('Richard') and natural kind terms ('water', 'gold', or 'tiger') refer successfully, it is not by virtue of being more or less adequate *descriptions.*[7] In other words, reference is possible without descriptive knowledge, and where these attempted descriptions are partial or erroneous.

We should consider, for example, how easy it is to be inducted successfully into the practice of using proper names to refer, even where descriptive knowledge is absent, incomplete, or erroneous. Consider the following example, which most people would regard as referring successfully, even if it is descriptively false:

> Peter is drinking martini (where Peter is drinking water).

In other cases, descriptive knowledge can be minimal. Imagine that I am walking across a crowded room, and I overhear a colleague saying the sentence: 'Barbara Tuchman was a significant twentieth-century historian'. Before this, I had never heard of Barbara Tuchman, but I can now immediately use this knowledge discursively, even without any further information or substance. In the opposite corner of the room, I join a group in conversation. One of the group points to a portrait of Barbara Tuchman and asks me 'do you know who that is?'. Immediately, I can employ my successful induction into the name-using practice: 'oh, that is Barbara Tuchman, she was an important historian'.

---

[7] Kripke, *Naming and Necessity.*

THE EXISTENCE OF THE WORD GOD   39

Kripke suggests that natural kind terms (such as 'water', 'gold', or tiger') enjoy 'a greater kinship with proper names than is generally realized',[8] in that reference can be achieved without full or accurate descriptions. This possibility is essential in order to explain the possibility of progress and continuity in science, and to account for agreement and disagreement within the development of a theory, and across theories. Consider the way in which a term such as the 'gene' gathers descriptive richness as our theoretical models develop. We might begin with a minimal account, such as 'whatever mechanism it is that is responsible for the inheritance of acquired characteristics'.[9] Speaking broadly, in the acquisition of natural language, our ability to refer to things such as 'lemons', 'tigers', 'cats' far exceeds our ability to give accurate descriptive accounts of these things.

In the case of natural kind terms, reference can be achieved with a sort of pointing into an unknown:

The natural kind x is that, whatever it is, which does this/has these effects/ features.

So, for example, with the concept of the 'gene', we can say the following:

The 'gene' is that, whatever it is, which is the mechanism responsible for the inheritance of acquired characteristics.

Another example frequently cited in the literature is that of 'water', where we can say:

'Water' is that, whatever it is, which is the clear colourless liquid in our seas and lakes, which we drink and is essential for life.

Our understanding of the 'gene' is constantly developing, in such a way that we enrich our descriptive accounts of it. Similarly, people referred successfully to 'water' for thousands of years before our understanding that water *is* H_2O. The technical term given to this way of referring to something is called 'rigid designation': the idea being that the natural kind term attaches rigidly to x, whatever x turns out to be, even considering the range of alternative ways in which the world might have been.

What about the suggestion, then, that the term 'the divine', or 'God', operates rather like a natural kind term? Such an extension is invited by Kripke himself, who suspects that something like his analysis of natural kind terms will apply to a wide range of general terms, including 'species names, whether they are **count nouns,**

---

[8] Ibid., 134.
[9] For this example, I am indebted to Soskice, *Metaphor and Religious Language*, 131.

40 NEGATIVE NATURAL THEOLOGY

such as "cat", "tiger", "chunk of gold", or **mass terms** such as "gold", "water", "iron pyrites"':

> It also applies to certain terms for natural phenomena, such as 'heat', 'light', 'sound', 'lightning', and presumably suitably elaborated, to corresponding **adjectives**—'hot', 'loud', 'red'.[10]

The seminal, and still unsurpassed, discussion of the possibility of understanding the concept of 'God' as a natural kind term, is provided by Soskice, in her 1985 text, *Metaphor and Religious Language*.[11] Soskice notices a striking and attractive feature of the discussion of natural kinds: that successful reference can occur even in the absence of direct acquaintance, or accurate theoretical description. This insight seemed to block a familiar line of philosophical attack, influenced by logical positivism, which had plagued academic theology throughout the 1950s, 1960s, and 1970s, lead to various forms of hand-wringing about the value of religious language and 'God-talk'. Consider, for example, this line of attack from A.J. Ayer:

> To say that something transcends the human understanding is to say that it is unintelligible. And what is unintelligible cannot be significantly described ... If one allows that it is impossible to define God in intelligible terms, then one is allowing that it is impossible for a sentence both to be significant and to be about God. If a mystic admits that the object of his vision cannot be described, then he must also admit that he is bound to talk nonsense when he describes it.[12]

Furthermore, the acknowledged element of 'unknowing' in the use of natural kind terms (we cannot describe what we refer to) resonates with some theological sensibilities about the unknowability and indescribability of God, which are particularly reflected on by negative theology, resonating with the humility that we are interested in modelling in this book. Soskice praises the 'agnosticism of our formulations', where we 'do not claim to describe God but to point through His effects, and beyond His effects, to Him':

> It is, hence, of the utmost importance to keep in mind the distinction, never remote in the writings of Anselm or of Aquinas, between referring to God and defining Him. This is the fine edge at which negative theology and positive theology meet, for the apophatic insight that we say nothing of God, but only point toward

---

[10] Kripke, *Naming and Necessity*, 134. The bold is original.
[11] Soskice, *Metaphor and Religious Language*.
[12] A.J. Ayer, *Language, Truth and Logic* (Harmondsworth: Penguin Books, 1971), 156. Cited by Soskice, *Metaphor and Religious Language*, 144.

THE EXISTENCE OF THE WORD GOD   41

Him is the basis for the tentative and avowedly inadequate stammerings by which we attempt to speak of God and His acts.[13]

If the concept of God/the divine is to be construed as a natural kind term, we do not need accurate theoretical descriptions, but, of course, we do need some sort of adequate rule to fix the reference of the natural kind, along the lines of those offered for the concept of the gene, or of water. We will need some sort of formulation along the lines of:

God is that, whatever it is, that $[x,y,z]$.

The difficult work remains of specifying what constitutes the content '$[x,y,z]$': what are the effects, impacts, and features which cascade from the natural kind identified, if the suggestion that the concept of divinity functions like a natural kind is feasible? Soskice explores three suggestions, which I will set out in turn, setting out some difficulties as we go along.

First of all, seeking a 'designation on which there is general agreement', Soskice explores Anselm's formula in the Proslogion:

God is that than which nothing greater can be conceived.

Soskice finds this 'unsatisfactory', not as a rule for thinking about God, but as a characterization of the mode of designation, along the lines of a natural kind, because 'its formal nature deprives it of any means of linking God causally to the world'.

This leads Soskice to a second suggestion:

God is that, whatever it is, which is the source and cause of all there is.

Even though this is Soskice's preferred 'causal' pathway, she acknowledges that the suggestion as it stands is 'crude', because 'it depends upon the belief that God is causally related to the world, at its origin or perhaps even in specific events and experiences within human history'. Nonetheless, Soskice takes comfort from the safety earned from the 'criticism customarily levelled at the theological realist, that he claims to describe God'.[14]

There are, though, more intractable difficulties with this suggested filling out of the concept of God as a rigid designator. Of course, a theist will indeed affirm that God is the source and cause of all there. Nonetheless, this will not work as

---

[13] Soskice, *Metaphor and Religious Language*, 140.
[14] Ibid., 139–140.

42   NEGATIVE NATURAL THEOLOGY

an account of how the term God refers, insofar as it functions like a natural kind, because there are possible sources and causes of all that there is, which it would be strange to call God. Importantly, the term God refers to the 'source and cause of all there is', *whatever the source and cause is.* This is how rigid designation works. Consider what happens if, in fact, the source and cause of all there is, is random chance, or a deep law of physics or metaphysics, with no particular salience for our existence—offering no hope, consolation or promise—except that it is the condition of possibility of our existence. If we have fixed the reference of God to mean 'that which is the source and cause of all there is', well then: this is God.

One could bite this bullet, and accept this result, but we are now offering a revisionist account of the function of the concept of the divine, which does not really match up with its use in natural language. It is a bit like the way in which theologians might receive talk from physicists about the 'God particle': I think, correctly, that theologians and religious believers do not get overexcited about this—or not on religious grounds—thinking that physicists are getting closer to the divine essence.

As a third route, Soskice suggests fleshing this out through attention to 'religious experience', through an initial 'pointing' to 'God through religious experience', which 'is of considerable importance to the faithful'.[15] The continuity of this reference is then secured through complex traditions, which, in the case of Christianity are mediated through textually based memory. At this point, Soskice is drawing on Kripke's quickly sketched suggestion about how reference might be fixed sometimes, in contexts that are more appropriate to names than natural kinds, where there is an original 'dubbing' or 'baptism', such that a name is given to something, and then continuity of reference is fixed:

> Someone, let's say, a baby, is born; his parents call him by a certain name. They talk about his to their friends. Other people meet him. Through various sorts of talk the name is spread from link to link as if by a chain.[16]

The phrasing is strange, 'someone, *let's say*, a baby'. When has anyone ever been born who is not a baby? In any case, the point is that, somehow, this chain can extend through vast tracks of space and time: enabling us to refer to Shakespeare, to John of Gaunt, to Julian of Norwich, to Jesus. Kripke claims that he is not offering an 'alternative theory', but simply offering a 'better picture' than is provided by those accounts that regard names as a type of description.

There are deep problems with Kripke's entire 'baptism and causal chain' picture, which I will come to in a bit. Even without questioning the fundamental picture,

---

[15] Ibid., 139.
[16] Kripke, *Naming and Necessity*, 91.

there are some more specific difficulties with Soskice's theological application. The problem is that it makes successful reference dependent upon an originary direct acquaintance with God. But, a persuasive account of the role of the concept of God and divinity in natural language should not *depend upon* a claim about the existence of God. This is, in part, because it will be radically unsuccessful as an account for non-believers and sceptics. The concept clearly has a meaningful role; whether or not God exists. This is not to deny, of course, that some religious believers will regard themselves as in communities and traditions which enjoy continuity with some originary religious experience. The point is, though, not to conflate a substantive belief with a theory of how a concept gets its meaning within ordinary language.

In fact, it is unclear quite why Soskice concludes her discussion with the positive allusion to religious experience, as, earlier in her account, she provides ample grounds, along the lines set out above, for not taking this route, commenting that 'we take it as given that no eye has seen God, and no finger pointed Him out':

> [S]ince such experiences cannot be replicated, fixing reference by means of them demands commitment to the validity of the experience as reported by the experience. But those who judge themselves to have experienced God may be mistaken, as theists freely admit.

Given this, Soskice admits that 'attempts to fix a reference in this way may fail to be widely convincing, given the contested nature of religious experience' such that it is 'unlikely to persuade the sceptic'.[17]

Soskice's emphasis upon inherited 'chains of communication' has been found to be attractive to many people doing constructive work in theology: it seems to stitch together philosophy of language with a positive regard for traditions, communities, and ecclesial and textual practices. This embeddedness within communities and traditions has a cost, though. One can see how Soskice's account could reach out to Judaism and Islam: both have textual traditions, in some sort of ostensible relationship with originary experiences and reported revelations. But, it is less clear how either of the approaches explored by Soskice—causal and experiential— would adequately address non-monotheistic traditions and movements, such as Buddhism, Daiosm, pantheism, or versions of Spinozism.

Consider, for example, the philosopher Timothy Sprigge. Sprigge is part of the surprising resurgence of panpsychism in analytical philosophy of mind. The details of Sprigge's argument do not concern us here, so much as his determination to use the concept of the divine in the context of his metaphysical theory. Sprigge argues for the reality of a pervasive and 'intense consciousness'. More local and

---

[17] Soskice, *Metaphor and Religious Language*, 138–139.

44   NEGATIVE NATURAL THEOLOGY

gathered centres of experience (you and me) are parts of this more cosmic consciousness. Sprigge identifies this pan-consciousness, eternally present to all of space and time, as 'the Absolute', or 'God'. Sprigge writes that 'if we believe in the Absolute it is hard not to accept the view that everything moves to *One far off divine event to which the whole Creation moves*'.[18] 'To live a fulfilled life', Sprigge suggests, 'requires that one somehow adapts to the universe, and to one's particular place in it', which can only be achieved through 'an appropriate relation to God, *qua* universal consciousness'.[19] Neither an originary dubbing/baptism, nor a particular experience handed down through a causal chain, would seem to account for this use of the word God. God, on Sprigge's conception, is not a personal source and cause of consciousness. God *is* consciousness, in which we, to a degree, participate. Nor is there a rich textual tradition of mediating beliefs about this God: God is experienced in the immediacy of consciousness.

Alternatively, we could look to reflections by Einstein, who affirmed 'I'm not an atheist'[20]:

> I believe in Spinoza's God who reveals himself in the orderly harmony of what exists, not in a God who concerns himself with facts and actions of human beings.[21]

Einstein is not writing of a 'religious feeling' just in a vague sense of 'being over-awed' or finding something marvellous. Nonetheless, Einstein finds 'alien' the 'idea of a personal God'.[22]

There is, of course, a possible 'robust response' to all this. One could say that the conception of God and divinity as espoused in monotheism is so different from that set out in impersonal and pantheistic (or panentheistic) accounts, that we should not expect to have a common account of the meaning of the concept of divinity. There are two problems with such a response.

First of all, it would seem to distort our actual experience of discourse in this area: the Christian theologian knows that she does not agree with Sprigge or Einstein about God, but any 'natural' conversation that occurred would proceed on the basis that there is a disagreement about a common topic. It takes an ideological act of the will to remove this conviction. We should recall that we are not

---

[18] T.L.S. Sprigge, 'What I Believe', in *The Importance of Subjectivity: Selected Essays in Metaphysics and Ethics*, ed. Leemon B. McHenry (Oxford: Oxford University Press, 2010), 4–14, 13.

[19] Ibid., 229.

[20] Einstein, *New York Times*, 25 April 1929, 60. Cited in Max Jammer, *Einstein and Religion: Physics and Theology* (Princeton: Princeton University Press, 1999), 48.

[21] Cited in Jammer, *Einstein and Religion*, 49. This is Einstein's cabled reply to a query from Rabbi Herbert S. Goldstein of the Institutional Synagogue in New York, 'Do You Believe in God? Stop. Prepaid Reply Fifty Words', 49.

[22] Einstein, Letter to Beatrice Frohlich, 17 December 1952, Einstein Archive, reel 59–797, cited in Jammer, *Einstein and Religion*, 121.

attempting to offer a revisionist account of the role of the concept God in ordinary language, but are taking up Rahner's invitation to dwell on the 'mere fact that this word exists', and to look non-judgementally at what role this concept actually has. In terms of some of the themes identified in the previous chapter, the 'robust' response here would seem to prioritize flag-waving, over and above an interest in exploring, on the ground, potential borderlands.

The second problem with the 'robust response' is that it seems to undercut the very motivation of drawing upon natural kinds at all. One of the chief advantages of fixing meaning in a Kripkean way, rather than by descriptions, is supposed to be that it facilitates both continuity of reference across theory change, and the possibility of different communities of investigation and practice making common reference, even where there is some disagreement. This honours both the humility and the intellectual freedom we wish to embody in the renewal of natural theology. So, we fix the reference of 'gene' by talking of 'this, whatever it is which is the mechanism responsible for the inheritance of acquired characteristics'. We fix the reference of 'water' by saying 'this, whatever it is, which is the clear colourless liquid in our seas and lakes, which we drink and is essential for life'. We then discover more about both genes and water. If the meaning of 'gene' and 'water' were given by a set of descriptions, we would be in danger on at least two fronts: first of all, of being locked into a sort of relativism within communities or 'language-games'. Secondly, we would fail to give an account of continuity in the progress of theories: if the meaning of 'gene' is fixed by a (flawed) description, and the description is then supplanted, then the meaning of the term shifts, such that we are talking about something different from one moment to the next.

The point is that when meaning is fixed by rigid designation, there is a continuity of reference, even where there can be radical shifts in our understanding. This enables humility and flexibility of thought. Perhaps we are content to allow the concept of the divine to balkanize into fragments of disconnected language games, or, into a loose family-resemblance at best; but, the decision to think about natural kinds at all is an initial marker to try not to let this happen. Certainly, it was a motivating consideration for Soskice that rigidly designated terms can indeed 'be coreferential across theories'.[23]

I've presented these criticisms as problems with Soskice's account, but, in truth, the problems lie deeper, with Kripke's own picture of how reference might work. Soskice searches for a causal link between the rigid designation of 'God' and a community of use: either through originary experience and acquaintance, or by talking of God as being 'the cause and source of all that is'. This reflected Kripke's suggestion that if reference is not fixed by definite descriptions, it must be

---

[23] These problems around co-referentiality, non-Christian religions, and the insularity of 'language games' are raised in a review of Soskice's book, written by Jamie Ferreira, 'Review of Janet M. Soskice: "Metaphor and Religious Language"', *The Thomist,* 51/4 (1987), 719–725.

46 NEGATIVE NATURAL THEOLOGY

secured through some sort of causal link: an original baptism, mediated through a causal chain.

The broad consensus in philosophy of language since the publication of *Naming and Necessity* in 1980 is that Kripke was more successful in his criticism of the descriptive account of proper names and natural kinds, than he was in providing an alternative 'causal chain' picture of how reference is achieved.[24] A significant problem is that 'causality' is just too pervasive and multi-faceted, in order to be a sufficient explanation of how reference is fixed. Take, for example, a reference to 'Cicero'. Michael Luntley observes that it 'does not take much to get into a Cicero-directed thought', but that 'the question that needs answering is whether being in a causal chain is sufficient'.[25] There are numerous causal chains that connect us to Cicero: the continuity of the Earth's atmosphere, for example, or the continuous existence of the star that is our sun. The physical universe is stitched together by infinite causal chains. We are only a few handshakes away, we are told, from everyone currently living, perhaps not so very many away from anyone who has ever lived: but handshakes are not supposed to be how reference is fixed:

> [T]here are doubtless innumerably many causal chains connecting my use of the name 'Cicero' and the Roman orator. In addition, there are probably a good few chains connecting my use to the use of a long-forgotten neighbour who named his dog 'Cicero'.

What matters has to be 'more than merely standing in a sequence of sound productions that are causally traceable back to Cicero'. But what is this more? Well, it has to be the particular nature of the causal chain that matters, and what we have in view must be that it is a causal chain that communicates some sort of relevant information. As Luntley comments:

> [I]f this is the notion that is at work, the causal theory is not a theory that is insensitive to information. Indeed, it is an informationally sensitive account of reference, and it is the informational links which you have, not the causal links, that do the work.[26]

This is revealed by what Luntley calls the 'famous names convention' in the literature on philosophy of language. The names chosen to illustrate how causal chains

---

[24] For my sense of the more recent 'state of the debate', I am indebted to the following: Scott Soames, *Beyond Rigidity* (Oxford: Oxford University Press, 2002); Michael Luntley, *Contemporary Philosophy of Thought* (Oxford: Blackwell Publishers, 1999); and chapters by Gauker, Sawyer, Robertson, Abbott, and Ludlow in *The Routledge Companion to Philosophy of Language*, ed. Gillian Russell and Delia Graff Fara (New York: Routledge, 2012).

[25] Luntley, *Contemporary Philosophy of Thought*, 274.

[26] Ibid., 274.

work are typically famous ones, such as 'Cicero'. Why do famous names feature so heavily? It is because 'everyone will know what the example is about!':

> In other words, writers use a famous name to ensure that we are party to a name-using practice before the discussion of what constitutes a name-using practice gets under way. This means that most of what constitutes a name-using practice goes unnoticed, because we are asked to consider an example with which we are familiar.

What makes the 'theory look good in the cases used to set up the picture' is that 'in such cases causal links are employed that happen also to be informational links'.

The heart of the problem is this: that Kripke assumes that theories of reference must be *either* descriptive, or causal. When Kripke finds that they are not descriptive, he concludes that they must, therefore, be causal. But, as Luntley shows, this is a falsely restrictive set of alternatives. We can accept that reference is not fixed descriptively, without having to conclude that reference must be causal, based on some sort of initial acquaintance, followed up by some sort of causal continuity. Instead, we should explore the possibility of accounts that are informationally sensitive and rich. Of course, such informational links are *also causal,* but, vitally, not 'all causal links are informational links',[27] and their being causal is necessary but not sufficient to account for reference.

These informational links can be highly various and fragmentary. Consider a reference to the 'theory of relativity', which many people achieve, with no more than a highly partial 'preliminary cache of information', which 'immerses' us in a 'web of information' that is somehow directed at the reference.[28] This points to the wider conceptual role of names and natural kinds, where, as Luntley puts it, the 'meaning of a term is a function of its systematic connectedness within a language'.[29]

If we pull things together for a moment, we can summarize what we may have learned from developments in philosophy of language about reference. Reference (which facilitates communication, agreement, and disagreement) can be fixed:

- Without extensive theoretical knowledge of what is referred to.
- Without originary acquaintance with what is referred to, involving a type of ostensive dubbing or 'baptism'.
- Without a detailed description of what is referred to.
- Without a specific causal chain of communication going back to something picked out by pointing, or direct acquaintance.

---

[27] Ibid., 279.
[28] Ibid., 281.
[29] Ibid., 290.

48 NEGATIVE NATURAL THEOLOGY

Reference requires some element of the following:

- Some sort of informational grasp of what is being referred to.
- This informational grasp can be fragmentary, various, and shifting.
- The informational grasp may be fixed by the conceptual role played by a term in a wider language, rather than being fixed by acquaintance, ostensive definition, or 'baptism'.

Although Martha Nussbaum is not responding to the criticisms of Kripke set out above, she does set out an approach that implicitly leans into the 'informationally-rich' conceptual space recommended by Luntley and others, in a way that may have lessons for philosophical theology. I will briefly discuss this, before reflecting on whether we might want to frame a looser and more inclusive attempt at capturing what the word 'God' might achieve, if thought of as akin to a rigid designator.[30] Nussbaum's suggestion is that virtue concepts can function as rigid designators, so that a virtue can be referred to in the following way:

> The virtue x is that, whatever it is, which is the proper attitude to take with reference to an area of human life—which area is both problematic and non-negotiable, requiring some sort of decided disposition towards it.

Take, for example, the virtue of 'fortitude'. This can operate as a rigid designator in the following way:

> 'Fortitude' is this, whatever it is, which is the proper attitude to take with reference to our shared physical vulnerability and exposure to risk and danger.

Drawing an analogy from Aristotle, Nussbaum observes that when the ancient Greeks heard a clash of thunder, they named it 'thunder', without any accurate description of what thunder is.[31] The successful reference without descriptive knowledge makes it possible to accrue descriptive knowledge over time, whilst talking continuously about the *same thing* (whether that be thunder, or a virtue), and not constantly changing topic. For our purposes, I note that the conceptual role being played by the virtue in no way relies upon an original baptism, or experience, or a chain of communication. Rather, it is richly characterized in terms of the role played by the concept in a wider life, in a way that needs several clauses and

---

[30] Martha Nussbaum, 'Non-relative Virtues: An Aristotelian Account', in *The Quality of Life*, ed. Martha Nussbaum and Amartya Sen (Oxford: Oxford University Press, 1993), 242–269.

[31] Ibid., 247. The Aristotle reference is *Posterior Analytics. Topica*, trans. Hugh Tredennick and E.S. Forster, Loeb Classical Library 391 (Cambridge, MA: Harvard University Press, 1960), II. 8, 93a21ff.

A proposal

Soskice had a particular context and motivation: to remove the obstacle in the road to talking about God *at all,* in the light of the robust and sweeping verificationist critique. If the pathway that opened up was rather 'restricted' to traditional text-based religions of the book, it was still a liberation, as before, no pathways at all were opened up. The context now is rather different. Traditioned systematic and constructive theology, and philosophy of religion, speaks with considerable confidence about God. But we might be able to glimpse other pathways that are less explored: this is the freedom to explore neglected and latent traditions, thinkers and movements, spoken of in the opening chapter. The revised conception of how natural designation might work could help us see our way to some of these pathways.

As I commented in the opening of this chapter, speaking in terms of rigid designation may assist us when regarding widely varying uses of the concept of God. We can hope to go beyond seeing equivocation, and, even, beyond a very loose sense of family-resemblance. The concern being addressed here is not the verificationist one (that language about the divine is strictly meaningless because unverifiable), but a different one, also with a link to a Wittgensteinian instinct (although more the latter than the early Wittgenstein).

I have in mind here Wittgenstein's warning not to seek a single set of necessary and sufficient conditions for the meaning of any significant concept (truth, justice, knowledge, freedom), but to be attentive to differences. There may be some patterns of continuity and overlap, but these will be more along the lines of a family-resemblance, or, using Wittgenstein's other image, like the intertwined cords that go into making a single rope: there will be some contact between some parts of the cords throughout, but not at every point. Taking the Wittgenstein warning here indicates that there may be something philosophically neurotic about trying to speak meaningfully about different applications of the *same* concept ('the divine'). Perhaps it is better to consider them different concepts, relative to each context of usage.

Against this, we might offer that it is un-Wittgensteinian to *assume a priori* that there is not more that can be said. Something like this claim was made by the Wittgensteinian philosopher Bede Rundle.[32] Rundle complained that the key Wittgensteinian virtue was being *attentive,* and that when we are attentive, Rundle

---

[32] Bede Rundle, *Wittgenstein and Contemporary Philosophy of Language* (Oxford: Wiley-Blackwell, 1990).

considered, we can often find more binding conceptual commonalities than sheer family-resemblance delivers.

The advantage of the rigid designation approach is that it seems to identify a common enough task and aspiration, whilst being infinitely open to the different substantive contents given to the concept of the divine. If there is to be an adequate version of the rigid designation formulation it will need to aim for something between totalizing control and sheer equivocation. Also, it need not cover every single use of the term/concept ever made: even the successful designation 'water is H_2O' does not do that. There are stray and non-standard uses of the concept of water ('the water of life' is a strong and illegal home-made spirit in the Republic of Ireland), and so there will be with the concept of God/the divine. One tries to find, somehow, a rich vein, which helps to bring us to the heart of the matter. Perhaps it helps to think of the task as being the heuristic one of using the notion of rigid designation as a lens (where there can be more than one legitimate lens), rather than as an exploration of an 'essence', which seems particularly inappropriate thing to look for, perhaps, when talking about 'the divine'. This is compatible with the epistemically humble intention, stated in the previous chapter, to undertake a sort of grammatical investigation into the use of the concept of the divine, rather than attempting to say something directly about 'the divine'.

In this spirit, therefore, I offer a constructive suggestion about *one possible way* of filling in the content of *x,y,z,* with a suggestion about two possible advantages this way of looking might provide for us.

The following, then, is (like Nussbaum's effort with virtues) a multi-claused attempt to describe one of the possible conceptual roles played by God/the divine, within a wider life, in a way that is capable of moving in very different substantive directions. It is not dependent upon originary baptisms, experiences, or causal chains, but carves out an informationally rich conceptual role within a language:

> God/the divine is that, whatever it is, which
> when we relate to it appropriately,
> promises the optimal attitude,
> which attitude offers consolation, hope, peace, courage, acceptance, humility, obedience, or promise,
> in relation to limits, tensions, conflicts, fragmentation, and disintegration,
> which are irreducible, non-negotiable, and problematic in our lives.

I will spend a bit of time unpacking the different parts of this suggestion. The formulation is open to exploring a range of relevant to limits, tensions, conflicts, fragmentation, and disintegration. By 'relevant', I mean, as said before 'likely to raise the question of whether or not to talk about God and the divine'. The final line is intended to unpack what might constitute such relevance. In order even to provoke an attraction, or resistance, to talking about the divine, a limit would need to be not only irreducible and non-negotiable (we cannot simply make the issue disappear through conceptual analysis, for example), but also problematic in our lives.

That there is a multiplicity of terms surrounding the 'optimal attitude' ('consolation, hope, peace, courage, acceptance, humility, obedience, or promise') is intended to offer alternative routes in a common terrain, which is apt, given the breadth and diversity of the work done by the concept of divinity. There are different ways of engaging with limits, from (Stoic) resignation, which I would read as a type of consolation and peace, to transformative hope, to a sort of courage and obedience, perhaps called for in some more fiery Calvinist visions.

One way of construing the chapters that follow, is in terms of offering various attempts to fill out the placeholder concept of 'whatever it is' that 'offers consolation, hope, peace, or promise, in relation to different types of limit, tension, conflict, fragmentation, and disintegration, which are irreducible, non-negotiable, and problematic in our lives'.

All the approaches that are discussed in this book fit, in some way, and to some degree, the formulation set out above. As commented in the opening chapter, I focus in this book on approaches that engage in some way with the distinction between the subjective and objective perspectives upon ourselves. This is the type of limit and tension explored here.

Possible advantages

In relation to the issues raised in philosophy of language, I think that the suggestion here meets the criteria of avoiding those things that are not helpful (originary baptisms and causal chains), and of approaching instead the information-rich conceptual role being played, where concepts get their meaning within contexts of use, within an environment. Perhaps the greatest benefit brought by the rigid designation framework is that it channels our attention onto the *role* of the concept within different embodied thought worlds, rather than attempting to codify and compare various theoretical or descriptive accounts of the nature of God and divinity.

The suggested formulation also addresses some of the concerns raised around Soskice's approach: that by routing the reference of the rigid designator 'God' so closely to Christian practices and traditions, Soskice was unable to account for either co-referentiality, or to give an adequate account of usages of the notion of the divine, such as we find in pantheism, Absolute Idealism, Spinozism, panpsychism, Stoicism and modern paganism, for example. The advantage of the formulation I offer here is that it says very little about how the concept of the divine is given substance: about how this reaching out to engage with the limits in our life is achieved, or, about the specific commitments or beliefs involved, with various underpinning metaphysics or ethics, and with different associated traditional affiliations.

52 NEGATIVE NATURAL THEOLOGY

The suggested formulation seems also to be applicable to polytheistic accounts, belief systems, and practice. A divinity that relates to one particular area of our life—either regionally or in terms of an area of concern, such as war, or healing, or motherhood—may offer something like this overcoming of tensions and fragmentations with respect to this area. But, if an approach is genuinely polytheistic, the substantive commitment this reflects might be that there is no overall and unifying hope, or consolation, that all these aspects of our lives will be drawn together into a whole. This may be received as reflecting a tragic account of reality, of a universe in violent tension, or, it may not: perhaps hope comes in more fragmentary, realist, and chaotic forms? Something like this finds some confirmation in the anthropological work done by Tanya Luhrmann on English witchcraft in the 1980s, and in the intellectual defence of contemporary polytheistic spiritualities provided by Ronald Hutton, both of which are explored in Chapter 5.[33]

An adequate account of the role(s) played by the concept of God in ordinary language needs to illuminate and resonate with the use of the concept in the utterances and practices of believers. But, the concept of God is also denied, avoided, doubted, and refuted, and a satisfactory account of the role of the concept will need to be able to resonate with these usages also. We might separate out here three different types of dissent and demurral:

(i) Where there are grey areas, and disagreements about whether a particular conception of something ought to be regarded as 'divine'.
(ii) Where there is an ambivalent reticence about employing the concept of the divine.
(iii) Where there is principled refusal to employ the concept of the divine.

The use of rigid designation as a tool would seem to offer something in each area.

Grey areas

Perhaps one person is inclined to call x divine, but another is not, maybe because she does not think that this particular x provides any sort of optimal or hopeful attitude towards the incommensurabilities in our lives. Sometimes, people claim to believe in God, or the divine, but other people say that they do not, even to the point of calling them atheists. Einstein, in places, is willing to call a traditional Christian believer superstitious, rather than religious. Why? Well, we might say, because he considers that the anthropomorphic projection (as he construes it)

---

[33] Tanya Lurhmann, *Persuasions of the Witch's Craft* (Cambridge, MA Harvard University Press, 1989); Ronald Hutton, *The Triumph of the Moon: A History of Modern Pagan Witchcraft* (Oxford: Oxford University Press, 1999), esp. ch. 20.

THE EXISTENCE OF THE WORD GOD   53

could not fit the formulation for the rigid designation of divinity: he does not consider that this would be in any sense a satisfactory resting place for us in relation to 'limits, tensions, conflicts, fragmentation, and disintegration' that we face.

Another example would be the systematic Christian theologian, immersed in premodern traditions of thought, richly suffused with Thomism. It has been known for such a theologian to look at what they consider to be the anthropomorphic construction (or so they find it) of some analytical philosophy of religion, and to find that whatever is posited there, is not, in any case *God*. Why? Again, I submit, in part because it does not provide an adequate resting place, the 'optimal attitude', which attitude is to some degree consoling and hopeful, towards the irreducible limits in our lives. Certainly, such a Christian believer would not find the Einsteinian conception of the divine to be an adequate candidate for the rigid designator, although such a believer has a range of theological attitudes available to her to such views, from the appreciative, to the derogatory.

Ambivalence and reticence

The formulation may also enable us to reflect on another interesting type of case, where something like the same conceptual space is pointed towards, but where the language of divinity/God is *not* used. We can imagine the same formulation, but with the word 'the divine/God' removed:

> XXXX is that, whatever it is, which when we relate to it appropriately, promises the optimal attitude, which attitude offers consolation, hope, peace, courage, acceptance, humility, obedience, or promise, in relation to limits, tensions, conflicts, fragmentation, and disintegration, which are irreducible, non-negotiable, and problematic in our lives.

As we have already seen, some of the most interesting recent philosophy leans precisely into this space, where philosophers are at pains to distance their approaches from religion, and concepts of the sacred, the divine, or God. In ways that will be explored in the next two chapters, this way of thinking about the concept of God can also give us more textured ways of characterizing a refusal to speak about God.

Working with this notion of rigid designation, we are able to pose a more precise question than simply wondering if there is 'something divine' about any philosophical approaches. We can ask: given that the role and function of a conceptual space has so many similarities with what the concept of divinity rigidly designates, what is at stake in calling it 'divine' or not? Are we suffering from an impoverished category of 'divinity', which means that people assume that any notion of the divine involves a 'supernatural being', a divine Nobodaddy? Or, does the translation work more corrosively in the other direction? The philosopher who styles herself as 'secular' can reply: 'yes, this is the important work that the concept of the divine did previously, but now we can do this work without this problematic concept'.

Refusal

There are several different ways of insisting that there is nothing to which such a rigid designation rule refers. We might deflate the issue in a Wittgensteinian way, and insist that no 'optimal attitude' to 'limits, tensions and fragmentations' is required or appropriate. The idea that there is some sort of 'problem' here, like the search for the 'meaning of life', is an understandable intellectual neurosis, which needs therapy and dispersion, rather than solutions. Or, an optimistic humanist (see Chapter 4) might insist that the tensions and limits are not so trenchant and final, and can be overcome by seeking objective truth, which uncovers the 'magic of reality'. Alternatively, we might accept the seriousness of our condition, but think that there is no peace, consolation, or hope, but only the possibility of defiant rebellion and courage, in the face of an 'absurd' situation (see the discussion of Albert Camus in Chapter 3). Possibly, in the end, even this might not help, and we need to accept simply, merely, that 'in the end truth, perhaps, is sad'.[34]

Concluding reflections

We began this discussion with some of Rahner's reflections on the mere existence of the word 'God', which we took up as an invitation to explore the role of the word 'God' or 'the divine' in natural language. By exploring the category of natural kinds, which refer through a type of rigid designation, we have looked at the conceptual role of the concept of God within natural language. One way of thinking about the concept of God, I suggested, is that it points to that, whatever it is, which engages hopefully and consolingly with limits in our lives. This is compatible with the fact that the concept of 'God' or the 'divine' are given many different substantive contents, many of which are contradictory with each other.

Rahner himself would seem to give some succour to this way of looking at the role of the word 'God', although, of course, he does not use the vocabulary of 'rigid designation'. Rahner describes an orientation to 'absolute mystery' as arising because of the 'distinction' and 'unity' between an objective and subjective perspective upon ourselves ('objective consciousness and subjective consciousness').[35] As I will explore further in the next chapter, he is even prepared to say that 'when we

---

[34] Paul Claudel, in a letter to Jacques Rivière, 24 October 1907, quoted in Josef Pieper, *Happiness and Contemplation*, trans. Richard and Clara Winston (South Bend, IN: St Augustine's Press, 1979), 31.
[35] Rahner, *Foundations*, 52.

THE EXISTENCE OF THE WORD GOD   55

use the term "God"', in certain contexts, we 'do not know what this term means *from any other source except through this orientation to mystery*'.[36] There is a sort of 'pointing' gesture here, rather as with rigid designation: the word 'God' is simply and only the name for this orientation towards the relationship between the subjective and objective perspectives.

'This word' (God), Rahner writes, 'is so very much without contour', and because of this, is 'obviously quite appropriate for what it refers to, regardless of whether the word may have originally been so "faceless" or not'.[37] There may then be further attempts to speak 'explicit language' about God, but 'in order to remain true', Rahner writes, 'all metaphysical ontology about God must return again and again to its source, must return to the transcendental experience of our orientation towards the absolute mystery'.[38]

In some ways, this way of looking at things has an eirenic and inclusive dimension: it can motivate all sorts of invocations of the divine. On the other hand, it may simply inflame annoyance and mutual antagonism: '*that* cannot possibly fulfil the role of God', one says to the other. It may inculcate greater respect and curiosity amongst thinkers who style themselves as secular, to see the range of things, in the world and beyond it, that have been evoked by the concept of the divine; or, it may deepen contempt, to see the disorder in the house when we consider the range of things that have been construed as playing the role. It may bring us, at least, to where some of the real difficulty and source of perplexity lies, in a way that, again, Rahner points to.

Rahner reflects on the tension between the breadth of horizon opened up by thinking of all that the word 'God' does, and in relation to particular traditional claims about God:

> As it is practiced in the concrete, religion always and inevitably seems to say: 'God is here and not there', or 'This is in accordance with his will and not that', or 'He has revealed himself here and not there'. As practiced in the concrete, religion seems neither willing nor able to avoid making God a categorical object.[39]

Rahner describes this as 'the basic difficulty for all of us today':

> It strikes us only too easily as an irreligious indiscretion, almost as bad taste vis-à-vis this silent and religious reverence before the absolute mystery when we not only talk about the ineffable, but when beyond that we point our finger as it were at this or that particular things among the usual pieties within the world of our

---

[36] Ibid.
[37] Ibid., 46.
[38] Ibid.
[39] Ibid., 82.

experience and say: there is God. It is obvious that the historical, revealed religion which Christianity is experiences its most fundamental and universal threat from this difficulty.[40]

But then, on the other hand, when religion 'does avoid this' seemingly arbitrary pointing, it seems 'to evaporate into a mist which perhaps does exist, but in practice it cannot be the source of religious life'. Even the 'atheist who is troubled and terrified by the agonizing nothingness of his existence' is able to 'be religious in the sense that we reverence the ineffable in silence, knowing that there is such a thing'. But is such religiosity worth the name? Is something that is everywhere, anywhere in particular?

Rahner dwells on the difficulty of standing between the bad taste of pointing to one piety amongst others, on the one hand, and evaporating into mist in the other. 'To do justice to this difficulty', Rahner concludes, 'we must proceed carefully and in several steps'.[41]

Perhaps employing the tool of rigid designation may us to avoid 'bad taste' and superstition, without evaporating into the mist. We take some first steps, in any case, in the next chapter.

[40] Ibid., 82–83.
[41] Ibid., 83.

3
Absurd and Holy Mystery
Karl Rahner and Albert Camus

In relation to the 'cosmic question', of 'how to live in harmony with the universe and not just in it?', Nagel's least committed possible response goes as follows:

> This may lead us to a sort of counterfactual theism (if there were a God, the question would have an answer), or to despair, or to a sense of the absurdity of life.

This chapter is concerned with this sense of the absurd. What is involved in feeling that life is absurd? And, if life is absurd, would the 'existence of God' help, and, if so, why and how?

The remaining chapters in this book consider different attempts to embrace, or resist, the concept of God/the divine, in relation to the various tensions between perspectives, as set out in the first two chapters. Clearly, some attempts to engage with the confrontation of perspectives will be more religious than others. In this chapter, I want to investigate the issue even before we have got to the level of offering 'resolutions', or 'responses'. My focus here is at a stage before we have even begun to look at attempts to 'resolve', or 'overcome' or 'move beyond'—resignedly or hopefully—the sense of alienation or tension between the subjective and objective perspectives. It concerns the way in which one attends simply to the problem itself, regardless of, and prior to, attempting, if we do, any sort of resolution.

I begin by showing that there are significant common features to Albert Camus' notion of the state of rebellion in relation to the absurd, and Karl Rahner's notion of the pre-apprehension of holy mystery.[1] I identify three similarities. First of all,

---

[1] Theological interest in Camus seems to have declined somewhat, after a high point of interest in the 1950s and 1960s. Significant treatments from this time include Thomas L. Hanna, 'Albert Camus and the Christian Faith', 36/4 (1956), 224–233; Henri Peyre, 'Albert Camus: An Anti-Christian Moralist', *Proceedings of the American Philosophical Society*, 102/5 (1958), 477–482, and 'Camus the Pagan', *Yale French Studies*, 25 (1960), 20–25; Charles Mueller, 'Albert Camus: the Question of Hope', *Cross Currents*, 8/2 (1958), 172–184; Nathan A. Scott, 'The Modest Optimism of Albert Camus', *The Christian Scholar*, 42/4 (1959), 251–274; John Loose, 'The Christian as Camus's Absurd Man', *The Journal of Religion*, 42/3 (1962), 203–214; and M.M. Madison, 'Albert Camus: Philosopher of Limits', *Modern Fiction Studies*, 10/3 (1964), 223–231. Notable more recent theological treatments of Camus include Sean Illing, 'Between Nihilism and Transcendence: Camus's Dialogue with Dostoevsky', in *The Review of Politics*, 77/2 (2015), 217–242, and David Newheiser, *Hope in a Secular Age: Deconstruction, Negative Theology and the Future of Faith* (Cambridge: Cambridge University Press, 2019). These commentators follow a number of routes. One predominant line is to read Camus as a (perhaps unknowing)

Negative Natural Theology. Christopher J. Insole, Oxford University Press. © Christopher J. Insole 2024.
DOI: 10.1093/9780198933007.003.0004

58   NEGATIVE NATURAL THEOLOGY

both Rahner's pre-apprehension and Camus's rebellion arise from the collision between the subjective and objective perspectives upon ourselves. At the heart of this
is a conception of freedom. Secondly, both the pre-apprehension and rebellion are
marked by what I call an 'irreconcilable completeness' (which is explained further
down). Thirdly, both the pre-apprehension and the state of rebellion are universally accessible, but not pervasively chosen: each needs to be continually chosen
and renewed, if we are not to sink into a state of forgetting.

I then turn to important differences between Rahner and Camus, in relation
to the confrontation between the subjective and objective perspectives. When
doing this, two of the themes that run throughout the book surface promin-
ently: humility and freedom. The nub of the difference between the two thinkers
is this: that where Rahner calls the irreducible confrontation 'holy', Camus calls
it 'absurd'. There is, I will suggest, a 'freedom of naming': holy, or, absurd. Rahner
embodies an attitude of worship, and Camus of vigilant rebellion. The comparison of two thinkers, looking for similarities and differences, can be, in itself,
a relatively futile and superficial exercise. This is not, at least, my aim. My aim,
which I bring to completion in the final part of the chapter, is to explore what
is at stake, theologically and philosophically, in the choice of how to name—or,
how to describe—the mystery that both point to, and which, I venture, is pervasively recognizable and salient to many people. I draw out some lessons about the
freedom of belief, and the humility and limitations of different types of thinking,
specifically, those types of thinking that tend to be characterized as being cases
of 'reason' or 'philosophy'. I have done this, here, through an engagement with
Camus and Rahner, but, of course, other representative thinkers could have been
chosen.

This chapter focuses on Camus' wrestling with the problem of the absurd,
with a particular focus on *The Myth of Sisyphus,* although also drawing on his
play *Caligula,* the novels *The Stranger* and *The Fall,* and a few other essays and
letters. In his later writing, Camus leans into a more divinely suggestive space,

---

fellow traveller with theologians, in that Camus exposes some idolatrous elements in Christianity as
practiced, which should be eliminated in the interests of renewing Christian theology: Loose focuses
on theodicy and over-anthropomorphic conceptions of God, and belief in an afterlife. Other commentators are more critical of Camus' understanding of Christian theology: Scott worries about Camus' 'in-
accurate firing' at an over-personal conception of God ('The Modest Optimism of Albert Camus', 252).
Another approach is to find elements of hope in Camus' philosophy: Moeller draws out Camus' appreciation of 'solar happiness' ('Albert Camus: the Question of Hope', 175), 'cities of sun' (177), and 'sunlit
beaches' (177); Scott also reflects on Camus' devotion to 'an inexhaustible sun' ('The Modest Optimism
of Albert Camus', 272) and the 'invincible summer' (272), which Scott aligns to Paul Tillich's 'absolute
faith' (272) in 'the power of being' (273), an 'at-one-ment with Being itself' (273). None of these treatments place Camus into conversation with Rahner, or align the concept of the absurd with Rahner's
notion of 'mystery'. In my focus on the relationship between the subjective and objective perspectives in
Rahner's thought, I find affinities between my approach and that set out by Thomas Sheehan, 'Rahner's
transcendental project', *The Cambridge Companion to Karl Rahner,* ed. Declan Marmion and Mary
E. Hines (Cambridge: Cambridge University Press, 2005), 29–42.

with some Neo-Stoic overtones.[2] This later orientation of Camus' is not my focus here.

Mystery

There are three shared features which can be identified in Camus' state of rebellion and in Rahner's pre-apprehension of holy mystery. I will summarize these features below, before setting them out in more detail:

- Self, world, and freedom. Both Rahner's pre-apprehension and Camus' rebellion arise from the tension and fragmentation between the subjective and objective perspectives. At the heart of this is a conception of freedom.
- Irreconcilable completeness. Both the pre-apprehension and rebellion are marked by what I call an 'irreconcilable completeness' (which I will explain).
- Universally accessible but not chosen. Both the pre-apprehension and the state of rebellion are universally accessible, but not pervasively chosen: each needs to be continually chosen and renewed, if we are not to sink into a state of forgetting.

Self, nature/world, and freedom

The pre-apprehension of holy mystery, and the state of rebellion, both arise from the collision between the subjective and objective perspectives, or, from the encounter between the self-as-agent and the self-as-object in the wider 'world' or within 'nature'. At the heart of this is a conception of freedom. I want to draw out here a strand that will do more work for us: the two-fold freedom of practical

---

[2] Some commentators describe a 'shift' here. So, for example, David Carroll claims that Camus comes to 'abandon Sisyphus and the Absurd', in 'Rethinking the Absurd: *Le Mythe de Sisyphe*', in *The Cambridge Companion to Camus*, ed. Edward J. Hughes (Cambridge: Cambridge University Press, 2007), 53–66, 66. Although I am not preoccupied here with Camus exegesis, it might be more apt to say that the absurd remains in Camus' thought as a constant reference point, and resource for thinking and living, which is not an endpoint, or a doctrine. This is suggested by Camus himself, in interviews given in 1946 and 1951: *Three Interviews*, in Albert Camus, *Lyrical and Critical Essays*, ed. Philip Thody, trans. Ellen Conroy Kennedy (Random House, New York: Vintage Books, 1970), 345–365. Camus comments that 'accepting the absurdity of everything around us is one step, a necessary experience: it should not become a dead end' (346). 'It arouses a revolt that can become fruitful', such that it 'could help us to discover ideas capable of restoring a relative meaning to existence, although a meaning that would always be in danger' (346). Later on in the same interview, Camus says that 'when I analyzed the feeling of the Absurd in *The Myth of Sisyphus*, I was looking for a method and not a doctrine. I was practicing methodical doubt. I was trying to make a "*tabula rasa*", on the basis of which it would then be possible to construct something' (356). There is a suggestive parallel here with Rahner's sense of mystery, where it is also the case that Rahner goes beyond this spare generative encounter, in order to 'construct something'.

60 NEGATIVE NATURAL THEOLOGY

reason, where *practical* reason is occupied with the question of 'how should one live?'.

The first dimension of this freedom becomes visible, when we consider a central way in which practical reason is distinct from theoretical reason. Theoretical reason does not typically have a choice as to whether or not to accept, say, Euclid's laws about the properties of the triangle. Although we can choose whether or not to study geometry, once this choice has been made, the discoveries of theoretical knowledge tend not to give much room for freedom of choice.

With practical reason, though, there is an irreducible moment of freedom, of commitment. There is the choice of a way of life, and an attitude towards the good. This choice can be explicit and discrete, a moment of epiphany, or resolution, or, more commonly, it can be piecemeal and rather haphazard, only brought to consciousness at certain points in a life. Such a choice might be expressed by a commitment to a philosophical way of life—as Pierre Hadot shows with Stoicism, Epicureanism, or Platonism—but often, it will be expressed more obliquely, by implicit consent to, or dissent from, certain practices and institutions: marriage, for example, or democracy, or the ethos of a school or university department.

We might talk of 'freedom' here independently of global metaphysical debates about what, precisely, *freedom* is, or whether we enjoy, say, non-determined freedom, given what we know (or think we know) about neurophysiology, or the cultural and social construction of human beings. All that is needed is a preparedness to use the notion of freedom in some sort of way. And everyone is, in the end, whatever they say about it in philosophy seminars. The internal phenomenology of agency is just too strong and all-consuming to allow us to do otherwise. All of this is well said by Camus, in his pithy comment: 'I have nothing to do with the problem of metaphysical liberty. Knowing whether or not man is free doesn't interest me. I can experience only my own freedom'.[3]

For Camus, the sense of absurdity arises from the possibility we have, as self-conscious and free, of regarding ourselves both from a subjective and an objective point of view. What is absurd then, is neither nature in itself, nor the self, but the encounter of the self and nature. As Camus puts it, 'if I were a tree among trees, a cat among animals':

> This life would have a meaning or rather this problem would not arise, for I should belong to this world. I should *be* this world to which I am now opposed by my whole consciousness and my whole insistence to all creation.[4]

It is the co-presence of the human self and nature that generates absurdity: 'the Absurd is not in [the human] ... nor in the world, but in their presence together'[5]:

---

[3] Albert Camus, *The Myth of Sisyphus,* trans. Justin O'Brien (London: Penguin Books, 2000), 42.
[4] Camus, *The Myth of Sisyphus,* 38–39.
[5] Ibid., 24.

ABSURD AND HOLY MYSTERY 61

What is absurd is the confrontation of the irrational and the wild longing for clarity whose call echoes in the human heart. The absurd depends as much on [the human] as on the world.[6]

The absurd is born of this confrontation between the human need and the unreasonable silence of the world.[7]

The sense of disunity emerges as the strangeness and 'density' of the world becomes manifest to us. Throughout Camus' writings, there is an evocation of our attraction to nature, as well as a sense of repulsion. 'Strangeness creeps in', Camus writes, in our 'perceiving that the world is "dense", sensing to what degree a stone is foreign and irreducible to us, with what intensity nature or a landscape can negate us':

At the heart of all beauty lies something inhuman, and these hills, the softness of the sky, the outline of these trees at this very minute lose the illusory meaning with which we had clothed them, henceforth more remote than a lost paradise ... The world evades us because it becomes itself again. That stage-scenery masked by habit becomes again what it is. It withdraws at a distance from us ... Just one thing: that denseness and that strangeness of the world is the absurd.[8]

The next move I make is a particularly important pivot in my thinking about Camus and Rahner: something recognizably similar to this (metaphysically low-ramification) 'freedom' has been called other names, such as, for example, 'spirit', the 'infinite', and, in particular, 'transcendence'. The concept of transcendence comes from the Latin *transcendere*, which means to 'go beyond'. Transcendence can enter our thinking not as a possession and foundation, but as a constant leaning into that which is beyond, into an unknowing, a freedom, a reaching past that which is now the horizon of our finitude. Such transcendence requires both a subject, and a world within which the subject is thrown: there needs to be a finitude that the subject reaches beyond. Not to be a 'tree amongst trees' is to go beyond, and to participate in an event of going beyond, of 'transcending', or 'transcendence'. 'Transcendence' here is the name of freedom. So, we do not have a subject, and wonder if it is involved in 'transcendence'. Rather, to be a subject, and not an object, an agent and not an object of observation, just is to be able 'to go beyond': to speak the next word, to think, or resist, the next thought, to act or desist from acting. Camus himself uses the language of transcendence:

I am thus justified in saying that the feeling of absurdity does not spring from the mere scrutiny of a fact or an impression but that it bursts from the comparison

[6] Ibid., 17.
[7] Ibid., 22.
[8] Ibid., 12–13.

between a bare fact and a certain reality, between an action and the world that transcends it.[9]

Rahner's notion of 'transcendence' parallels Camus' sense of the absurd. For Camus, the sense of the absurd requires both self and world, the 'wild longing for clarity' meeting the 'unreasonable silence of the world'.

Rahner describes the orientation to 'absolute mystery' as arising because of the 'distinction' and 'unity' in 'objective consciousness and subjective consciousness', or in 'willed will and willing will'.[10] This latter distinction, 'willed will', and 'willing will', maps onto the distinction drawn out by Bilgrami, between conceiving the self as an object of observation and prediction, and the self as an engaged agent.

To become aware of oneself as an engaged agent, as subjective consciousness, Rahner writes, requires that one 'becomes conscious of himself as the product of what is radically foreign to him':

> This element, namely, that man also *knows* about his radical origins in these causes, is not explained by these origins.[11]

We might recall here Camus' reflection that the sense of absurd arises from the encounter between the world and the self, where the 'world evades us', that it goes beyond us, transcends us, 'because it becomes itself again',[12] and where the human spirit seeks to transcend this evasion of the world in her 'wild longing for clarity'.[13] It is Rahner, not Camus, who writes that the person who 'has the experience of emptiness, or inner fragility', has the experience of the 'absurdity of what confronts him',[14] but in this experience finds a 'movement towards liberating freedom, and the responsibility which imposes upon him real burdens and also blesses them'.[15] This freedom and responsibility can be re-described, without further metaphysical commitment, as 'an ever-present knowledge of the infinity of reality'.[16] This 'infinity' arises simply because of the possibility of questioning, of the self and the world:

> In the fact that he affirms the possibility of a merely *finite* horizon of questioning, this possibility is already surpassed, and man shows himself to be a being with an *infinite* horizon.[17]

---

[9] Ibid., 24.
[10] Ibid., 52.
[11] Ibid., 29.
[12] Ibid., 12–13.
[13] Ibid., 17.
[14] Ibid., 33.
[15] Ibid.
[16] Ibid.
[17] Ibid., 32.

The sophisticated computer working through an algorithm may have a vast horizon, but it will be finite—determined by the task, albeit in all its complexity and quantity. But, when we face the creature who can be burdened with the futility of all tasks, all complexity, and all quantities: then we encounter a subject not bound by what is in front of it, who does not have only a finite (a determined and measured) horizon. We know this without metaphysics, and without physics.

Rahner's sense of absolute mystery, like Camus' sense of the absurd, needs an encounter between the self and the world. Both Camus and Rahner, in different ways, explore how different types of 'suicide' (literal and philosophical) evade this encounter. The sense of the absurd arises from a seemingly irreconcilable tension between the subjective and objective perspectives upon human life. One way to do away with a tension, or a conflict, between two sides or perspectives, is to abandon, or render harmless, one of the perspectives. And that, for Camus, is effectively what suicide aspires to.

In the case of literal physical suicide, the subject removes the problem of the absurd, by removing, as far as he or she is concerned, the subjective, engaged and interior perspective altogether. The opening line of the *Myth of Sisyphus* engages precisely with this possibility:

> There is but one truly serious philosophical problem and that is suicide. Judging whether life is or is not worth living amounts to answering the fundamental question of philosophy. All the rest—whether or not the world has three dimensions, whether the mind has nine or twelve categories—comes afterwards. These are games; one must first answer.[18]

The absurd arises become of the joint co-presence of the human self and the world. If we eliminate the self, we also destroy the Absurd. 'Negating one of the terms of the opposition on which he lives amounts to escaping it', writes Camus. 'Living is keeping the absurd alive', whilst to 'abolish conscious revolt', with death, is 'to elude the problem'.[19]

Observing the influence of Dostoyevsky on Camus, Sean Illing notes parallel reflections from Dostoevsky and Camus on the 'logic of suicide'.[20] First of all, Dostoyevsky:

> I condemn this Nature, which so brazenly and unceremoniously inflicted this suffering, to annihilation along with me . . . Since I am unable to destroy Nature, I am destroying only myself, solely out of the weariness of enduring a tyranny in which there is no guilty party.[21]

[18] Ibid., 5.

[19] Ibid., 40.

[20] Sean Illing, 'Between Nihilism and Transcendence: Camus's Dialogue with Dostoevsky', 222–223.

[21] Madison, 'Albert Camus: Philosopher of Limits', 226.

64   NEGATIVE NATURAL THEOLOGY

And, then, Camus:

> Living, naturally, is never easy. You continue making the gestures commanded by existence for many reasons, the first of which is habit. Dying voluntarily implies that you have recognized, even instinctively, the ridiculous character of that habit, the absence of any profound reason for living, the insane character of that daily agitation and the uselessness of suffering.[22]

One strand of the 'response' that Camus offers to suicide is to point out that it constitutes a 'solution' (if that it be) only for the individual, leaving the problem of the Absurd for others. As the commentator Madison puts it, 'killing oneself' destroys 'the Absurd for that individual only':

> The Absurd will continue as long as there are men. Suicide then merely escapes the problem; it does not solve it.[23]

If the 'individualism', the lack of collective thinking, is really thought to be the problem with suicide, rather than, say, there being something intrinsically wrong with self-destruction, then there are wild and murderous ways of escaping individuality. Such a collective option is modelled in Camus' description of Caligula, who after the death of his beloved Drusilla feels the emotional force of an encounter with the Absurd, not only 'grief', as the commentator Scotts puts it, but 'rage and anger and indignation',[24] encapsulated in the terse statement:

> Men die; and they are not happy.[25]

Caligula's murderous and arbitrary rampage can be understood as a type of unilaterally made but collectively enforced suicide pact, decided upon by him on behalf of a non-consenting humanity. As Scott puts it, Caligula becomes 'a kind of missionary in behalf of absurdism, deciding that the service he shall render Rome will be that of making known the metaphysical anarchy that dominates existence'.[26] Caligula announces that 'the world has no importance; once a man realizes that, he wins his freedom', and choose to wear 'the foolish, unintelligible face of a professional god',[27] and, as Scott puts it, 'arranges a drama that is intended to be a terrifying simulacrum of the unconscionable arbitrariness of fate itself'.[28] Through

---

[22] Camus, *The Myth of Sisyphus*, 7.

[23] Fyodor Dostoevsky, *A Writer's Diary, Volume 1: 1873–1876*, trans. Kenneth Lantz (London: Quartet Books, 1994), 656.

[24] Scott, 'The Modest Optimism of Albert Camus', 260.

[25] Albert Camus, 'Caligula', in *Caligula and Other Plays*, trans. Stuart Gilbert (London and New York: Penguin Books, 2013), 1–62, 7.

[26] Scott, 'The Modest Optimism of Albert Camus', 260.

[27] Camus, 'Caligula', 12, 38–39.

[28] Scott, 'The Modest Optimism of Albert Camus', 260.

this 'campaign against creation' Caligula hopes to 'give men access to the real facts of their condition in this world'.[29]

In his 'Letter to a German Friend' (July 1944) Camus brings this analysis to bear on the take over of Germany by the National Socialists. 'Tired of fighting heaven', Camus writes to his 'friend', 'you gave up the lucid view and considered it more convenient [. . .] for another to do your thinking for you and for millions of Germans'. This entailed the 'exhausting adventure in which you had to mutilate souls and destroy the world'; 'you saw the injustice of our condition to the point of being willing to add to it', and 'you turned despair into intoxification':

In short, you chose injustice and sided with the gods.[30]

Rahner has a version of the question of suicide posed by Camus. As we saw, suicide, for Camus, involves 'negating one of the terms of the opposition'[31] involved in the state of the absurd. When the self is annihilated, as with suicide, 'everything is over'.[32] Suicide 'settles the absurd'; it is 'living' that keeps the 'absurd alive'.[33] Rahner's suicide is a more technical one, where the person 'discovers either to his horror or to his relief that he can shift responsibility from himself for all the individual data that make up his reality':

[He] can place the burden for what he is on what is not him. He discovers that he has come to be through what is other than himself.[34]

'All particular anthropologies', Rahner writes, attempt to do away with the self, by explaining it 'after the model of a self-regulating multiple system'.[35] Rahner's way of refuting such suicide is different from Camus'. Rahner exposes a type of contradiction, performed by the self-negating person, who claims to have no freedom or responsibility. Let a person try to 'explain himself away':

Even when man would want to shift all responsibility for himself away from himself as someone totally determined from without, and thus would want to explain himself away, *he* is the one who does this and does it knowingly and willingly. *He* is the one who encompasses the sum of all the possible elements of such an

---

[29] Ibid., 260–261.

[30] Camus, 'Letters to a German Friend: Fourth Letter', in *Resistance, Rebellion, and Death,* trans. Justin O'Brien (New York: Random House, 1960), 3–25, 21–22.

[31] Camus, *The Myth of Sisyphus,* 40.

[32] Ibid., 41.

[33] Ibid., 40–41.

[34] Karl Rahner, *Foundations of Christian Faith: An Introduction to the Idea of Christianity,* trans. William V. Dych (New York: Crossroad, 2016), 27.

[35] Ibid., 31.

66 NEGATIVE NATURAL THEOLOGY

explanation, and thus *he* is the one who shows himself to be something other than the subsequent product of such individual elements.[36]

So, 'even when a person would abandon himself into the hands of the empirical anthropologies':

[H]e still remains in his own hands. He does not escape from his freedom, and the only question can be how he interprets himself, and freely interprets himself.[37]

[H]uman action is condemned to mediacy, thrown ineluctably into relatedness, but without the actor ever losing the ability to see and say 'I' and 'myself'. Even the attempt to deny the self-other bivalence ends up replicating it.[38]

Irreconcilable completeness

Both Camus' state of rebellion and Rahner's apprehension of absolute mystery have what I am calling an 'irreconcilable completeness' to them. In the state of rebellion, there is a clear-eyed acknowledgement that *both* the exterior and internal perspectives upon our lives cannot be reconciled, and must both be held to attentively. It is 'irreconcilable', insofar as we are unable to reconcile, harmonize, tessellate, or overcome the tension of these perspectives. It is a type of 'completeness', insofar as we do not turn our attention away from either the subjective or objective perspective.

One aspect of the irreconcilability of the tension is that there is no higher or transcendent resolution: 'I continue to believe that this world has no higher meaning', Camus writes. Camus then immediately follows up in a way that affirms the element of 'completeness', the inability to remove either the objective or subjective perspective:

I know that something in it has meaning and that is [the human], because he is the only being to insist upon it.[39]

The sense that there is a tension at all, the irreconcilability, is parasitic upon an always frustrated desire for completeness. As the commentator Madison puts it:

[I]f the Absurd continues, so must the tension it creates. Nature will forever be man's dire antagonist. Rebellion, then, is the ethical key to authenticity, for the

---

[36] Ibid.
[37] Ibid., 39.
[38] Ibid., 30.
[39] Camus, 'Letters to a German Friend: Fourth Letter', 22.

human being must resist his environment to maintain his identity. In the words of Camus, 'In order to exist, man must rebel'.[40]

This language of nature being a 'dire antagonist' is notable. In Chapter 1, I commented that a focus on the tension between the subjective and objective perspectives maps particularly well onto certain types of worldview: teleological and free subjects trapped within a deterministic world, for example. In *The Myth of Sisyphus,* there is a hostile and alienated patina to Camus' references to 'nature' and the 'world', the self as seen from the objective perspective. This could be challenged, or transformed, if we understand the non-human world as in some sense suffused with value, or as making some sort of demand or call on us, or as being less alien to us. Pantheism, paganism, and panpsychism all offer something along these lines. Camus himself, in his later writings, leans into a more enchanted and value-laden space, in his wistful, yet grateful, evocations of sun-blanched beaches and empty Mediterranean squares at noon. Here, it is simply worth noting that the characterization of our 'problem' is itself philosophically committed in contestable ways.

Rahner describes something of the irreconcilable completeness when talking about the person experiencing 'himself as being at the disposal of other things, a disposal over which he has no control'. The 'mystery' of our transcending self in the world is one that 'constantly reveals itself and at the same time conceals itself'. The self and world relationship is 'grounded' elsewhere than in the subject itself:

> By its very nature subjectivity is always a transcendence which listens, which does not control, which is overwhelmed by mystery and opened up by mystery.[41]

The alternative is for the self to 'mistake itself for an absolute subject and divinize itself'. The irreconcilability is met constantly as the self finds that it 'is not at its own disposal', as 'for all its infinity it experiences itself as radically finite'.[42] The self is a 'finite infinity',[43] nicely encapsulating the conceptual space carved out by the notion of irreconcilable completeness.

For both Rahner and Camus, the tension between the subjective and objective perspectives, the external and internal, can never be removed, tessellated, or harmonized, because we can never locate our inside-known freedom within the external and objective perspective. The freedom, the transcendence, the ability to go beyond, in Rahner's vocabulary, 'the term of transcendence' is 'indefinable', because 'the horizon itself cannot be present within the horizon'.[44]

---

[40] M.M. Madison, 'Albert Camus: Philosopher of Limits', 227. The Camus reference is *L'Homme Révolté* (Paris: N.R.F Gallimard, 1951), 35.
[41] Rahner, *Foundations,* 58.
[42] Ibid.
[43] Ibid.
[44] Ibid.

68 NEGATIVE NATURAL THEOLOGY

Accessible but not chosen

A third feature of Camus' sense of the absurd is that although universally accessible to all self-conscious finite beings, it is not universally and always dwelt upon, such that an awareness of the absurd, and of rebellion in relation to it, must be continually chosen and renewed.

The universal accessibility of the sense of the absurd can give a sense of levelling and solidarity: 'in an absurd world', the 'rebel still has one certainty':

> It is the solidarity of men in the same adventure, the fact that both he and the grocer are baffled.[45]

This is within the context where the possibility of forgetting, of obscuring, the sense of the absurd is too tempting. Camus has his character Jean-Baptiste Clamence muse about the situation 'all over Europe', where 'future historians' will say of the average European 'he fornicated and read the papers', such that 'after that robust description', 'there will be no more to say on the subject'.[46] Rahner's sense of pre-apprehension of absolute mystery is also something that is universally accessible, but temptingly forgettable. As Rahner writes, 'a person can, of course, shrug his shoulders and ignore this experience of transcendence':

> He can devote himself to his concrete world, his work, his activity in the categorical realm of time and space, to the service of his system at certain points which are the focal points of reality for him.[47]

So, 'most people' live 'at a distance from themselves', ensuring that 'they have enough to do',[48] including, one supposes, reading newspapers and fornicating. Others might postpone ultimate questions in 'silence and in a perhaps sensible scepticism',[49] or there can be a 'despairing involvement in the categorical realm of human existence':

> One goes about his business, he reads, he gets angry, he does his work, he does research, he achieves something, he earns money. And in a final, perhaps unadmitted despair he says to himself that the whole as a whole makes no sense, and that one does well to suppress the question about the meaning of it all and to reject it as an unanswerable and hence meaningless question.[50]

---

[45] Albert Camus, 'La Remarque sur la Révolte', in *Existence* (Paris: Gallimard, 1945), 18. For this reference I am indebted to Scott, 'The Modest Optimism of Albert Camus', 262.

[46] Albert Camus, *The Fall* trans. by Robin Buss (London: Penguin Random House UK, 2013), 5.

[47] Rahner, *Foundations*, 32.

[48] Ibid.

[49] Ibid., 33.

[50] Ibid.

A twice-appearing freedom

I spoke previously of a 'two-fold freedom': that is, first of all, freedom appears as the experience of transcending itself. But, there is also a freedom about how to regard, and how to name, this fundamental freedom. Rahner associates the 'transcendental experience', outlined above, with the name of God:

> If man really is a subject, that is, a transcendent, responsible and free being who as subject is both entrusted into his own hands and always in the hands of what is beyond his control, then basically this has already said that man is a being oriented towards God.[51]

This identification is written of in a rather minimalist way—reminding us of the way in which 'rigid designation' works, as explored in Chapter 2—exemplified by the ancient Greeks hearing the clash of thunder, and naming it 'thunder', without much contour or theoretical description of what thunder actually is.[52] We can remind ourselves here of Rahner writing about the mere 'existence' of the 'word God'. Rahner emphasizes that the word 'God' names the space, whatever it is, of the subjective finite encounter with the infinity, with freedom, and the mystery of our thrownness in the world:

> To understand man in this way, of course, does not mean that when we use the term 'God' in such a statement, we know what this term means from any other source except through this orientation to mystery.[53]

It is worth reflecting on the strength of this claim. 'When we use the term "God" in such a statement', Rahner reflects, we 'do not know what this term means *from any other source except through this orientation to mystery*'.[54] The word 'God', here, is simply and only the name for this orientation towards the relationship between the subjective and objective, the internal and the external, where the relationship involves an irreconcilable completeness, and needs to be constantly and vigilantly chosen and renewed, lest it be forgotten. In this aspect of the usage of the word God, there is a lack of any contour to the concept.

'This word', Rahner writes, 'is so very much without contour', and because of this, is 'obviously quite appropriate for what it refers to, regardless of whether the word may have originally been so "faceless" or not'.[55] It seems that Rahner's

---

[51] Ibid., 44.
[52] As commented in the previous chapter, I am indebted here to Nussbaum, 'Non-relative Virtues', 247.
[53] Rahner, *Foundations*, 44.
[54] Ibid.
[55] Ibid., 46.

70 NEGATIVE NATURAL THEOLOGY

contourless word stands rather like Camus' 'meridian of thought' in the face of the absurd, the 'vigil of the mind'. As with this vigil, the word 'God' does not, at first, lean into either hope, or resignation:

> The concept 'God' is not a grasp of God by which a person masters the mystery, but it is letting oneself be grasped by the mystery which is present and yet ever distant.[56]

There may then be further attempts to speak 'explicit language' about God, but 'in order to remain true', Rahner writes, 'all metaphysical ontology about God must return again and again to its source, must return to the transcendental experience of our orientation towards the absolute mystery'.[57]

With Camus' sense of the absurd, there is always freedom, but also, a friction and resistance from the world, a thrownness to the freedom. Rahner's minimalist word 'God' also gestures to this resistance. 'By its very nature', Rahner writes, 'subjectivity is always a transcendence which listens, which does not control, which is overwhelmed by mystery and opened up by mystery'.[58] The 'mere fact that this word exists', Rahner observes, 'is worth thinking about',[59] although in comments that follow it seems that it is not the 'word', but the concept:

> Whether we say *Gott* or 'God' or the Latin *deus* or the Semitic *El* [...] that makes no difference here.[60]

Other words can circle around this conceptual and existential space. Although the 'term and source by which transcendence is born can be called "God"', we can 'also speak' of 'being, of ground, of ultimate cause, or illuminating, revealing logos, and we can appeal to what is meant by a thousand other names'[61]:

> When we say 'God' or 'primordial ground' or 'abyss', then of course such a word is always fraught with images which go beyond what the word really wants to say, and which have nothing to do with what it really means. Each of these notions always has the patina of history on it, including the individual's history, so much so that what is really meant by such a word is hardly discernible any more.[62]

---

[56] Ibid., 54.
[57] Ibid.
[58] Ibid., 58.
[59] Ibid., 45.
[60] Ibid.
[61] Ibid., 60.
[62] Ibid.

My suggestion is that Rahner's minimalist application of the concept of God, of absolute mystery and primordial ground, maps onto the same conceptual space articulated by Camus' sense of the absurd.

If this is correct, then it helps to make sense, I would suggest, of Rahner's repeated insistence that there is something 'self-evident' about the reality of God, at least when conceived in a minimalistic way, as the 'a priori openness of the subject to being as such', where the 'silent and uncontrollable infinity of reality is always present as mystery'.[63]

If God is the name for our transcendence, encountered in the unresolved meeting of the internal and external perspectives, then God will indeed be 'self-evident'. This does not amount to a proof for the existence of something over, above, and beyond this encounter, this lived transcendence. Although the 'holy mystery' has a 'self-evident nature', this is not a 'reflexive proof for God's existence'.[64] Also, perhaps, the 'self-evidence' only stands if the encounter between the internal and external perspectives is thought to be problematic and unresolved.

Here we see the potential of the rigid designator approach, as set out in Chapter 2, to identify the meaningful point of difference between positions, as well as similarities. Rahner points at this conceptual space, and recommends worship as an optimal attitude. Camus follows the same arrow into a similar space, but identifies a different optimal attitude, recommending a state of rebellion in the face of the absurd. Such an attitude is bracing and requires courage, but it is neither hopeful nor tragic. Alternatively, there might be a more radical challenge to Camus and Rahner.

We might venture that there is nothing to which the act of rigid designation refers. If we are Wittgensteinian quietists, we might say that no 'optimal attitude' to any of these tensions or fragmentations is required or appropriate: the search for such an attitude is a type of intellectual neurosis, a little like the radical sceptic unnecessarily searching for a 'proof' that she is not a brain-in-a-vat. One might also think that no optimal attitude is required, if one is a sort of humanist optimist (to be discussed in the next chapter): the 'magic of reality' is so invigorating, and the scientific search for truth so transformative and significant, that consolation and hope is not needed. Alternatively, we might not think the tension between the perspectives is as trenchant and final as presented here: they can become unproblematic by being therapeutically dispersed, either through philosophy, or actual therapy. As commented above, and in Chapter 1, there may be accounts of the self in the world that do not generate the anxious sense of there being a problem, or, which, at least, seek to undermine this sense. For now, though, we continue to inhabit Rahner and Camus' shared thought-world, where the perspectives encounter each other in a way that generates, at least initially, tension and anxiety.

---

[63] Ibid., 35.
[64] Ibid., 69.

The freedom of naming

Although Rahner often writes of 'holy mystery', he is also careful to differentiate the two terms. There is, he insists, an 'intrinsic difference' between the two words, 'holy' and 'mystery', even though he will understand them 'as a unity'.[65]

This thought helps us take stock of where we are. Putting aside whether I am exegetically 'on target' with Rahner or Camus, the reading of these figures has allowed a particular question to emerge. If, in the encounter of self and world, we are faced with a mystery, what should we say about this mystery? How should we regard it? As 'holy', or as something else? For example, as 'absurd'? And, what is at stake in different attitudes, and how does one come to one position over another?

I suggest that the sheer encounter of the subjective and objective perspectives is sufficient for a sense of 'bare mystery', where this involves an irreconcilable completeness, arising from the juxtaposition of our desire and a non-responsive silence, and the need for a difficult and chosen vigilance of mind, in order to keep the mystery in sight. It is in the chosen, or given, attitude toward this mystery that we find the key difference in the adjective, 'absurd' or 'holy'.

Camus is drawn to an attitude of rebellion in the face of mystery, and is explicit about the non-coercive freedom in this choice. As well as 'rebellion', alternative options are canvassed by Camus, in relation to this mystery. What unites these alternatives, and differentiates them from rebellion, is that they invoke, somehow, ethically or despairingly, *divinity*. The most familiar is the 'leap of faith', which Camus finds in Kierkegaard and Chestov. About Kierkegaard, Camus writes that 'the very thing that led to despair of the meaning and depth of this life now gives it its truth and its clarity':

> Christianity is the scandal, and what Kierkegaard calls for quite plainly is the third sacrifice required by Ignatius Loyola, the one in which God most rejoices: 'The sacrifice of the intellect'.[66]

'God is maintained', Camus observes, 'only through the negation of human reason':

> Like suicides, gods change with men. There are many ways of leaping, the essential being to leap. Those redeeming negations, those ultimate contradictions which negate the obstacle that has not yet been leapt over, may spring just as well (this is the paradox at which this reasoning aims) from a certain religious inspiration as from rational order. They always lay claim to the eternal and it is solely in this that they take the leap.[67]

---

[65] Rahner, *Foundations* 66.
[66] Camus, *The Myth of Sisyphus*, 29.
[67] Ibid., 32.

ABSURD AND HOLY MYSTERY 73

Such leaping towards divinity need not be through an explicit appeal to the 'irrational', but can be done in the name of 'reason':

> From the abstract god of Husserl to the dazzling god of Kierkegaard the distance is not so great. Reason and the irrational lead to the same preaching. In truth the way matters but little, the will to arrive suffices.[68]

Both 'the abstract philosopher' and the 'religious philosopher' start out 'from the same disorder and support each other in the same anxiety':

> [T]he essential is to explain. Nostalgia is stronger here than knowledge.[69]

Here, Camus accuses not only Christianity, but the 'Greeks':

> From Pandora's box, where all the ills of humanity swarmed, the Greeks drew out hope after all the others, as the most dreadful of all. I knew no more stirring symbol; for, contrary to the general belief, hope equals resignation. And to live is not to resign oneself.[70]

There can also be a darker side to 'divinity', and to aligning oneself with it. Camus points to this in what he writes about 'the gods'. This is exemplified, as we saw above, by the murderous despair of Caligula, putting on the 'the foolish, unintelligible face of a professional god'[71], and by parts of the German nation 'siding with the gods', choosing despair, in supporting National Socialism.

Two lessons can be drawn from this account of references to divinity in Camus: first of all, that divinity is always invoked in at attempt (sunlit or dark) to resolve and escape, through flight and fantasy, or death, despair, and destruction, the absurd condition. Secondly, that it is a *choice* always whether to make leaps into the divine, an act of freedom, where the highest and only argument, really, that Camus produces is a free choice. To his 'German friend' Camus writes: 'you chose injustice and sided with the gods'[72], 'I, on the contrary, chose justice in order to remain faithful to the world'.[73]

There seems to be here an act of freedom, rather than a justificatory argument. Admittedly, the reference to 'justice' might constitute a type of argument, but not, it would seem for Camus. Camus shares with his 'German friend' the conviction that there is no 'human or divine code'.[74] Camus asks, 'where lay the difference?'

---

[68] Ibid., 36.
[69] Ibid.
[70] Ibid., 111.
[71] Camus, 'Caligula', 12.
[72] Camus, 'Letters to a German Friend: Fourth Letter', 22.
[73] Ibid.
[74] Ibid., 21.

74 NEGATIVE NATURAL THEOLOGY

between the two of them, responding 'simply that you readily accepted despair and I never yielded to it':

> Simply that you saw the injustice of our condition to the point of being willing to add to it, whereas it seemed to me that man must exalt justice in order to fight against injustice, create happiness in order to protest against the universe of unhappiness.[75]

It is not that Camus first accepts the principle of justice, and then chooses to act. It is the act of choice that brings about justice. Justice simply is the act of choice for solidarity and rebellion:

> And, to tell the truth, I, believing I thought as you did, saw no valid argument to answer you except a fierce love of justice which, after all, seemed to me as unreasonable as the most sudden passion.[76]

The choice of justice does not come after an argument, but is a 'fierce love', 'as unreasonable as the most sudden passion'.[77]

A similar lack of argumentation, a free choosing, can be found in Camus' critique of less murderous suicidal courses of action. Consider: although Camus opens *The Myth of Sisyphus* with the declaration that 'there is but one truly philosophical problem and that is suicide', it might not be evident to the reader that there is much of a 'philosophical' answer given to this problem. It is true that Camus offers a number of reactions to suicide. As we have already seen, Camus points out that suicide only removes the problem for the individual who undertakes it, and not for others. But, this in itself does not seem to get to the heart of the matter. My act of suicide lacks solidarity with others. But, we might ask, 'so what?'.

In the face of the Absurd, what is that? It is for others, and them alone, to determine their response to the same Absurd. What, after all, could I do for others in the face of the abysmal irresolvability of the situation? Camus himself seems to inhabit this attitude in the character of Merseult in the *Stranger*:

> From the dark horizon of my future a sort of slow, persistent breeze had been blowing toward me, all my life long, from the years that were to come. And on its way that breeze had leveled out all the ideas that people tried to foist on me in the equally unreal years I then was living through. What difference could they make to me, the deaths of others, or a mother's love, or his God: or the way one decides to live, the fate one thinks one chooses, since one and the same fate was bound

---

[75] Ibid.
[76] Ibid.
[77] Ibid.

to 'choose' not only me but thousands of millions of privileged people who, like him, called themselves my brothers ... All alike would be condemned to die one day ...[78]

As we saw in the case of Caligula, there can be disastrous consequences if one does have a more extravert disposition, a desire to 'involve others'. This concern might be expressed by involving them, somehow, in my suicidal and despairing course of action. In another strand of his reaction to suicide, Camus takes another tack, which is to complain that suicide annuls or avoids the problem, rather than re-solving it. 'If I attempt to solve a problem', Camus reflects, then 'at least I must not by that very solution conjure away one of the terms of the problem'.[79] The com-mentator Nathan Scott glosses this passage by explaining that suicide, for Camus, would be to 'annul' the problem, and not to 'solve' it:

> And, what is more, it would be for man to consent to his own defeat, for, in the desperate leap out of the Absurd into the spurious relief of nothingness, he re-pudiates himself: he consents to his humiliation, himself becomes the agent of it and, in thus succumbing to his impotence effectively, abdicates his humanity.[80]

But, again, we might ask: 'so what?'. The concerns expressed here do no look much like a reason, or an argument. What is wrong with wanting to avoid or annul prob-lems, rather than resolving them? Especially, we might think, when the problem is judged to be irresolvable. Indeed, whole traditions of philosophy, such as those going back to Wittgenstein, encourage us to seek to avoid and 'conjure away' any 'philosophical' problem that is, in principle, unsolvable, although the examples chosen are usually less dramatic, along the lines of 'how do I know that I was not created five minutes ago, complete with memories?'. A Wittgensteinian would be, perhaps, more likely to refuse to accept that the 'problem of the absurd' is a prop-erly formed problem, before accepting that suicide is a valid avoidance of a well-formed and irresolvable problem. But the point stands: if I accept the problem of the absurd as well-formed, and choose to avoid and annul it, well: why not? Suicide, I am told, is a 'repudiation'[81], and an avoidance, a humiliation, and an ab-dication. Yes, but perhaps, in the face of inevitable defeat, these are apt and valid forms of action.

I might put the point as follows. It is almost as if Camus intends to offer in-sulting reactions to the option of suicide, rather than refuting it. But, if you do not mind the insults, or, you do not receive what is intended as an insult to be such,

---

[78] Albert Camus, *The Outsider,* trans. Stuart Gilbert (London: Hamish Hamilton, 1965), 125–126.
[79] Camus, *The Myth of Sisyphus,* 24.
[80] Scott, 'The Modest Optimism of Albert Camus', 254.
[81] Camus, *The Myth of Sisyphus,* 41.

well, then, you may not be moved. At the same time, I have a sense that Camus might not be much troubled by these observations, because of his devotion to a more classical and originary sense of philosophy, which involves an approach to the Socratic question of 'how should I live?', where the answer to this question must involve a degree of non-coerced freedom. That is, as we saw above, the answer to such a question will never be non-negotiable, in the way that following a Euclidean proof delivers a non-negotiable conclusion, if one accepts the axioms and premises. The geometer has no freedom to choose. This relates to our reflections on the freedom that attaches itself to philosophy: the stretch of freedom in relation to the question of how to live, especially when engaging the problem of the absurd. Such freedom does not mean that 'anything goes', or that recommendations are not made, and reasons given. But it can transform our sense of what sort of thing counts as a reason.

Immediately after declaring that 'suicide' is the 'one truly serious philosophical problem', Camus gestures towards an originary conception of philosophy as a 'way of life', by supporting Nietzsche's claim that 'a philosophy, to deserve our respect, must preach by example'.[82] Perhaps, then, it is by virtue of examples, of virtuous exemplars, that a way of life is sketched out and recommended, by a sort of 'showing' that goes beyond saying, by drawing attention, as Camus puts it, to 'facts the heart can feel', through a 'balance between evidence and lyricism', achieving simultaneously 'emotion and lucidity'.[83] The way of life suggested and recommended by Camus, is characterized by a courageous 'consciousness and revolt', and a celebration of 'everything that is indomitable and passionate in a human heart'.[84]

We should note that the terms on which this way of life are recommended are irreducibly practical and ethical, and that the criteria for evaluation are chosen in freedom, and not in response to a non-negotiable chain of argumentation. It is this that gives such philosophy both its modesty and its significance, as Camus puts it, 'at once so humble and so heavy with emotion'.[85] Furthermore, perhaps we might venture to say that when a piece of philosophy claims to engage with that which is of the greatest significance, if it spurns the humility that accompanies the self-conscious element of freedom, there such philosophy disqualifies itself from attaining the very significance that it aspires to. Of all pieces of philosophy of religion, the ontological argument (when presented as a proof) is the most geometrically coercive in its form: accept the axioms and premises, and the conclusion that necessarily God exists must follow. As Camus observes, 'I have never seen anyone die for the ontological argument', but 'many people die

---

[82] Ibid., 5.
[83] Ibid., 6.
[84] Ibid., 41.
[85] Ibid., 6.

because they judge that life is not worth living'.[86] Camus recommends rebellion as a way of life, and the recipient of this recommendation can only accept or reject it in freedom.

Camus is drawn to rebellion in response to the absurd, but canvasses other responses, if only to reject them. But, does Camus acknowledge the act of freedom that has already occurred in naming this conceptual space 'the absurd' in the first place? In relation to a similar existential conceptual space, Rahner is drawn to worship. It is because of the attitude of worship that the mystery is named holy, and not absurd: the difference is between absurd mystery, and holy mystery. We can speak of a difference that arises from a choice of naming, where the naming comes downstream of the free reaction to it. We might consider, here, Rahner's choice of words, evocative of the freedom of naming, when he writes (emphasis mine): '*we want to call* the term and source of our transcendence "the holy mystery"'[87]:

> For what else would we call that which is nameless, that at whose disposal we exist and from which we are distanced in our finiteness, but which nevertheless we affirm in our transcendence through freedom and love, what else would we call this if not 'holy'? And what could we call 'holy', if not this, or to whom would the name 'holy' belong more basically and more originally that to this infinite term of love, which love in the presence of the incomprehensible and the ineffable necessarily becomes worship.[88]

We have a differentiation between mystery and holy mystery, and then, also, a sense that the identity of 'holy mystery' and the word 'God' is not obvious. The term 'holy mystery' must be 'understood, deepened, and then gradually shown to be identical with the word "God"'.[89] This will need to be done by reverting 'frequently to other terms' which are 'available elsewhere in the humane and philosophical traditions'.[90]

One clear implication of this is that the conceptual space of something such as 'holy mystery' can be opened up within thought, without using, at least, at first, the concept of God or divinity. This is a lesson we took from the discussion of rigid designation. Another possibility is that the word 'God' can be employed, without any origin in, or reference to, a sense of holy mystery. When this happens, we have the danger of a type of supernatural object, a being alongside other beings.

---

[86] Ibid., 5.
[87] Rahner, *Foundations*, 60.
[88] Ibid., 66.
[89] Ibid., 61.
[90] Ibid.

Just as Camus denies that the existence of a supernatural being would make any difference, fundamentally, to his sense of the absurd, so Rahner also underlines that the 'original experience of God is not an encounter with an individual object *alongside of* other objects'.[91] We do not 'have an experience of God as we have of a tree, another person and other external realities', which objects 'evoke their name by themselves because they simply appear within the realm of our experience at a definite point in time and space, and so by themselves they press immediately for a name'.[92] Rahner finds that both 'atheism and a more naïve form of theism labor under the same false notion of God', with the former denying it, and the latter believing in it. Such a God 'operates and functions as an individual existent alongside of other existents'. This conception of God is 'basically very unreligious', because 'it understands God as an element within a larger whole, as a part of the whole of reality'.[93] Once again, the discussion of rigid designation is helpful here: the word God can be used in an over confident and anthropomorphic way, in such a way that, for some, the concept loses its deeper resonances, which should offer consolation, hope, peace, courage, humility, obedience, or promise. Instead, we worry, we are offered a fantasy, an imaginary friend.

Camus writes of a silent world meeting our desire for meaning. Such a silence, I would suggest, is not unknown to Rahner, just because 'we do not know God by himself as one individual object alongside others, but only as the term of transcendence'.[94] There is an absence of God from the world. Because God is an 'ineffable and incomprehensible presupposition, as ground and abyss, as ineffably mystery', God 'cannot be found in his world':

> He does not seem to be able to enter into the world with which we have to do because he would thereby become what he is not: an individual existent alongside of which there are others which he is not. If he wanted to appear in his world, he apparently would immediately cease to be himself: the ground of everything which appears but itself does not appear.[95]

For this reason, Rahner writes that the divine 'is present only in the mode of otherness and distance':

> It can never be approached directly, never be grasped immediately. It gives itself only insofar as it points wordlessly to something else, to something finite as the object we see directly and as the immediate object of our action.[96]

[91] Ibid., 54.
[92] Ibid., 44–45.
[93] Ibid., 63.
[94] Ibid., 64.
[95] Ibid., 81.
[96] Ibid., 64–65.

Faith and life

Drawing upon the discussion so far, I will conclude with two reflections: first of all, on the satisfactory but unsatisfying nature of philosophy, when it shows a proper humility. Secondly, I will reflect on what wider lessons we might draw, from the discussion of Camus and Rahner, about the relationship between traditioned Christian theology and philosophy that engages with the divine.

Philosophy: Unsatisfying But Satisfactory

I have suggested above that when the mystery is declared to be absurd, the associated attitude is one of rebellion, and that when the mystery is characterized as holy, the associated attitude is one of worship, and a type of awful gratitude. When Camus recommends the state of rebellion, there is not much in the way of *argument,* or reasons given, for the vigilant and tensive state of mind that Camus evokes. There is, rather, a performative embodiment of one answer to the Socratic question of 'how to live?', whose recommendation cannot be disaggregated from the living of a whole life, and the weight, love, and movement of a whole personality. I am drawn then to the, perhaps unsatisfying, suggestion that the choice as to whether or not to name the mystery as absurd or holy can similarly not be separated out from the movement, weight, and love of a whole personality and life.

The answer may be unsatisfying, in that we cannot find a reason, a piece of contested evidence, a move in reasoning or argument, around which we can try to lever one worldview into another. But, is it not the case that we cannot, in truth, do that, and that when theology or philosophy pretends that it can, it becomes foolish? So, an unsatisfying answer may not be, therefore, an unsatisfactory one. The only satisfactory answer, that is, the only apt and defensible position, may, in truth, be unsatisfying. We should show a proper humility. And that is tied up with the very limits of reason and philosophy, about which theology has something to say, as does reflexive and critical philosophy, as witnessed to, for example, by philosophers such as Kant.

Christian theology and philosophy that leans into the divine

Can thinking alongside Rahner and Camus help us to make any progress in reflecting upon the relationship between philosophy that speaks of the divine, and more traditioned Christian theology? Rahner gives us some lines of reflection. Let us say that it is true that the contours of 'mystery' do map on to Camus' sense of the absurd. What, then, does the Christian theologian make of this? Well, of course, there are different types and varieties of Christian theologian. But one possibility

80   NEGATIVE NATURAL THEOLOGY

is witnessed to by Rahner, who draws attention to a strand of Catholic theology which is prepared to speak of the 'light of natural reason'. So, Rahner affirms that in the encounter with transcendence and mystery, we find an 'unthematic and ever-present experience', a 'knowledge of God which we always have even when we are thinking of and concerned with anything but God'.[97]

Drawing upon the work of the theologian Karen Kilby, I want to distinguish two different ways in which we might interpret this sort of claim about the 'universality' of the pre-conceptual and unthematic experience of God.[98] The first way considers the experience to be as raw and unmediated, say, as our perceptual experience of redness, or solidity. Insofar as any experience can be free of cultural and interpretative saturation, such an experience of redness might be thought to be so. Some cultures will then associate redness with violence and warfare, others, perhaps with fraternity, or celebration. So, the first way of construing the 'universal experience of God' claims that this experience is a universal experience, which Christian theology can *build upon* and use as a type of prolegomenon, in order to move towards a more specific and explicitly realized metaphysic and worldview.

The second way to construe Rahner's claim does not make recourse to a raw and unmediated experience (akin to 'redness'), but already embeds itself in a matrix of interpretation. Here, we might say, the 'experience' is more like an encounter with elegance, beauty, or humour, which is already a thoroughly interpreted and mediated experience. From within this interpretative matrix, a certain claim is made that human beings have an unthematized awareness, a 'universal experience' of God. But, this is not a claim that can be made from outside of this theological framework. Some passages in Rahner seem to incline more in this direction. For example, where Rahner writes that 'from a theological point of view, the *concrete* process of the so-called natural knowledge of God in either its acceptance or its rejection is always more than a merely natural knowledge of God'.[99]

Kilby concedes that Rahner can be read in either way, but suggests that the second way is the 'better reading', in that it ascribes a more plausible and nuanced position to Rahner. I agree. The second construal also resonates with the emerging motif of epistemic humility, and the freedom of naming (note, again, the phrasing above, 'we call this orientation grace'). From within a Christian thought world, the encounter with mystery is called 'holy', and received through grace; from within the absurdist thought world, the encounter is called 'absurd', and received rebelliously.

There can be a tendency to worry, perhaps more on behalf of philosophers than by them, that co-opting philosophy within Christian theology is 'condescending'.

---

[97] Ibid., 53.
[98] Karen Kilby, 'The relation of philosophy to theology: a nonfoundationalist reading', in *Karl Rahner: Theology and Philosophy* (London and New York: Routledge, 2004), 70–99.
[99] Rahner, *Foundations*, 57.

But, why should mere reason expect to arbitrate here about the framing, one way or another—absurd or holy—of an entire thought-world? This is an expression of the satisfactory but unsatisfying quality of philosophy, and of reason. Analogously, we might say that it is a limit of mathematics that it cannot give us a lesson in life about happiness; but, such a limit is not a limitation. It is a proper designation of scope. This, perhaps, parallels pervasive concerns about Rahner's notion of 'anonymous Christians' (those that theology may regard as Christians, even when this is not their self-description). The freedom of the believer to choose such naming may be an expression of the *limits* of reason and philosophy, and not a condescending attitude towards the *limitations* of philosophy or 'secular reason'. The absurdist may also, of course, exercise this freedom, and name believers as unconscious fellow travellers, crypto-rebels, albeit in denial, and lacking, perhaps, in courage or vigilance. We must all name the world from within our limits, employing the freedom that we have within these limits.

In terms of the discussion of borderlands and flags, set out in Chapter 1, we are in interesting territory here. Both Rahner and Camus occupy the same landscape, and share some of the same movements, but they regard their situation very differently. It is as if we are looking at the same range of mountains. But someone, Rahner or Camus, without knowing it, is looking at the mirrored reflection of the mountain range in a deep and dark lake, whilst the other is looking at the original. They must each regard the other, whether with compassion or contempt, as seeing only the derivative reflection, either of Holy Mystery, or of our absurd condition.

To paraphrase Kant, we identify the limits of reason, to make space for freedom, and the freedom to call such freedom grace, made manifest across the whole warp and weave of a life.

4

Humanism Not Mysterious

The Happy Human

The third possible response to Thomas Nagel's 'cosmic question', of 'how to live in harmony with the universe and not just in it?', is as follows:

> The question has an 'inside-out' answer: perhaps, for example, meaning is to be found from human nature.

One prominent variant of this response is what has been called 'humanism', and this chapter looks at this movement, in the light of the framing question about the attraction (or aversion) to speaking about the divine when engaging with limits, tensions, and fragmentations in our lives.

It is difficult to write about humanism. This is because it can mean so many things. Accordingly, the first section of this chapter addresses the problem of discussing something as broad and multivalenced as 'humanism'. I will look at three mainstream characterizations of 'humanism', offered by Thomas Nagel ('humanism as the search for immanent meaning'), Jean-Paul Sartre ('humanism as theological anthropology without God'), and John Gray ('humanism as secularized Christian eschatology'). I express some misgivings about the armchair essentialism involved in such accounts, and prefer, instead, to attend to the concrete practices and activities of self-identified humanists. For help here, I turn to a recent anthropological study of the British Humanist Association (since 2017 known as Humanists UK), undertaken by Matthew Engelke. Drawing upon Engelke's observations, I will cover two key humanist commitments: the search for happiness, and the importance of being good without God and religion (discussed in the second section).

In the third section, I explore a potential tension in the practices and commitments of humanists: being happy is a key ideological commitment for humanists, *but* religious belief and practice is not permitted, even if, and where, it contributes (demonstrably and significantly) to happiness. Understanding why this is the case helps us to unearth, I will claim, two undergirding humanist commitments: first of all, that to hold a belief rationally, we must have warrant and evidence equivalent to knowledge. This, I suggest, is by no means an uncontroversial and unproblematic claim. The second assumption is that genuinely secure and 'permitted' happiness arises only from contemplating and understanding objective truth. This

Negative Natural Theology. Christopher J. Insole, Oxford University Press. © Christopher J. Insole 2024.
DOI: 10.1093/9780198933007.003.0005

relates, I will argue, to the most fascinating and generative humanist assumption of all: that objective truth is, in the end, somehow, good for us, beautiful, and inducive of ethically transformative behaviour. As such, my suggestion will be (in the fourth section), that there is an attempt to deny the fundamental reality of what some other thinkers (Nagel, Bilgrami, Camus, and Rahner, discussed so far in the book) have insisted is an irreducible tension between the subjective and objective perspectives on our lives, which tension can be a generating source of both religious worship, and of atheistic rebellion. As commented in Chapter 1, this perceived tension is not universally felt: it can be dissolved or reframed in other ways, and other tensions and fragmentations can arise, either within the perspectives themselves, or in relation to different second-person perspectives upon ourselves. That said, from within a particular post-Kantian strain of thinking, and affect, the tension between the subjective and objective perspectives is received as important. Some key humanist commitments and practices, I will be suggesting here, are illuminated by considering how they engage with the purported tension between objective and subjective perspectives.

If this is correct, then the deepest disagreement in this neighbourhood is not between humanist and 'religious' perspectives, but between approaches that endorse such 'humanism' about objective truth, and those (such as Camus) who suspect, or affirm, that to some degree objective truth may be 'inhuman'. In the concluding part of the chapter, I explore both atheistic and religious versions of such 'inhumanism', and admire the difficulty and bravery of the humanist position.

Humanism

As already observed, in any discussion on humanism, it will quickly be pointed out just how vague and multifaceted the term is. So, we might note that humanism has its origins in renaissance philosophy. We could also draw attention to theological varieties of humanism,[1] either appreciatively, or with a wry aside, as expressed by Bernard Williams, when he observes that for Christianity, 'the cosmos may not be looking at human beings, in their fallen state, with much admiration', but 'it is certainly looking at them':

> If man's fate is a very special concern to God, there is nothing more absolute than that: it is a central concern, period.[2]

---

[1] See, for example, David E. Klemm and William Schweiker, *Religion and the Human Future: An Essay on Theological Humanism* (Oxford: Wiley-Blackwell, 2008).

[2] Bernard Williams, 'The Human Prejudice', in *Philosophy as a Humanistic Discipline*, ed. A.W. Moore (Princeton and Oxford: Princeton University Press, 2006), 135–152, 136.

There is, though, I would submit, a usage of the term 'humanism' that is both narrower and more concrete. The philosopher Thomas Nagel approaches this usage when he writes that humanism is the 'view that we ourselves, as a species or community, give sense to the world as a whole':

> The significance of an individual life does depend on its embeddedness in something larger, but it is the collective consciousness of humanity rather than the cosmos that plays this role. Our self-consciousness and our place in cultural, cognitive, and moral history make membership in the human community a significant larger identity. The universe does not offer any sense to our lives, but we are not alone in it.[3]

Although humanism 'does not show us how to live lives that are more than human', it 'does argue that living a human life should be something much more than living the life of the individual human being one is',[4] whilst at the same time, underscoring that 'there is no universe other than a human universe, the universe of human subjectivity'. As Nagel puts it:

> [W]e are the source of all value, which replaces the value not given to our lives by the nonexistent creator.
> The point of humanism [...] is that no such endorsement or external support is needed. It is we who give sense to the universe, so there is no need for a higher principle to give sense to us.[5]

Nagel draws on William James to help draw a distinction between the religious and the non-religious. Paraphrasing James, Nagel writes that 'were one asked to characterize the life of religion in the broadest and most general terms possible':

> [O]ne might say that it consists of the belief that there is an unseen order, and that our supreme good lies in harmoniously adjusting ourselves thereto.[6]

'Humanism denies this', writes Nagel, and 'finds our supreme good in harmony not with an unseen but with a visible order—one that is universal in a sense, but not unduly unfamiliar'.[7] Humanists take 'self-conscious life as a self-contained source of value'.[8]

---

[3] Nagel, 'Secular Philosophy and the Religious Temperament', 10.
[4] Ibid.
[5] Ibid.
[6] Ibid.
[7] Ibid., 11.
[8] Ibid., 12.

HUMANISM NOT MYSTERIOUS   85

Nagel makes the, initially plausible, suggestion that 'humanism and its relatives take us outside of ourselves in search of harmony with the universe, but not too far outside':

> Since the universe cannot be identified with the human world, they do not really give us a way of incorporating our conception of the universe as a whole into our lives and how we think of them.[9]

On an initial drive past, this would seem to be correct, obvious even. In this chapter, I will suggest, though, that this could be questioned: that the deepest humanist commitments, as revealed in the conduct, utterances, and practices, of living self-identifying humanists, do suggest that the universe has a particular shape and structure, and that without this, key humanist practices are jeopardized, or, at least, they are robbed of some of their motivation.

The claim will be that humanist practices, habits, values, and discourse, seem to rely on 'objective truth' being fundamentally good for us: morally, aesthetically, and hedonistically. As such, my suggestion will be, there is an attempt to deny the fundamental reality of what some other thinkers have insisted is an irreducible tension between the subjective and objective perspectives on our lives.

This line of thought is distinct from other claims about the subterranean theological springs of secular humanism. For example, one venerable tradition of critique accuses humanism of an essentialism about human nature, and an optimism about that nature, which has a distinctively theological shape. This optimism, the charge is, becomes difficult to motivate, when God is no longer in the picture. Such a critique can be found in both Sartre and Heidegger.[10] Writing about the 'philosophical atheism of the eighteenth century', Sartre comments that 'the notion of God is suppressed, but not, for all that, the idea that essence is prior to existence':

> [S]omething of that idea we still find everywhere, in Diderot, in Voltaire and even in Kant. Man possesses a human nature; that 'human nature', which is the conception of human being, is found in every man; which means that each man is a particular example of an universal conception, the conception of Man ... the essence of Man precedes that historic existence which we confront in experience.[11]

This, Sartre fears, is a type of theological anthropology without God. Such an essentialism about human nature has its natural place in a theological framework,

---

[9] Ibid., 11–12.
[10] Martin Heidegger, 'Letter on Humanism', in *Basic Writings* (London and New York: Routledge, 2008), ed. David Farrell Krell, 141–182.
[11] Jean-Paul Sartre, *Existentialism and Humanism* (York: Methuen, 2017), trans. Philip Mairet, 29.

where 'the conception of man in the mind of God is comparable to that of the paper-knife in the mind of the artisan':

> God makes man according to a procedure and a conception, exactly as the artisan manufactures a paper-knife, following a definition and a formula. Thus each individual man is the realisation of a certain conception which dwells in the divine understanding.[12]

This type of essentialist humanism 'upholds man as the end-in-itself and as the supreme value':

> Humanism in this sense appears, for instance, in Cocteau's story *Round the World in 80 Days,* in which one of the characters declares, because he is flying over mountains in an aeroplane, 'Man is magnificent!' This signifies that although I, personally, have not built aeroplanes I have the benefit of those particular inventions and that I personally, being a man, can consider myself responsible for, and honoured by, achievements that are peculiar to some men. It is to assume that we can ascribe value to man according to the most distinguished deeds of certain men.[13]

Sartre finds this 'kind of humanism' to be 'absurd' (and not in an interesting way):

> [F]or only the dog or the horse would be in a position to pronounce a general judgement upon man and declare that he is magnificent, which they have never been such fools as to do—at least, not as far as I know. But neither is it admissible that a man should pronounce judgement upon Man . . . we have no right to believe that humanity is something to which we could set up a cult, after the manner of August Comte. The cult of humanity ends in Comtian humanism, shut-in upon itself, and—this must be said—in Fascism. We do not want a humanism like that.[14]

More recently, John Gray finds in humanism a belief in progress which resembles a secularized eschatology:

> [S]ecular humanists believe that the growth of knowledge can somehow make humans more rational.[15]

---

[12] Ibid., 28–29.
[13] Ibid., 65–66.
[14] Ibid., 65.
[15] John Gray, 'An Illusion with a Future', *Daedelus* (Summer 2004), 8.

Such humanists 'seek in the idea of progress what theists found in the idea of providence—an assurance that history need not be meaningless'[16]: 'the idea of progress is a secular version of Christian eschatology'.[17]

I do not deny that these two suspicions, of submerged essentialism and secularized eschatology, may have some purchase on some strands of humanism. Also, there is something obviously right about Nagel's claim that humanism involves, at the very least, an immanent and 'non-religious' way of finding value in being human. But, the alternative suggestion that I develop here arises from thinking of humanism not only as a philosophical system, with submerged propositional foundations that do hidden work, but also as a set of lived and embodied practices, which are shaped by and express fundamental values, attitudes, and dispositions. By doing this, we might avoid the danger of a sort of armchair essentialism about the nature of 'humanism', with a tendency to carve out conceptual strawmen. 'The humanist is an essentialist'. Is she, really? In which statement, or practice, is this demonstrated or evidenced? 'The humanist has a secularized eschatology'. Does he? How would this be revealed? The problem with such projected accounts of the essence of humanism is that they offer, effectively, a critique of humanism as a description of its core. It would be like beginning a discussion of Christianity by *describing* it as the means by which the oppressed are kept in their servitude, or, as an infantile strategy for evading the reality of death. One might, of course, come to these judgements, in particular cases, on the basis of extended attention and observation, but it would be unfair to start out with these as accounts of the essence of Christianity. Just so with humanism.

My intention here is to embody a two-pronged approach, set out in Chapter 1, where humility leads us to two types of instinct. First of all, to seek for 'what is at stake' in a broad and deep sense: not only attending to explicit arguments and justifications, but also looking to affect, formation, practices, virtues and habits. But, also, at the same time, not to become quasi-behaviouristic about this, in a way that so prioritizes practices as observable behaviour, that we no longer attend to more interior practices and realities: thinking (in diverse forms and ways), hoping, and the secret half lights of the mind and soul.

To assist with the first part of this two-pronged movement, I draw on the work of the social anthropologist, Matthew Engelke, who spent time observing 'in the field' the meetings, practices and beliefs of the British Humanist Association.[18] Since 2017, the British Humanist Association has gone under its new name, 'Humanists UK', but I will follow Engelke's discussion, and call the movement by its former name (its name when Engelke conducted his study). By drawing on this work we facilitate, with respect to humanism, a necessary turn, and corrective, in recent

---

[16] Ibid., 3.

[17] Ibid., 4.

[18] Matthew Engelke, '"Good without God": Happiness and Pleasure Among the Humanists', in *Values of Happiness: Towards an Anthropology of Purpose in Life,* ed. Iza Kavedzija and Harry Walker (London: Hau Books, 2017), 144–161.

academic theology. This is the renewed attention to practices and habits as central to religious life and identity.[19] The insight here is that an exclusive obsession with propositional beliefs skews the actual significance of religion as a way of life, which shapes and transforms habits, practices, values, and affections at least as much as it offers 'explanations'. A similar 'practical turn' can assist us in unlocking what is distinctive and pervasive about the cultural movement, and the set of practices and belief, which constitute humanism.

In employing the notion of a 'practice' I mean to evoke the broad Wittgensteinian sense of a structured activity governed by implicit or explicit rules or expectations: this could include games, rituals, meetings, types of discussion or debate, and celebrations, as well as 'practice' in the more precise sense, as described by Clare Carlisle, when considering the way in which a musician or athlete hones their skill through repetitive 'self-forming and self-enhancing behaviour'.[20]

Invoking the broadly Wittgensteinian concept of a practice helps draw our attention to his insight that what people really believe can be revealed by their practices, more than it is by their own metalevel reflection on their beliefs. The identification of these deeper assumptions will be less of an armchair speculation, a creation of straw figures, and will arise instead after careful listening and attention. I hope that drawing on the observations of an anthropologist writing about actual humanist meetings, conversations and discourses, we can overcome some of the difficulties of writing sensibly, and fairly, about humanism.

Honouring also the claim that thinking, in its many forms, is a distinctive and important human practice, I will use this anthropological work to identify and comment on three key dimensions of humanist thinking:

(a) the centrality of happiness
(b) no God, and no religion
(c) the orientation towards 'objectivity' and 'truth'

Happiness, and no God, and no religion

At the time of Engelke's research (2011), the British Humanist Association (BHA) could boast twelve thousand members, paying an annual fee of £35, and a further eighteen thousand supporters, who receive updates of BHA events and meetings.[21]

---

[19] This renewed attention has taken a wide variety of forms: including, for example, a focus on the ecclesial, political, and social dimension of faith, as well as an interest in habits, practices, desire, and affections. For the former, see Stanley Hauerwas, *The Hauerwas Reader* (Durham, North Carolina: Duke University Press, 2001). For the latter, see fn.30.

[20] See Clare Carlisle, 'Habit, Practice, Grace: Towards a Philosophy of Religious Life', in *New Models of Religious Understanding*, ed. Fiona Ellis (Oxford: Oxford University Press, 2017), 97–115.

[21] For all these details I am drawing directly on Engelke, '"Good without God"', 136.

Amongst high-profile members of the BHA, Engelke lists Richard Dawkins and Stephen Fry, media scientists Jim Al-Khalili, Brian Cox and Alice Roberts, the journalist Polly Toynbee, the philosopher A. C. Grayling, and fiction writers such as Philip Pullman and the late Terry Pratchett. Amongst supporters are the actors Patrick Stewart and Ricky Gervais. More broadly, Engelke reports that the demographic of the BHA is largely 'white', 'male', and 'well-educated':

> Just shy of 89 percent of members are 'White British' [. . .] just over 69 percent are male, and 72 percent of members have a university degree; 13 percent of these degrees are from Oxbridge.[22]

Of this number, 24 percent are 'members of a political party', and 80 percent 'donate at least monthly to one or more charities', 'giving some indication that this is a demographic with high levels of civic engagement'.[23]

The group identified by Engelke for study is, it must be said, a relatively small group, and a strikingly nondiverse one at that. To an extent, for our purposes, there may be a trade-off here: we have identified a narrow enough target so as to talk meaningfully about 'humanism', but, in doing this, we have constrained and limited the significance of this discussion. This just has to be faced, I think. Two mitigating reflections can be offered, though. First of all, according to Engelke's figures, there were, in 2011, 30,000 humanist members or associates. In 2017, the British Humanist Association (BHA) renamed itself as 'Humanists UK', and claims now to have 100,000 members and supporters. One would not think twice about writing a chapter about Kantian ethics, although it is unlikely that one could find anything like even the smaller number of 30,000 'Kantians' signing up to any network or association. Secondly, for good or ill, the humanist movement has a public intellectual profile in the UK which far outstrips the size of its membership base. This is revealed in the celebrity list given by Engelke, of humanists who are, to some degree, noisy and articulate about their humanist commitments. In ways also detailed below (for example, the atheist bus campaign), the humanist attack on religion, and on belief in God, is perhaps the most public, conspicuous, and highly esteemed challenge that we can find in the wider culture. Many more people find that humanist beliefs and commitments resonate with their worldview and aspirations than ever sign up to be card-carrying BHA members. On this basis, a discussion of the BHA would seem warranted, given that it represents wider cultural assumptions and commitments.

Engelke summarizes the three main areas of activity for the BHA: 'promoting humanism in policy and public debates', 'servicing and fostering local humanist

---

[22] Matthew Engelke, 'The Coffin Question: Death and Materiality in Humanist Funerals', *Material Religion,* 11/1 (2015), 26–49, 32.
[23] Ibid.

groups', of which there are around sixty, ranging in size from six to sixty people, and the 'provision of ceremonies', such as 'weddings, naming ceremonies, and, above all, funerals'.[24]

Engelke draws attention to the logo for the humanist movement, which was selected, in 1965, out of 150 entries in a competition: the 'happy human', which features in the lapel pins of some BHA members, which read '"Happy Humanist" or "Good without God"'.[25]. Happiness, here and now, is important to humanists. Engelke considers a project put together by the humanist Andrew West, 'a series of portraits of humanists accompanied by their answers to the question:

'What are you happy about?'

Each entry begins: 'I am happy today because'.[26] Following this tag is a wide list of entries: including children, food, drink, flowers, birds, consumption, 'television shows, clothes, a new pair of stilettos—even the purchase of a camper van'.[27] As Engelke summarizes it, happiness is displayed as an 'admixture of sentiments, affects, demeanor, and declarations, even actions'.[28] Engelke cites a line written by the nineteenth-century American agnostic Richard Ingersoll, often used at humanist meetings:

> Happiness is the only good. The time to be happy is now. The place to be happy is here. The way to be happy is to make others so.[29]

Such happiness 'contains both hedonic and eudaimonic components'.[30] For example, in a BHA video Stephen Fry talks of the importance of living '*fully* and *well*', embracing both 'pleasures (wine, gardening) and purposefulness (political commitments, social justice)'. Fry states that 'for every humanist I met, the two had to be seen as of a piece'.[31] 'Harry from London' expresses the same point more pithily, writing that the two things that make him happy are 'making love', and 'progress in moral philosophy'.[32]

The celebration of 'happiness' and the 'here and now' is contrasted with approaches that, it is thought, do not lead to happiness, or locate happiness in the

---

[24] Engelke, '"Good without God"', 136.
[25] Ibid., 133.
[26] Ibid., 134.
[27] Ibid., 140.
[28] Ibid.
[29] Ibid., 139.
[30] Ibid., 141.
[31] Ibid.
[32] Ibid.

beyond, in the supernatural. A negative reference to religion is part and parcel of this commitment to happiness. As Engelke puts it, 'it is the language of the Enlightenment that dominates', where:

> [O]ne particular version of the Enlightenment story has pride of place: that in which reason snuffs out religion and gives rise to a modern world governed by science.[33]

This approach is exemplified by the 2008 Atheist bus campaign, which was itself an understandable response to an advertisement by a Christian organization, proclaiming that only Jesus can save you from hell. The Atheist bus slogan stated:

> There's probably no god. Now stop worrying and enjoy your life.[34]

As well as having an hedonic, and a eudaimonic element, the happiness of the humanist is also an implied critique of religion. When the humanist proclaims that 'she loves her new heals', this is not 'at core to betray her entrapment by the "hedonic treadmill" of consumption. Or, at least, it is not only ever that':

> For what such embracement of earthly pleasures is also supposed to suggest is that there are only earthly pleasures to be had—that we are each our own makers. Humanists use their stilettos to beat God over the head; they use their camper vans to run him down the road. They use their chances to explain why they're happy to be happy here and now in a way that underscores its ethical valences.[35]

For this reason, Engelke insists that 'we need to approach happiness as an ideological commitment'.[36] We have, then, 'not hedonism for hedonism's sake'.[37] Rather, it is 'about being good without God'.[38]

The critique of religion, or, at least, of certain strands of Christianity, is that it is inimicable to happiness. For example, Engelke writes that 'humanists often express dismay and sometimes disgust at the thought that the master sign of Christianity is not a happy human but a suffering man':

> How, they ask, could any community orient themselves by a crucifix?[39]

---

[33] Ibid., 137.
[34] Ibid., 132.
[35] Ibid., 142.
[36] Ibid.
[37] Ibid., 145.
[38] Ibid.
[39] Ibid., 146.

92 NEGATIVE NATURAL THEOLOGY

This might provoke the question: what, about, then 'happy religion'? If religious belief and practice evidently contributed to happiness, even, demonstrably, according to social scientific criteria, would this change things? Indeed, some social scientific studies do seem to indicate that religiosity correlates 'scientifically' with a high degree of happiness.[40] The answer seems to be that it does not fundamentally change the humanist reaction. As Engelke reports:

> There are equal measures of opprobrium, then, for Christians and other believers who don't dwell on the crucifixion or suffering. The stereotyped 'happy-clappy' Christian is considered just as problematic as what some BHA members would gloss as the guild-laden, crucifix-wearing Catholic.[41]

There is some unhappy stereotyping here ('guilt-laden Catholic'), and considerable overlooking of eudaimonistic strands within Christian, indeed, Catholic theology, with the Thomistic central focus on the joy and happiness of the participation in God's own life, in the beatific vision. But, Engelke is, presumably ventriloquizing attitudes here, and not thereby endorsing them.

I want to pause here, because this is an important moment in our discussion of humanism. It indicates a significant tension in a core set of humanist practices and priorities. The tension is this: that religion contributing to happiness is not permitted, by the humanist, to give warrant for holding religious beliefs. It would not be permissible to submit a line to Andrew West's happy humanist exhibition that reads: 'I am happy today because Jesus loves me', or 'because platonically-infused Thomism is a cognitively and emotionally rich framework for living and loving'.

This prohibition even on happiness inducing religious commitment, given the humanist focus on happiness, is interesting, and takes us into deeper waters. I deliberately use the term 'tension', as it is not, in itself a contradiction. In calling this a tension, and not a contradiction, I disagree with other commentators who have found more startling 'paradoxes' in the humanist attitude to religion. One of the more surprising critiques in this area comes from the avowedly *atheist* philosopher, Bernard Williams, who launches a scathing assessment of 'humanism in the sense of militant atheism', that it 'encounters an immediate and very obvious paradox':

> Its speciality lies not just in being atheist—there are all sorts of ways of being that— but in its faith in humanity to flourish without religion; moreover, in the idea that religion itself is peculiarly the enemy of human flourishing. The general idea is that if the last remnants of religion could be abolished, humankind would be set

---

[40] Olga Stavrova, Detlef Fetchenhauer, and Thomas Schlösser, 'Why are Religious People Happy? The Effect of the Social Norm of Religiosity Across Countries', *Social Science Research,* 42, 90–105; Amy C. Wilkins, '"Happier than non-Christians": Collective Emotions and Symbolic Boundaries Among evangelical Christians', *Social Psychology Quarterly,* 71/3 (2008), 281–301.

[41] Engelke, '"Good without God"', 146–147.

free and would do a great deal better. But the outlook is stuck with the fact that on its own submission this evil, corrupting, and pervasive thing, religion, is itself a *human* invention: it certainly did not come from anywhere else. So humanists in this atheist sense should ask themselves: if humanity has invented something as awful as they take religion to be, what should that tell them about humanity? In particular, can humanity really be expected to do so much better without it?[42]

Bernard Williams' comments here are characteristically witty, but, slightly off-target. The principle seems to be this: insofar as one invests significance in a well-functioning x, one is unable to accept or initiate critique of the practices, behaviour, or implications of anything involving x. So, a member of the Catholic church could not critique the Catholic church. A believer in free-market economics could never be concerned about the operation or outcomes of such economies. In fact, and *pace* Williams, it would seem to be that investing in the notion of a well-functioning x would necessarily entail wanting to critique poorly-functioning versions of x. The connoisseur of football will appreciate fine playing, and critique shoddy versions. Having high expectations in a particular area is, in fact, likely to generate critique and concern. The humanist can, of course, consistently uphold the value of humanity, whilst being concerned by de-humanizing tendencies arising from the human spirit itself, which is capable of denaturing itself, insofar as it participates in superstition, and the supernatural hope offered by religion.

The humanist's attitude to religion does not contradict the humanist's high view of humanity. But, the question remains: where and when religion seems to humanize, and to make people happy, what then, for the humanist, is wrong with it? Williams' broader instinct is correct, I think: there is something going on in this neighbourhood, an unacknowledged and unargued for positivity somewhere, but not perhaps in humanism's view of 'humanity'.

Objectivity and truth

The problem seems to be this: happiness, for the humanist, is inextricably linked with a conception of *objective truth*. As Engelke puts it, 'religion frustrates eudaimonia',[43] even if it makes people happy, *because* 'evidence is a precondition for eudaimonia, because the good life can only be lived with due regard for science':

> And 'evidence' does mean scientific evidence: objective, verifiable, and replicable. *Evidence means knowledge rather than belief*: fact rather than feeling.[44]

[42] Williams, 'The Human Prejudice', 135.
[43] Engelke, '"Good without God"', 148.
[44] Ibid. Italics mine.

94 NEGATIVE NATURAL THEOLOGY

This is an important claim: that happiness is linked to evidence, which is indexed to *knowledge rather than belief.* That is to say, there is no 'freedom of practical reason'. The 'freedom of practical reason' emerges when we realise, in a moment of humility, that knowledge has reached its limits, but that thinking goes on. For example, thinking engages with the cosmic question, of 'how to live in harmony with the universe and not just in it?', or with the more concrete form of this question, 'how should one live?'. Those who support the validity of such a claim to freedom, arising from humility, point out that practical reason is distinct from theoretical reason in the following way: theoretical reason does not usually have a choice as to whether or not to accept, say, the geometrical properties of a triangle. As we observed in the previous chapter, we might choose whether or not to study geometry, but once this choice has been made, we do not have much freedom of choice in relation to the principles of geometry. With practical reason, though, there is a moment of choice, of commitment. There is the choice of a way of life, and an attitude towards the good.

Crucially, such freedom involves the ability to frame beliefs and commitments, where we have limited knowledge, in contexts where such beliefs help us to engage in a way of life, and to answer the question, 'how should I live?'. Therefore, the humanist restriction on the freedom of practical reason ('evidence', 'knowledge' and 'proof' alone) is a stark and vital epistemic principle, which runs far deeper than the hostility to religion, although it is mainly manifested in this hostility. It would seem fair to say that for the humanist, it is not so much epistemic humility that is meditated and acted upon, but a strenuous commitment to epistemic discipline: not to hold any convictions that do not have an evidential base that warrants knowledge. The humanist looks at the religious believer, and sees a lack of discipline, and the believer looks at the humanist, and sees a lack of humility. Both perspectives lack a certain charity and generosity, failing to see the good that each side seeks.

The denial of the freedom of practical reason—'knowledge and evidence alone'—cuts across religious and non-religious divides: in terms of the discussion of borderlands and flags in Chapter 1, we might say that citizens of two countries, however far from the border, can share values and commitments, and be closer to each other than to some of their immediate neighbours. Globalists and internationalists across the world are more similar to each other than patriotic nationalists living in the same neighbourhood, who themselves share more in common with patriotic nationalists from different nations all over the world.

There might be two sorts of justification given for the freedom of practical reason, in contexts where theoretical knowledge has no jurisdiction or reach. The first type of justification could be more 'descriptive', centred on the observation that our ordinary epistemic practices simply do involve the exercise of such freedom. Even if this observation is accepted, there would be a further debate to be had about the task of epistemology. That is to say: is it the task of epistemology to reflect our actual practices, or should epistemology involve widescale, or piece-meal, reform of our practices?[45]

The second consideration is more 'normative', and involves the claim that—whether or not our actual epistemic practices do involve such freedom—we ought to embrace and exercise it. In favour of this suggestion, the argument might be made that the freedom of practical reason is essential for our flourishing, in a context where truth is complex and only partially disclosed, and our capacities finite. That is: even if we do not, in actual fact, employ the freedom of practical reason very much, or, even if we can 'get along' without it, we *ought* to be open to this freedom. I am aware that to defend this claim, as I am inclined to do, there would be a lot of work to do, and many criticisms to consider. To defend the position, one could draw on a venerable tradition of maintaining the freedom of practical reason, found in Pierre Hadot, and, if Hadot is correct, in classical philosophical schools. It is also an important commitment for Kant, with his notion of the 'priority of practical reason'[46]: that is, where theoretical reason meets its in principle limits, practical reason can make its own moves, with a mixture of humility and confidence. This is at the heart of Kant's self-proclaimed project of denying 'knowledge' to 'make room for belief' (Bxxx).[47]

In a more constructive and contemporary key, one might work through the analytical literature on the notion of 'pragmatic encroachment'.[48] The term arises insofar as 'pragmatic' considerations (how to live/engage with a significant life project) are permitted to 'encroach' upon the types of warrant one is required to have to hold beliefs: those who support pragmatic encroachment think that such considerations can encroach on the type of warrant we need, lowering the epistemic bar, or changing the nature of the bar altogether, to pragmatic considerations alone. Those who oppose pragmatic encroachment disagree with this claim. There is a lot more that one could say here, but, whatever one says, it is clear that the BHA humanist is at a far end of a spectrum of possible positions, in denying the permissibility of any sort of pragmatic encroachment, and that this is a vital humanist epistemic commitment, in some ways more fundamental than an opposition to

---

[45] The debate around 'naturalized epistemology' circles around this contestable claim. Those who defend 'naturalized epistemology' support the idea that epistemology should begin with, and remain answerable to, our ordinary epistemic practices. See, for example, Hilary Kornblith, 'In Defense of a Naturalized Epistemology', in John Greco and Ernest Sosa (eds.), *The Blackwell Guide to Epistemology* (Malden MA: Blackwell, 1999), 158–169, and Jennifer Nagel, 'Intuitions and Experiments: A Defense of the Case Method in Epistemology', *Philosophy and Phenomenological Research*, 85/3, 495–527. For a critical account of naturalized epistemology, see Laurence Bonjour, 'Against Naturalized Epistemology', *Midwest Studies in Philosophy* XIX, 283–300, and for a response to some criticisms, see Hilary Kornblith, 'Naturalistic Epistemology and its Critics', *Philosophical Topics*, 23/1 (1995), 237–255.

[46] For a more extensive discussion of Kant on this point, see my *Kant and the Creation of Freedom: a Theological Problem* (Oxford: Oxford University Press, 2013), ch. 7.

[47] For full details of Kant referencing and abbreviations, see Chapter 7, fn.4.

[48] For an excellent overview of the recent debate, see Brian Kim and Matthew McGrath (eds.), *Pragmatic Encroachment in Epistemology* (London: Routledge, 2019).

religion. It is an opposition to the freedom of practical reason. Kant can be hailed by humanists as a fellow spirit. For example, Stephen Law writes that 'modern humanism clearly involves a commitment to Enlightenment in Kant's sense'.[49] But, on this point, at least, the humanist disagrees with Kant: in setting the limits to knowledge, the humanist does not make room for belief. For the humanist, the limits of knowledge are also the limits of belief. Belief and knowledge occupy the same space.

The humanist's only warrant for holding beliefs is something that achieves the status of knowledge. Engelke is struck by the frequency with which the notions of 'proof' and 'evidence' are celebrated in humanist writings and statements:

> If immortality or the supernatural could be 'proved' in the same way as the value of the antioxidants in blueberries, then humanists would alter their positions. Striving after truth in such terms, according to strict and well-defined evidentiary protocols, is a central aspect of humanist virtue. 'I care passionately about the truth because it is a beautiful thing and enables us to lead a better life', says Dawkins, in a promotional statement on the BHA's homepage.[50]

This immediately brings something to light. It is clear that an ethical eudaimonic element is vital to the bloodstream of humanism. Recall Harry from London, who enjoys 'progress in moral philosophy', as much as he relishes 'making love', and Stephen Fry's celebration of 'purposefulness (political commitments, social justice)'. But, we might ask, how are ethical principles 'proved'? Not in the same way 'as the value of the antioxidants in blueberries'. Even there, it is unclear how we can prove the 'value' of the antioxidants. We can prove their existence, but their value is ordered to a purpose, an end. It is not transparent how the humanist celebration of objective evidence will lead us to discover or endorse *purposiveness* or *value* (normative or otherwise).

In part, the humanist shares here the wider difficulty of how to give naturalistic accounts of value and normativity. Derek Parfit is a notable example of a recent philosopher who claims that naturalism is limited to description, which description can never generate something 'that matters' in a normative way.[51] The standard naturalistic response is to say something along the following lines: that we can generate all the normativity and value that we need, or could ask for (or are entitled to), through our subjective caring about, and valuing of, things.[52] There

---

[49] See, for example, Stephen Law, *Humanism: a Very Short Introduction* (Oxford: Oxford University Press, 2011), 20.

[50] Engelke, '"Good without God"', 148.

[51] Parfit, *On What Matters* (Oxford: Oxford University Press, 2011), esp. vol. 2.

[52] See, for example, David Copp, 'Normative Naturalism and Normative Nihilism', and J.L. Dowell and David Sobel, 'Advice for Non-Analytical Naturalists', in *Reading Parfit on What Matters*, ed. Simon Kirchin (London and New York: Routledge, 2017), 28–53, and James Lenman, 'Naturalism

is much more that can be said here, but what we can immediately see is that it will not be straightforward for the humanist to draw on this line of defence ('subjective caring and valuing'), precisely because it would involve endorsing a freedom of belief, or, at least, a freedom of attitude, that goes beyond knowledge and 'objective evidence'. I am not denying the possibility of coming up with a cogent humanist conception of value, but the challenge will always be this: to find a conceptual space between hard 'objective evidence', on the other hand, which will deliver no more than more elaborate description, and, on the other hand, a notion of 'subjective valuing', which, if it is to deliver what the humanist needs, might also permit even religious belief, if such commitment is, indeed, of value to the subject. The humanist faces the challenge of protecting the possibility of value, without permitting some strands of religious belief.

An example of an appeal to subjective valuing is given by Bernard Williams in his defence of the 'human prejudice'. It is worth while attending to this, to see the sort of bind the humanist might find herself in. 'Suppose', Williams writes, that 'we accept that there is no question of human beings and their activities being important or failing to be so from a cosmic point of view':

> That does not mean that there is no point of view from which they are important. There is certainly one point of view from which they are important, namely ours: unsurprisingly so, since the 'we' in question, the 'we' who raise this question and discuss with others who we hope will listen and reply, are indeed human beings.[53]

This opens up an alternative response to the encounter between the subjective and objective perspective upon our lives. It can be easy to adopt a rather sniffy and aloof attitude to anyone who chooses not to engage, at least sometimes, with the profundity of the encounter between the subjective and objective perspective. This is especially so when spending time with the likes of, say, Albert Camus. When Camus writes about the 'average European', that it 'will be said of him "he fornicated and read the papers"',[54] he does not intend this as a compliment. But, why insist on such a profound reckoning with our predicament? Is mooning about one's significant insignificance compulsory? Is it, even, good for us, and, for those around us? Constantly mooning and moaning about our cosmic insignificance could be a depressing, unhealthy, and energy-sucking distraction. We could become tedious and burdensome to our loved ones. Perhaps, it is better to inculcate

---

without Tears', in *Essays on Derek Parfit's On What Matters* (Oxford: Wiley-Blackwell, 2009), ed. Jussi Suikkanen and John Cottingham, 21–38.

[53] Williams, 'The Human Prejudice', 138.
[54] Albert Camus, *The Myth of Sisyphus*.

habits that encourage a healthy, robust, and earthy occupation of the human prejudice, a preference for our subjective perspective, which, nonetheless, knows that this is what it is. This is not the more usual Wittgensteinian claim that such 'cosmic doubts' are (in some obscure way revealed by philosophical therapy) 'meaningless'. It is, more, that they are harmful, sometimes pastorally disastrous, hindering our happiness.

Perhaps the humanist could occupy something like Williams' 'human prejudice', but, I think there are two difficult nearby areas here. First of all, there is the problem of how to stop Williams' defence of the 'human prejudice' being applied to some strands of religious belief, perhaps, especially, those that are not primarily grounded on confident, or brittle, explanatory 'extra-scientific' claims about fundamental reality. In truth, this will include quite a wide range of theological commitment, reflecting the 'practical' turn mentioned above, and could range in different ways across more 'grammatical' postliberal approaches to doctrine, approaches that emphasize the formation of habit and desire, and to approaches with a hint of fictionalism, or anti-realist construals of truth and justification. The suggestion might be made, at this point, that the humanist could perhaps be permitted to turn to religion, or, at least, to a suitably nuanced version of it. Of course. But, could a BHA humanist do this, qua remaining a BHA humanist? Could a fiscal conservative remain a conservative, if they endorse, in peacetime, radical socialist policies? If there is a need, here, for a reminder, Engelke's anthropological work reveals antipathy to religion as one of the core pillars of BHA humanism. This is not just found in celebrity intellectuals such as Dawkins and Grayling. Consider the humanist celebrant (of funerals and weddings), 'Mary', a 'vibrant and vivacious older woman, raised Catholic, who thought Dawkins didn't go nearly far enough in his criticisms of faith':

> She told me at great length how valuable it would be for humanists to help engineer a mass occupation of the nation's churches: reclaiming the shared spaces of community had to be part and parcel of any enlightenment project.[55]

It seems as if, on the one hand, Williams' minimalist position (endorsing what we subjectively value) could be too generous, with no clear rationale for excluding types of religious commitment. But, looked at from another perspective, the minimalism seems to be not enough, when one considers the humanist discourse around the beauty, goodness, and transformative power, not of subjective valuing, but of *objective truth*. Williams' human prejudice does not reach the characteristic humanist fascination with, and constant seeking of, a morally rich and truth-oriented happiness. Consider Dawkins' claims that 'truth' is 'a beautiful thing and

---

[55] Matthew Engelke, 'The Coffin Question', 35.

enables us to lead a better life'. But, is the truth beautiful? Some have thought that, 'in the end truth, perhaps, is sad'.[56]

It might be possible to step back from quite such a literal construal of the notion of objective truth being in itself transformative, good, and beautiful. Perhaps, it is more that the discipline involved in the search for such truth is good, and conducive to happiness, such that we can therefore *choose* to adopt an attitude towards objective truth as, in itself, a great and happiness generating good. Maybe. But, it seems to me, this still involves a contestable confidence in what seeking out objective truth will do for us. Also, the notion that we *choose to believe* that truth is transformative (without *really* thinking this) is problematic for the humanist to adopt, given that a core commitment undergirding humanist practices and habits is the emphasis on proof and evidence, and the sense that we do *not* have the freedom to choose to believe things, for example, religious frameworks, where we lack knowledge. If the humanist can choose to believe something about truth, because it makes life better to do so, it will be difficult to prevent this principle permitting some types of religious belief.

There are two directions one can go in, having observed these features of humanism, which seem to be in tension: the lack of freedom for practical reason, and the claim that the sheer truth is 'beautiful' and moral. The more negative path is to ask what grounding the humanist has for her ethics: to demand a notion of value that avoids the Scylla of mere description and the Charybdis of mere subjective valuing. As we have seen, Sartre finds the end point of eighteenth-century humanism ('hooray to the essence of the human being!') in fascism. That seems too strong, but we might worry about the resilience and depth of humanist resources actively to resist appalling ethical and social projects, if humanistic epistemology is indexed always to 'evidence' and 'knowledge'. Nazi doctors had evidence and knowledge. The problem was not that they did not know their science. All of this needs saying, and worrying about. But it is not my focus here. It should be noted, perhaps, that drawing attention to an inconsistency or a lack of grounding can in itself go two ways: one can look for better grounding, or one can drop the unsubstantiated commitments. I would always prefer the ungrounded humanist who cares for social justice, than the consistent humanist who did not. Consistency is not everything, and, it is not always beautiful, or truth tracking.

I do not intend, here, to 'trip up' the humanist, or to refute humanism. I take it as read that every variety of worthwhile commitment and worldview has its own weaknesses, pathologies, tensions, and paradoxes. A premise running through the whole book, in a way, is the view that such *aporiae* are an inevitable consequence of the richness of the truth, and the limitations of our grasp of it. In other words,

---

[56] Paul Claudel, in a letter to Jacques Rivière. 24 October 1907, quoted in Josef Pieper, *Happiness and Contemplation,* trans. Richard and Clara Winston (South Bend, IN: St Augustine's Press, 1979), 31.

100   NEGATIVE NATURAL THEOLOGY

a worldview without problems is probably too simplistic and reductive, and not worth defending or inhabiting. No one who values the religious perspective could think otherwise. Becoming aware of the complexities and tensions within the humanist thought-world makes it go up in my estimation.

I suppose the humanist, who does not particularly value the religious perspective, might be more troubled than I am by having attention drawn to certain tensions and fissures in the humanist worldview. Nonetheless, my intention here is not to bring down the humanist edifice, but to understand where some of the load-bearing beams are. I want to ask: what needs to be in place to support the humanist confidence in objective truth? What must the universe be like, if it were to be the case that reflection on sheer truth alone would deliver the good, the beautiful, and happiness? What are the 'conditions of possibility' of such a claim? And, here, we do seem to have a slightly eighteenth-century vibe. One way in which the 'conditions of possibility' would be met, would be if the universe itself were ordered and harmonious, and plenitudinous, such that there was indeed a tessellation, a harmony, between the 'objective' perspective ('truth') and the subjective perspective (with its strong hedonic elements). At this point, the frequent appeal to Enlightenment values has deep resonance. As Engelke puts it:

> Enlightenment is man's release from his self-incurred tutelage. Tutelage is man's ability to make use of his understanding without direction from another. Self-incurred is this tutelage when its cause lies not in lack of reason but in lack of resolution and courage to use it without discretion from another (and so on).[57]

In the expression of the 'ideological commitment to happiness', Engelke finds, there is a constant 'working to articulate, and live out, Enlightenment values'[58]:

> British humanists understand happiness as the struggle for, and promise of, enlightenment. Humanists see themselves as children of the Enlightenment, as taking up the mantle of reason, the tools of science, and the potentials of free thought. Being happy and being 'good without god' is a commitment both to pleasure and to progress.[59]
>
> The happy life is, in this important respect, the good life.[60]

Engelke cites 'one of contemporary humanism's heroes (and a committed member of the BHA-as-then for much of his adult life)', Bertrand Russell, who writes in *The Conquest of Happiness*:

---

[57] Engelke, '"Good without God"', 135.
[58] Ibid.
[59] Ibid., 134.
[60] Ibid., 141–142.

The happy life is to an extraordinary extent the same as the good life.[61]

The orientation towards the Enlightenment is illuminating. It points to more than just a 'belief in reason'. It is for this reason that I suggested earlier that Nagel was not quite correct to say that the humanist makes no claim about the wider universe, beyond human nature. If truth is to be both hedonic and eudaimonic, in the ways endorsed by the practices and speech of humanists, the universe does, in fact, need to have a particular sort of shape and structure.

One way in which the sheer truth can be beautiful, and for happiness to also be goodness, is for the universe to have the shape ascribed to it by Leibniz, or the early Kant. That is to say, the universe is, in its deep structure, beautiful, good, and happiness inducing, although, for the humanist, the order, harmony and plenitude of the universe will be its own end, and not an emanation, as it was for Leibniz and Kant, of the order, harmony and plenitude of the godhead. It is the sort of universe you will get with a particular conception of God, but, the humanist has it without God, finding the addition of God to wreck the picture entirely.

At this point in my discussion, I have to confess to a slight sense of unease. Am I becoming overexcited? Are my reflections on the role played by 'objectivity' in humanist discourse overblown (eighteenth-century vibes, and so forth)? All the humanist intends, we might think, is to praise epistemic virtues of impartiality, critical openness, and responsiveness to, and responsibility in the face of, *evidence*. I'm sure that the humanist does intend to praise these epistemic virtues, and that one can do this without donning an eighteenth-century costume. I worry a little, but I'm inclined to hold my ground, and, indeed, to dig in somewhat.

First of all, at the level of discourse, it is not me but (the much revered and quoted) Bertrand Russell who assures us that the happy life and the good life are the same, and it is Richard Dawkins who talks of the 'magic of reality',[62] and who claims that truth is beautiful. None of these assertions have seemed, for many people, historically and recently, to be obvious or uncontestable. Indeed, it is because of a startling or tragic gap between happiness and goodness, or truth and beauty, that some have been drawn to religious hope: such hope marks a lament that things are not as they ought to be.[63] Even where the hope has gone, or the will to hope has finally flagged, the *lament* can remain (witness Camus). To cut this off, before it all begins, by gesturing towards an identification between truth,

---

[61] Bertrand Russell, *The Conquest of Happiness* (London: Allen & Unwin, 1930), 173, quoted by Engelke, '"Good without God", 142.

[62] Richard Dawkins, *The Magic of Reality: How We Know What's Really True* (London: Black Swan, 2021).

[63] Arguably, for all its complexity, it is this that is at the heart of Kant's moral proof for the existence of God. See my *Kant and the Divine: From Contemplation to the Moral Law* (Oxford: Oxford University Press, 2020), ch.11. For a powerful recent expression of this willed hope, incorporating and never abandoning lament, see Newheiser, *Hope in a Secular Age*.

goodness, and happiness, seems to involve a step beyond 'the evidence', and, as such, to constitute something like a foundational ideological commitment for living.

Secondly, I return to my promise, made earlier, to attend not only to explicit propositional commitments, but to well observed patterns of habit, desire, and practices. It is here—in humanist meetings and practices—where the deep belief in 'objectivity', and the good that it will deliver, is most evident. Engelke writes about his experience of a humanist 'ethical jury', held in Green Vale in September 2012, where a group of humanists pay attention to one member's personal dilemma, attempting to come to an ethical resolution. The case being discussed concerns 'Gran's cat'.[64] The grandmother has asthma, and the much loved cat is making it worse, raising the question of 'how much should her children and grandchildren intervene?'.[65]

Ralph wants to know:

> [D]o you put pressure on her to get rid of the cat? Or do you just say something?[66]

The facilitator draws an arrow on the whiteboard, under the words 'Pressure vs. Suggestion':

The problem with pressure (perhaps, even, suggestion) is that by removing the cat, the loneliness will do more harm than the asthma would have.

A 'bearded man with glasses' states that it is the 'GP's job to interfere',[67] which leads to this:

> A woman in a floral-patterned shirt, who had been totally quiet to that point jumped in quickly: 'And he's objective!'[68]

Engelke reflects more broadly about the meeting that 'turning the matter over to the doctor—making it a scientific rather than a social issue ... kept recurring until the very end of the session':

> I was struck by the after-the-fact contribution by the woman in the floral-patterned shirt. It was as if she had to say it—she had to point to what she

---

[64] Engelke, '"Good without God"', 152.
[65] Ibid., 153.
[66] Ibid., 154.
[67] Ibid., 156.
[68] Ibid.

perceived as a doctor's objectivity. Objectivity really does matter to humanists; where it is perceived, it must be pursued.[69]

A humanist at a certain sort of Christian gathering might be perturbed by frequent recourse to the actions, influence, and guidance of the Holy Spirit. Outside of the circle of commitment, such invocations can seem, no doubt, like a case of magical thinking, made when we are at a loss to know what to do. For those outside of the circle of humanist commitment, though, I suggest that references to 'objectivity' can seem similarly magical and perplexing.

The suggestion being put here, about the role of objective truth, does not stand or fall, necessarily, insofar as it identifies the actual psychological motivation of particular humanist individuals. In some cases, I suspect the comments about 'objectivity' do capture actual psychological motivations. But, the claim still stands, I would maintain, as a more genealogical and conceptual claim about the origins, and conditions of possibility, of certain observed practices, utterances, and expressed values. The claim is that such a commitment to 'objective truth' has its natural home and original conceptual motivation in a particular conception of the way the world is, even where it is one no longer shared or explicitly owned by humanists. Nonetheless, it may be that the commitment continues to do active work in the life, practices, and utterances of humanists, even when we have lost sight of these unconsciously disavowed origins.

Two comparisons come to mind. First of all, the cartoon character Road Runner, running out of road, but remaining mid-air on a horizontal trajectory, at least for a while, through sheer energy and unknowing. The moral is: even if the 'ground' originally supporting the hope for objective truth is no longer there, the legs can keep moving, at least until the panicked realization kicks in. Secondly, and more substantively, I am put in mind of Alisdair MacIntyre's striking and 'disquieting suggestion' in the opening to *After Virtue*, where he asks us to imagine a post-apocalyptic world, where systematic knowledge of the natural sciences has been lost. All we find are broken remains: 'instruments whose use has been forgotten; half-chapters from books, single pages from articles, not always fully legible because torn and charred'.[70] Nonetheless, people seize hold of the fragments such as they find them, and recite them, argue about them, speculate about them, and build meaning and identity around them. MacIntyre's suggestion is that the world we do in fact live in, with respect to our moral lives, is equivalent to this post-apocalypse scenario, such that we argue arbitrarily and passionately about largely meaningless, because decontextualized, fragments. For our purposes here, the analogous point might be this: that people's practices can continue to be fragmentarily shaped by something

---

[69] Ibid.
[70] Alisdair MacIntyre, *After Virtue: A Study in Moral Theory* (London and New York: Bloomsbury, 2011), 1.

from hundreds of years ago, even where the overarching and meaningful framework, as a liveable whole, has been lost to memory.

If I am anywhere near the mark in all this, a curious and rather paradoxical question begins to emerge. Although humanism is avowedly 'non-religious', in being opposed to religion and the supernatural, is there a 'low ramification' way in which humanism is, in fact, in the end, 'religious'. That is to say, to a degree, to the extent that humanist practices and discourse point to the 'belief' that objective truth is somehow *for us*, and that the universe is such that the truth about it is good, and beautiful, and happiness inducing? This might be considered religious in a 'low ramification' sense, to the extent that there seems to be an aspiration towards, indeed, an optimism about achieving, a sort of unalienated life.

I am inclined, though, to say that humanism is not, in this sense, religious. Rather, it seems more accurate to say that the humanist refuses the sense of tension between the subjective and objective perspective to emerge at all. That is to say, the humanist seems to push away any intimation of alienation, before it gains an existential momentum. To explain what is meant by this, we should recall what has already been set out in describing the 'tension' between the subjective and objective perspectives.

The subjective and objective perspectives upon ourselves

Thinkers such as Nagel, Bilgrami, and Camus, consider that we are each of us capable of adopting both a subjective and objective perspective upon ourselves.

As set out a few times already in the book, by a subjective perspective, I mean the sense we have of our own significance. As we saw Thomas Nagel puts it:

> Humans have the special capacity to step back and survey themselves, and the lives to which they are committed, with that detached amazement which comes from watching an ant struggle up a heap of sand.[71]

We are able to regard ourselves, and all the effort, as if we were not ourselves. And it looks 'at once sobering and comical'.[72]

A strand of concern in this book has been the way in which a great deal of thinking engages with this confrontation of the subjective and objective perspectives: either leaning into faith in relation to it, or refusing to do so. An apprehension of this tension has been described, as we saw in the previous chapter, by Albert Camus, as a sense of the absurd, to which we are called to adopt the attitude of rebellion. Camus considers that living in the state of rebellion is the way to avoid

---

[71] Nagel, 'The Absurd', 15.
[72] Ibid.

leaping into either literal or philosophical suicide. Literal suicide removes the subjective perspective altogether, thus brutally 'resolving' the tension between the subjective and objective. Philosophical suicide, for Camus, involves claiming that the universe is somehow, deeply, religiously, 'for us', and that our subjective sense of significance is, or will be ratified, by some sort of supernatural agency, structure, or power. If literal suicide eliminates the subjective perspective, philosophical suicide, for Camus, projects the subjective onto the universe, thus eliminating (or softening in our favour) the 'objective perspective'.

The humanist, I suggest, does not need to find any sort of way, religious or otherwise, to harmonise the conflicting objective and subjective perspectives. Rather, the humanist refuses to allow that there is an opening mystery or absurdity: there is, instead, the beautiful, good, happiness inducing objective perspective, from which cascades subjective flourishing. In the end, then, the humanist does not lean into the space of mystery, seeking somehow to overcome or tessellate the irreconcilable and irreducible subjective and objective perspectives, *because* they claim to start from a place where a harmonious tessellation of the subjective and objective perspectives has *already occurred*. There is no mystery. There is no hope, because there is already a plenitude, if only we can sufficiently draw on the deep wellspring of 'objective truth'. Being religious, for Camus, is not the only way of committing what he calls 'philosophical suicide', which involves claiming that the objective perspective is deeply *for us.* If I am correct about humanism, then it would, for Camus, constitute a form of 'philosophical suicide'. Some of Camus' remarks about humanism, which I will come to further down, suggest that this speculation might have some purchase.

At this point, we might reflect again on the claim, as made by John Gray, that the humanist believes in 'progress', and that this is a secularized version of Christian eschatology. Maybe. But, it seems to me that the commitment to a tessellation between the subjective and objective perspectives is the deeper commitment, from which the belief in the possibility of progress arises. It is because, as Dawkins puts it, truth is 'beautiful' that greater and greater insight into (scientific) truth *will* lead to moral progress. Humanists know perfectly well that societies and cultures can go backwards, and they worry about this a lot. The belief in progress is more a belief in the inevitability of progress if and when truth is pursued. The universe is as we are called to be: 'good without God'.[73]

The more commonly observed standoff is between humanism and religious belief. My reflections here indicate that this might not be the most interesting contrast, when one has in sight the humanist attitude to the pregiven harmony between the objective and subjective perspectives. Some religious worldviews (Leibniz, the early Kant, perhaps also the critical Kant) endorse a similar view.

---

[73] Engelke, '"Good without God"', 159.

Inhumanism

The sharpest challenge to the type of humanism we have been talking about will not be the claims of religious believers: indeed, these will not be felt to be sharp at all by humanists. The harder challenge might be from those who consider 'objectivity' and 'truth' to be less intrinsically transformative, ethical, and reconcilable with the subjective perspective, from those who resist the notion that the truth is good for us, beautiful, and happiness generating. Such 'inhumanist' perspectives can be non-religious, or, religious in alternative and pantheistic ways. Unsurprisingly, perhaps, 'inhumanism' is not a term that has caught on (to be 'inhumane' is hardly decent), but it is a description that was given to a moment in twentieth-century thought. Camus, for example, in *The Plague,* writes that:

> Everybody knows that pestilences have a way of recurring in the world; yet somehow we find it hard to believe in ones that crash down on our heads from a blue sky. There have been as many plagues as wars in history; yet always plagues and wars take people equally by surprise.[74]

'In this respect', Camus has his narrator continue, 'our townsfolk were like everybody else, wrapped up in themselves':

> [I]n other words they were humanists; they disbelieved in pestilences. A pestilence isn't a thing made to man's measure; therefore we tell ourselves that pestilence is a mere bogey of the mind, a bad dream that will pass away. But it doesn't always pass away and, from one bad dream to another, it is men who pass away and, and the humanists first of all, because they haven't taken their precautions.[75]

Common to a certain sort of religious perspective, but also manifest in Camus' sense of the absurd, is an acknowledgement that the objective and subjective perspectives upon our lives cannot be reconciled, and must both be held to attentively. The situation is 'irreconcilable', insofar as we are unable to reconcile, harmonize, tessellate or overcome the tension of these perspectives. Common to both the sense of the absurd, and to religious yearning, is a commitment to a type of unresolved

---

[74] Albert Camus, *The Plague* (London: Penguin Books, 1984), 34.
[75] Ibid.

'completeness', insofar as we do not allow our attention to turn away from either the objective or subjective perspective.

We might be struck here by the thought that much religious and theological thinking is really quite sceptical and nihilistic, at least about the sufficiency of most purported and suggested 'solutions' to our various predicaments, which might be expressed in terms of limits, tensions, and fragmentations. At least one striking feature of religiosity is not credulity, optimism, or confident knowledge claims about the absolute, but a sense of how partial, broken, and fragmented our condition is, where a sense of 'wholeness' or 'healing' is only gestured to in the faintest way, but where this gesturing constitutes (for some people) one of our most important 'ecstatic' moments. On this front, at least, atheistic absurdism and religious belief occupy a similar borderland, albeit that the inhabitants either side of the border believe they are walking in different directions, to rather different outcomes.

The critique of humanism can also come from alternative religious sources, which find a sort of immanent divinity in the whole natural world. The North American poet Robinson Jeffers (1887–1962), associated with 'inhumanism', lived in a self-built stone house (the 'Tor') on the Californian coast, writing about 'earth and sea and sky and wheeling seasons and the evolutionary processes that made trees and salmon runs and hunting hawks'.[76] Jeffers frequently makes reference to the divine and to God, although his framework is explicitly pantheistic, rather than Christian:

> ... [W]e know that the
> Enormous invulnerable beauty of things
> Is the face of God[77]

In 1934, Sister Mary James Power writes to Robinson Jeffers, inviting him to contribute to an anthology of religious poetry, and enquiring about his 'religious attitudes'. The poet responded, 'a plain question deserved a plain answer'[78]:

> I believe that the universe is one being, all its parts are different expressions of the same energy, and they are all in communication with each other, influencing each other, therefore parts of one organic whole. (This is physics, I believe, as well as religion). The parts change and pass, or die, people and races and rocks and stars, none of them seems to me important in itself, but only the whole. This whole is in all its parts so beautiful, and is felt by me to be so intensely in earnest, that I am compelled to love it, and to think of it as divine. It seems to me that this whole

---

[76] Robinson Jeffers, *The Wild God of the World: An Anthology of Robinson Jeffers,* selected with an introduction by Albert Gelpi (Stanford: Stanford University Press, 2003). The quotation here is from Robert Hass' comments on the back cover of the book.

[77] Robinson Jeffers, 'Nova', *The Wild God of the World,* 161.

[78] Jeffers, 'Letter to Sister Mary James Power' (1 October 1934), in *The Wild God of the World,* 189–190, 190.

alone is worthy of the deeper sort of love; and that here is peace, freedom. I might say a kind of salvation, in turning one's affection outward toward this one God, rather than inward on one's self, or on humanity, or on human imagination and abstractions—the world of spirits.

I think that it is our privilege and felicity to love God for his beauty, without claiming or expecting love from him. We are not important to him, but he to us.[79]

The commentator, Albert Gelpi, writes of the way in which 'consciousness', for Jeffers, is 'the original sin that separated us from the divine processes of nature', rather than being 'the distinguishing and crowning glory of humans'.[80] Consciousness, which makes possible the subjective perspective, is that which makes us aware of the sense of separateness, which gives rise to a sense of the absurd and mystery. There is, in Jeffers' poetry, a desire to annihilate this difference, this alienating consciousness. Consider these lines from 'Carmel Point':

> ... Meanwhile the image of the pristine beauty
> Lives in the very grain of the granite,
> Safe as the endless ocean that climbs our cliff.—As for us:
> We must uncenter our minds from ourselves;
> We must unhumanise our views a little, and become confident
> As the rock and ocean that we were made from.[81]

Gelpi comments that 'some readers see Jeffers' inhumanist pantheism as resolving the dualism of mind and nature, subject and object in a pantheistic or ecological holism'.[82] In line with a sense of the irreconcilibity of the subjective and objective perspectives (which irreconcilability is implicitly denied by humanists), Gelpi counters that 'in fact' the 'tragic exultation of the poetry arises from the necessity and impossibility of resolving that dualism':

> Jeffers'[...]inhumanism makes his pantheism [...] a divine tragedy, not a divine comedy.[83]

Gelpi draws attention to the way in which Jeffers is only able to say: 'We must uncenter our minds from ourselves;/We must unhumanise our views a little': the 'tell tale verb is "must"; not here or ever: "I *have* uncentred my mind from myself"'.[84] Although Jeffers desires to 'become confident / As the rock and ocean that

---

[79] Ibid., 189.
[80] Albert Gelpi, 'Introduction: Robinson Jeffers and the Sublime', 1–19, 11.
[81] Jeffers, 'Carmel Point', in *The Wild God of the World,* 175.
[82] Gelpi, 'Introduction', 14.
[83] Ibid.
[84] Ibid.

we are made from', we are 'not made from rock or ocean, and confidence or lack of confidence is a human experience, projected here onto rock and wave out of human need'.[85]

In contrast to the humanist satisfaction in objective truth, Jeffers's thinking has the striving and aspiring quality of leaning into mystery, and into a desired wholeness, in this case, through a sort of wilfull self-annihilation:

> ... As for me, I would rather
> Be a worm in a wild apple than a son of man.[86]

Sometimes, Jeffers writes as if consciousness is something that must be worn reluctantly, and, thankfully, temporarily. Contemplating the corpse of a deer, Jeffers writes:

> ... The deer in that beautiful place lay down their
> bones. I must wear mine.[87]

This desire for the annihilation of consciousness is complex. Consciousness for Jeffers is both the source of alienation, and the way in which we are able to strive to uncentre ourselves, and to overcome the alienation. Also, consciousness is, itself, a wakening expression and moment of the very nature with which Jeffers desires oblivious union, 'man, you might say, is nature dreaming':

> ... but rock
> And water and sky are constant—to feel
> Greatly, and understand greatly, and express greatly, the natural
> Beauty, is the sole business of poetry.[88]

What Jeffers witnesses to here, is that what is most distinctive, perhaps, about our 'humanity', is our constant leaning into the 'inhuman', into the transcendent: God, or mystery, or rebellion, or, for Jeffers, into oblivious union with nature. We might say: a true human-ism desires to transcend the human, to become inhuman.

Jeffers watches himself being contemplated by vultures:

> ... 'My dear birds we are wasting time here.
> These old bones will still work; they are nor for you.' But how beautiful he'd
> looked, gliding down

---

[85] Ibid., 14.
[86] Jeffers, 'Original Sin', in *The Wild God of the World,* 172.
[87] Jeffers, 'The Deer Lay Down their Bones', in *The Wild God of the World,* 180.
[88] Jeffers, 'The Beauty of Things', in *The Wild God of the World,* 175.

110 NEGATIVE NATURAL THEOLOGY

On those great sails; how beautiful he looked, veering away in the seal-light
over the precipice. I tell you solemnly
That I was sorry to have disappointed him. To be eaten by that beak and
become part of him, to share those wings and those eyes—
What a sublime end of one's body, what an enskyment; what a life after
death.[89]

In Jeffers' desire for 'enskyment', there is a longing to be consumed, and devoured,
by winged divinity. Jeffers would not be found submitting comments about happiness involving new shoes, or, even, making progress (in making love or moral
philosophy). And, one would not find in the humanist photo exhibition the line, 'I
am happy today because I will become the main course for this magnificent avian
diner'.

The inhumanist impulse gestures to a far less comfortable relationship between
'truth' and our happiness:

The beauty of things means virtue and value in them.
It is in the beholder's eye, not the world? Certainly.
It is the human mind's translation of the transhuman
Intrinsic glory. It means that the world is sound,
Whatever the sick microbe does. But he too is part of it.[90]

In fact, we know Jeffers' attitude to humanism, in something like the sense we have
been discussing here. Jeffers writes a letter to the American Humanist Association
in 1951.[91] After pointing out that 'the word Humanism' refers 'primarily to the
Renaissance interest in art and literature rather than in theological doctrine', Jeffers
writes that '"Naturalistic Humanism" in the modern sense—is no doubt a better
philosophical attitude than many others', but that 'the emphasis seems wrong':

'[H]uman naturalism' would seem to me more satisfactory, with but little accent
on the 'human'.[92]

The suggestion is that the most significant aspect of the human condition is to
reach beyond the human:

Man is a part of nature, but a nearly infinitesimal part; the human race will
cease after a while and leave no trace, but the great splendors of nature will go

---

[89] Jeffers, 'Vulture', in *The Wild God of the World*, 183.
[90] Jeffers, '*De Rerum Virtute*', in *The Wild God of the World*, 176.
[91] Jeffers, 'To the American Humanist Association' (25 March 25 1951), in *The Wild God of the World*, 201.
[92] Ibid.

on. Meanwhile most of our time and energy are necessarily spent on human affairs; that can't be prevented, though I think it should be minimized; but for philosophy, which is an endless research of truth, and for contemplation, which can be a sort of worship, I would suggest that the immense beauty of the earth and the outer universe, the divine 'nature of things', is a more rewarding object. Certainly, it is more ennobling. It is a source of strength; the other of distraction.[93]

In exploring, and appreciating, the 'inhumanist' response, I do not mean to imply that the humanist position lacks its own courage and panache, or, even, lyricism. Another type of humanist practice is worth attending to here, when probing the deep commitments underlying (in several senses, psychological and conceptual) humanist desires and habits: the humanist funeral. The humanist's turning away from mystery, and from hope, because of an already given plenitude, is not an easy thing to do. It requires its own sort of tensive holding, with its own striving and bravery, as the inclination to disbelieve in the harmony of the subjective and objective is a strong one. The humanist must strive against the possibility of being deeply unhappy, and deny the claim that such unhappiness is, sometimes, an appropriate and measured response, given that the truth is often 'sad'. A reflection here by Engelke about humanists and funerals is striking. Engelke comments about BHA funerals that they are often 'joyful and irreverent in ways which, for the celebrants at least, are part of their ethical and ideological commitments to "the one life we have"':

> Within the funeral industry more generally, there is increasing talk of 'the happy funeral', which is juxtaposed to the 'solemn' nature of the traditional church counterpart. These days, jocular and ironic Monty Python and Frank Sinatra tunes are more likely to be heard than Anglican hymns or live organ music. BHA celebrants see themselves at the vanguards of this shift, of helping effect a more general transformation away from suffering, sin, and the horizon of happiness being set in an afterlife.[94]

To be a giggle at a funeral is a clear marker of ideological intent and commitment to the happiness project. It is not easy. It requires, sometimes, a turning away of the gaze. This is made manifest in what Engelke calls the 'coffin question':

> [M]any celebrants saw the presence of the coffin at the funeral as a potential rent in the immanent order, an object that could be imbued by the mourners with an agency or animate presence, and prompt emotional breakdowns (the figure of the widow who refuses to let go of the coffin, drowning in tears).[95]

---

[93] Ibid.
[94] Engelke, '"Good without God"', 150.
[95] Ibid.

112 NEGATIVE NATURAL THEOLOGY

Organ donation is understood by many humanists as an expression of this repulsion to the 'animate presence' of the corpse: where just under 30 percent of Britons are registered organ donors, the figure amongst BHA is 65 percent.[96]

Engelke describes how some of the more '"hardline"' BHA celebrants and members instruct 'loved ones' not 'to display or present a coffin or even an urn of ashes' at a BHA funeral:

> The best place for a dead body in this view is not the crematorium chapel but the medical school theatre.[97]

It is hard to resist the temptation to construe this postmortem offering as a beautifully apt act of devotion to 'objective science', which devotion is the drum beat of a virtuous BHA life:

> The right thing to do—the rational thing to do—is turn one's remains over to science.[98]

---

[96] Engelke, "The Coffin Question: Death and Materiality in Humanist Funerals', 36.
[97] Ibid., 36.
[98] Ibid.

5

William James' Radical Empiricism and Modern Paganism

In a lecture given in 1909, William James declares that absolute idealism has for some time 'reigned supreme' at Harvard, and at Oxford, and in the Scottish universities.[1] James comments that this movement was 'derived in the first instance from Germany', rather like a 'moist wind from far away, reminding us of our pre-natal sublimity', bringing with it a 'little vastness, even though it went with vagueness'.[2]

The way in which James comments on the ubiquity of absolute idealism is a little like the way in which someone might today begin a lecture by commenting on the prevalence of a certain strand of reductive naturalism. If someone were to do this today, it would be a safe bet that they are about to advocate for an alternative position: an enlarged naturalism, perhaps, or a position that goes beyond naturalism. Just so, James is advocating for a type of revised and enlarged empiricism, which he calls 'radical empiricism':

> [N]ow there are signs of [absolute idealism] giving way to a wave of revised empiricism.[3]

This empiricism, as we will see, has an openness and fluidity that is not associated with some other types of empiricism that come before and after James. There is something poignant in James' reflections here:

> I confess that I should be glad to see this latest wave [of radical empiricism] prevail; so—the sooner I am frank about it the better—I hope to have my voice counted in its favour.[4]

What we now know, of course, is that absolute idealism would largely disappear, but that, so also, would James' enlarged and 'radical' empiricism, replaced instead with what Mary Midgley called the 'pure weedkiller' of a much more repressive

---

[1] William James, 'A Pluralistic Universe: Hibbert Lectures at Manchester College on the Present Situation in Philosophy', in *William James: Writings 1902–1910* (New York: Library of America, 1987), 627–819, 633.

[2] Ibid., 632.

[3] Ibid., 633.

[4] Ibid.

Negative Natural Theology. Christopher J. Insole, Oxford University Press. © Christopher J. Insole 2024.
DOI: 10.1093/9780198933007.003.0006

and destructive empiricism, advocated in Oxford, for example, by A.J. Ayer.[5] This reductive empiricism would demand a high level of verifiable 'evidence'. As it turned out, even our ordinary beliefs in a common sense world come under suspicion, when the demand for evidence is so high.

As already set out, part of my purpose is to uncover some forgotten textures in the history of thought, in order to enlarge our freedom of thinking. We attend to some apparently dying (or dead) shoots, we might say, in order to see whether they might blossom again. In fact, though, we might, here, be doing something slightly different: attending to see if the trees have not, already, and unobserved, breathed some seedlings onto the moist wind, and given life, or at least, supportive nourishment to things that do now live. To this end, in this chapter, I look at William James' account of 'radical empiricism', which he understands to undergird his well known pragmatism, and his less well known advocacy of a 'pluralistic pantheism'. I put this into relationship with some of the practices of contemporary paganism, by engaging with some anthropological fieldwork, unearthing some hidden epistemological and metaphysical commitments, and drawing on some of the writings of the twentieth-century American poet and essayist Wallace Stevens.

In reflecting upon radical empiricism and modern paganism, and absolute idealism and non-naturalistic accounts of normativity, I consider that I am moving to the 'outer edge' of approaches that might be captured by Nagel's fourth response to the cosmic question:

IV   The question has an 'outside-in' answer, in terms of our place in a wider reality or purpose, although we do not need to go beyond a sufficiently rich understanding of immanent reality, of the world.

I say that they are at the 'outer edge' of this type of response, because it can be difficult to know when we step into the territory of stage V:

V   The question has an 'outside-in' answer that appeals to a dimension beyond the world, a transcendent realm or reality.

As I commented in the Chapter 1, I have become uncertain about the immanent/transcendent distinction. What is 'the world'? And, so, what is a 'sufficiently rich understanding' of all that is immanent? At what point is our conception of the immanent world so transformed that we effectively enter a type of transcendent realm or reality?

---

[5] Mary Midgley, *The Owl of Minerva: A Memoir* (London: Routledge, 2006), 120. For this quote and reference I am indebted to Clare Mac Cumhaill and Rachael Wiseman, *Metaphysical Animals: How Four Women Brought Philosophy Back to Life* (London: Penguin, 2022), 50.

I do not propose to offer a clear definition of 'the difference' between IV and V. In fact, the difficulty of knowing this will be one of the things we reflect upon, and return to at points in our remaining discussion.

When pairing James' radical empiricism with modern paganism ('modern' as in current, recent, contemporary), there may not be as big a leap here as initially appears. This is indicated by James' own explicit insistence that radical empiricism leads him to embrace what he calls 'pluralistic pantheism'. James embraces pantheism because he wishes to 'identify human substance with the divine substance', and it is pluralistic because 'the substance of reality may never get totally collected, and some of it may remain outside of the largest combination of it ever made'.[6] When presented with any worldview, James' first question is always what difference it makes to how a life is lived. Pluralistic pantheism, he finds, gives the most vitality to, and recognition of, life as lived:

> It surely is a merit in a philosophy to make the very life we lead seem real and earnest. [Pantheistic] pluralism, in exorcizing the absolute, exorcises the great de-realizer of the only life we are at home in, and thus redeems the nature of reality from essential foreignness. Every end, reason, motive, object of desire or aversion, ground of sorrow or joy that we feel is in the world of finite multifariousness, for only in that world does anything really happen, only there do events come to pass.[7]

For my account of some of the practices and experiences that characterize modern paganism, I draw on two main sources. First of all, I use the ethnographic work of the North American anthropologist Tanya Luhrmann, who spent time embedded in a number of pagan groups in the UK in the 1980s. There are a range of such groups. In this paper, I focus on Luhrmann's account of Wicca (witchcraft), and of a group called the 'Western Mysteries'. Secondly, I draw on the work of the historian of religion, and self-identified pagan, Ronald Hutton.

At the time of Luhrmann's study, she reports estimates of there being around 6,000–10,000 practicing pagans in the UK, and 80,000 self-identified pagans in America. Since then, the movement has grown in popularity and in cultural visibility. The 2021 UK Census recorded 74,000 people self-identifying as pagan. In the USA, a recent study found that 1.5 million people regard themselves as practicing pagans.[8] There are now many bespoke stores offering pagan goods, including spells, crystal balls, and regalia. Typically, they are found in more fashionable, quirky, and prosperous areas of cities such as London ('13 Moons', 'Witchfest'), or in York ('The Society of Alchemists', 'The York Ghost Merchants'), or in towns

---

[6] James, 'A Pluralistic Universe', 645.
[7] Ibid., 652.
[8] https://www.nationalgeographic.com/culture/article/where-to-go-to-explore-pagan-culture#:~:text=At%20least%201.5%20million%20people,explainer%20of%20these%20groups%20below.) Accessed 2 December 2023.

116 NEGATIVE NATURAL THEOLOGY

such as Sassafras in Victoria, Australia ('Elfhame', 'The Witchwood Grove'). These shops are often rather boutique and luxurious, like an expensive perfume or jewellery shop, with strong gestures to a type of nostalgia. They can evoke highly polished mahogany pharmacists from the 1920s: floor to ceiling drawers full of herbs and trinkets, with cabinets and shelves stacked with glass vessels containing colourful potions ('Dragon's Blood and White Sage', 'Anxiety and Depression Spell').

These wares are typically offered half playfully, half seriously, enabling a range of customers and voyeurs to engage in the experience, some with wry distance, others with more passion and commitment, some with a yen for Harry Potter style make believe, others for a little more occult *frisson,* or, maybe, something in between, and a bit of both.

What emerges strongly from both Hutton and Luhrmann is that there is a notable lack of concern in modern paganism with 'correct belief', or 'orthodoxy'. There seems to be little interest in any sort of alignment of, or conformity in, beliefs about fundamental reality. When treating the metaphysical commitments involved in references to deities made in Wicca, Ronald Hutton writes:

> [A] literal belief in the existence of those deities is not necessary to practitioners. Among pagan witches I have found people who think of their goddess and god as archetypes of the natural world or of human experience, others who regard them as projections of human need and emotion which have taken on life of their own, others who see them merely as convenient symbols, and yet others who have a belief in them as independent beings with whom relationships can be made. Some of the latter see themselves as having been 'called' by those divinities, and having been guided by them subsequently.[9]

About the pagans she encounters, Luhrmann writes that they are 'ordinary, well-educated, usually middle-class people':

> They are not psychotically deluded, and they are not driven to practice by socio-economic desperations.[10]

As will become clear, as this chapter unfurls, Luhrmann and Hutton generally find pagans to be creative, expressive, and imaginative, with a strong love of nature, often accompanied with principled ecological concerns, and a commitment to 'a tolerant and pluralist society with maximum potential for individual choice and self-expression'.[11]

---

[9] Hutton, *Triumph of the Moon,* 391–392.
[10] T.M. Luhrmann, *Persuasions of the Witch's Craft: Ritual Magic in Contemporary England* (Cambridge, MA: Harvard University Press, 1989), 7.
[11] Hutton, *Triumph of the Moon,* 404–405.

There is a slightly tired observation that might be made here: that paganism, so characterized, is markedly suited to a liberal, individualistic, consumerist, capitalist culture. The tonal implication, when such comments are made, is not typically intended to be positive: 'and isn't that just fine?'.

I am going to eschew this line of attack. It seems to me that it does not go deep enough, or wide enough. It is not deep enough, because we want to know which strands of the 'liberal, individualistic, consumerist' culture we are taking about. This same culture also produces atheistic materialists, agnostics, alcoholism, depression, TikTok addiction, gambling, premiership football, amusement arcades, nice restaurants, luxury hotels, evangelical Christians, and platonically infused philosophical theologians. Perhaps, insofar as we can trace the deep springs of pagan practice back to something liberal, consumeristic, and individualistic, this might incline us to be more positive about the potential that lies untapped in such individualism. These sorts of instant genealogies are implicit but lazy critiques, because they do not do the hard work of showing what is wrong, or harmful, with the supposed deep springs.

Secondly, the 'paganism is individualism' critique is not wide enough, because we could look through the same lens at so many religious, theological, and philosophical options. At the core of the matter may just be Charles Taylors' insight, from *A Secular Age*,[12] that for many people now, in a way that was not true in the past, whether to believe, and what to believe, are matters of choice.

With all that said, I think we can put some pressure on the claim made by Hutton and Luhrmann that there are no deep and shared beliefs or premises undergirding a variety of contemporary pagan practices. And, here, the parallel with an interest in 'tolerant and pluralist' societies does have some purchase. It is a common observation, as well rehearsed as it is well made, that there are significant and contestable—defendable, also—deep assumptions undergirding tolerant and pluralist societies, and that these deep commitments may come into conflict with other traditions, which in themselves are valid and rational, albeit more traditioned, communitarian, and oriented to a shared vision of the truth.

From the accounts given by Hutton and Luhrmann, one *can* find, I want to suggest here, some shared implicit epistemological assumptions and practices—which in turn imply a particular type of metaphysics—undergirding the various and diverse expressions of modern paganism. The commonality, the 'orthodoxy' may not initially appear at the level of propositional beliefs about the world, where a group of people share the same beliefs, say, about the reality of the gods. Rather, pagan orthodoxy emerges at the level of what they believe—explicitly or implicitly—about beliefs and experiences, and about how beliefs and experiences constitute, or interact with, reality. Perhaps, we might speak here of a type of

---

[12] Taylor, *A Secular Age*.

meta-orthodoxy: not at the level of agreeing on which propositions are justified, but at the level of a consensus about how justification for beliefs and experiences emerges at all.

Consider, for example, what Luhrmann goes onto say about pagan practitioners of magic:

> By some process, when they get involved in magic—whatever the reasons that sparked their interest—they learn to find it eminently sensible. They learn to accept its core concept: that mind affects matter, and that in special circumstances, like ritual, the trained imagination can alter the physical world.[13]

Now, this 'core concept' is *interesting*, and is not nothing: it requires some sort of epistemology and metaphysics, perhaps, quite a sophisticated one, if and when it is not simply crazy. Luhrmann reassures us, pagans are not typically 'more crazy' than any other group. Reading William James' on radical empiricism may help us to identify what some of these sophisticated and implicit assumptions might be. My discussion progresses, therefore, through two main headings, where themes from James and aspects of modern paganism are interwoven and placed in relationship. These headings are: the breadth of experience, and the humanizing of truth.

The breadth of experience

James' account of radical empiricism is motivated by a simple thought: what we immediately know of the world is given by 'experience', but that 'experiences' are far more varied and textured than the basic perceptual experiences that emerge in a certain sort of philosophical discussion. We do not simply have experiences of the form:

> I perceive a table
> I perceive a red patch

James encourages us, instead, to consider the whole range of sensations: 'to be radical', he writes, 'an empiricism' must not 'exclude' any 'element that is directly experienced'.[14] A radical empiricism takes everything 'that comes without disfavour',[15] 'at its face value, neither less nor more'[16]:

---

[13] Luhrmann, *Persuasions of the Witch's Craft*, 7.

[14] William James, 'A World of Pure Experience' (1904), in *Pragmatism and Other Writings*, ed. Giles Gunn (London: Penguin, 2000), 314–336.

[15] Ibid., 316.

[16] Ibid., 318.

Sensations are forced upon us, coming we know not whence. Over their nature, order and quantity we have as good as no control. *They* are neither true nor false; them simply *are*.[17]

When we 'hold fast' to experience 'just as we feel it', then we do not 'confuse ourselves with abstract talk *about* it, involving words that drive us to invent secondary conceptions in order to neutralize their suggestions and to make our actual experience again seem rationally possible'.[18] Amongst the most important features of sensation to present itself to us, James considers, are *relations*:

> [T]he relations that connect experiences must themselves be experienced relations, and any kind of relation experienced must be accounted as 'real' as anything else in the system.[19]

One way, then, in which radical empiricism differs from 'ordinary empiricism' (of the Hume and Locke variety), is that this 'ordinary empiricism' tends to do 'away with the connections of things, and to insist most on the disjunctions'.[20] Although some relations are merely 'mutable and accidental' such as those 'of date and place',[21] other 'conjunctions' are as fundamental a part of experience as anything else, and against the 'tendency to treat experience as chopped up into discontinuous static objects, radical empiricism protests':

> It insists on taking conjunctions at their 'face-value', just as they come. Consider, for example, such conjunctions as 'and', 'with', 'near', 'plus', 'towards'.[22]

This means that 'experience as a whole wears the form of a process in time'.[23] We 'live in such conjunctions' such that 'our state is one of *transition* in the most literal sense':

> We are expectant of a 'more' to come, and before the more *has* come, the transition, nevertheless, is directed *toward* it.[24]

James wants to go beyond discrete and rather static experiences ('there is a red patch in front of me'), to include our experience of continuous and shifting relations.

---

[17] James, 'Pragmatism' (1907), in *Pragmatism and Other Writings*, 1–132, 107.
[18] James, 'Pure Experience', 318.
[19] Ibid., 315.
[20] Ibid.
[21] James, 'Pragmatism', 107.
[22] James, 'Is Radical Empiricism Solipsistic?' (1905), in *Pragmatism and Other Writings*, 337–340, 337.
[23] James, 'Pure Experience', 324.
[24] James, 'Is Radical Empiricism Solipsistic?', 337.

This is a sort of horizontal extension of the category of fundamental experience. In the spirit of James, but going beyond his explicit argument, we might also search for a vertical depth extension of the category of experience, so as to include the entire flower and fauna of our experiential and phenomenological lives: including perceptions (auditory, tactile and visual) certainly, but, also, dreams, imagination, premonitions, moods, reverie, and memories. With a bit of tilting, we could see this as a legitimate extension of radical empiricism.

At this point, we can make a connection with a distinctive feature of Wicca: a fascination with *experience* broadly conceived. Hutton finds, in Wicca, an 'emphasis' upon 'personal experience as the final arbiter of truth or reality', with a 'stress on holistic conceptions of reality'.[25] There is a 'belief' amongst Wiccans that 'it is both possible and desirable to gain a better understanding of how the world functions as a whole, by discerning its inner workings and symbolic patterns'.[26] We find an openness to a diverse range of forms of experience, including 'clairvoyance, prophecy, psychokinesis, and magical healing'.[27] This is admittedly an expansive extension of James' 'radical' and non-hierarchical interest in experience, but it is continuous with it: once we have removed the idea that some experiences intrinsically wear their credentials on their sleeves, independently of their relation to other experiences within a life, then we may become open to, say, clairvoyant experiences, or dreams and reverie.[28]

Tanya Luhrmann's seminal study of practices of magic in modern witchcraft frequently draws attention to the centrality of experience construed broadly and deeply, encompassing the imagination and the inner life. Luhrmann comments that it is the 'mark of a good priestess to trust her responses and dreams and to understand when they serve as knowledge and when they are only the personal fantasies of a tired soul',[29] and that there can be a 'psychoanalytic feel' to a lot of conversations between Wiccans.[30] Luhrmann underscores that a key element to 'modern magic', is a 'private imaginative absorption', an almost childlike state where 'dreams, fantasies and personal emotion seem all-encompassing'[31]:

> It is as if magical practice returns the practitioner to the early stages of negotiating the boundaries between imaginative solipsism and the social, physical world.
>
> Magicians themselves freely draw the comparison between magician and child. This is a period of imaginative creativity and play, of exploration and self-discovery. Magicians repeatedly described themselves as having a

[25] Ibid.
[26] Ibid., 392.
[27] Ibid.
[28] Ibid.
[29] Luhrmann, *Persuasions of the Witch's Craft*, 90.
[30] Ibid., 80.
[31] Ibid., 103.

'childlike-wonder' at the world, a continual surprise at the diversity of nature, and they talk about the need for and value of playful fantasy.[32]

The humanizing of truth

The Drake ritual

In 1985, at a Wiltshire manor house called Greystone, Tanya Lurhmann attended a pagan gathering, a meeting of a group called the 'Western Mysteries'. The weekend event was ostensibly 'devoted to the works of C.S. Lewis'.[33] The meeting comes after months of planning for a 'big ritual', the group in constant contact with each other, discussing dreams and meditations. The group feel a common experience emerging, an attempted contact from some more evolved and non-earthly human beings. The pressure for the ritual is understood as being 'externally inspired',[34] and the group check the reliability of their individual dreams and imaginings, 'making sure that their interpretation was reliable and their contact trustworthy', 'neither a personal fantasy nor an evil being masquerading as a benevolent contact'.[35] We see here the non-hierarchical esteem for all manner of experiences, which maps onto some of James' concerns. We see also that 'reality' is measured against 'fantasy', by checking whether the experiences are shared.

Consensus emerges in the group: amongst the 'contacts' are Sir Frances Drake, Elizabeth I, and the court magician John Dee. The ritual is now called 'the Drake ritual', and the group research Drake and Elizabeth, 'meditating on maps, globes, ships and star maidens'.[36] When it comes to the rite itself, different members of the group 'mediate' or 'carry' Drake, Elizabeth, Dee. The room becomes the *Golden Hind*, a table with a candle the stern, other parts of the room, also marked by candles, are starboard, port, and prow. The following hours are dedicated to meditations, to narratives about historical voyages undertaken by Drake, with the 'listeners sitting eyes shut, in the dark'.[37] Some of them begin to sway to the swell of the sea, afterwards claiming to be seasick, and to have tasted the salt spray. Again, the experience was checked, and found to be in common, with the following all comments from the day:

> I found it difficult to walk, and found myself swaying with a rolling gait.
>
> I don't usually get seasick, but this was an exception. Didn't they have stabilizers?

---

[32] Ibid.
[33] Ibid., 205.
[34] Ibid., 207.
[35] Ibid., 208.
[36] Ibid.
[37] Ibid., 206.

Every time I looked across at Ted he was going up, and I was going down. And when I looked at Peter, he was going up. I came damn close to putting the port light out.

The power came in very strongly, even when the hall was being prepared for this working.

During the setting out of the room, the ship began to materialize, almost, and with the most unexpected power.[38]

At the climax of the rite the ship's 'pilot' narrates the death of Drake at sea, and then reads, emotively, the following lines written by Newbolt:

> Take my drum to England
> Hang it by the shore
> Strike it when your powder's running low.[39]

The ritual ends, and the pilot says, 'in a throaty voice':

Ye can open the door, Mr. Duncan, and let 'em all ashore.[40]

The group, previously, were not 'entirely sure what the ritual was "meant" to be about',[41] but after the rite, there is now more clarity:

[T]hey thought of themselves as helping, slightly, to bring heaven and earth together and to strengthen the inner life of their country.[42]

What are we to make of this unusual act of patriotism? It is, I think, more a John le Carré style 'Britain can make it' moment—amidst the materialism and division of the Thatcherite decade—than a populist rally. We might wonder what it has to do with C.S. Lewis, or what Lewis would make of it all. The 'two martyrdoms of Aslan' are mentioned at one point in the ritual, when it is noted that the *Golden Hind* was previously called the *Pelican,* which bird, pecking its own chest and making itself bleed, can symbolize the sacrifice made by Christ.

Whatever else one thinks of it, the rite comes over as an intense piece of make believe, something between a game played by children and a piece of immersive theatre. The participants in the ritual are not experiencing hallucinations. Luhrmann

---

[38] Ibid., 209.
[39] Ibid., 206.
[40] Ibid.
[41] Ibid., 208.
[42] Ibid., 207.

comments that the members of the group use a 'literal language to describe a let's-pretend account'[43]:

> The participants' impression that the sword or boat was real implies that the let's-pretend narration in the ritual was somehow as large as life, that it was different from ordinary narration, because the power flowed. Likewise, the poetic, symbolic responses are meant to identify a ritual so powerful that it elicited those associations. None of these reports lie, or consciously misrepresent the experience. The sense that there are 'contending forces' or a rocking ship was no doubt very 'real' and the experiential gist of these descriptions is no doubt accurate. And no doubt, the experiential intensity is heightened by the language.[44]

I want to see if pushing deeper into James' account of radical empiricism helps us to provide some epistemological illumination on this realistic let's pretend. When it comes to experience, for James, and modern pagans, so much is thrown up by experience: not just the perception of physical objects, but the flow of relations, and the works of the imagination, dream, and reverie. After spending some time on James' notion of the 'humanizing of truth', I will return to Luhrmann's account of pagan ritual.

James is preoccupied with how much human freedom is at work in our reception of what is given to us by the world for 'however fixed these elements of reality may be, we still have a certain freedom in our dealings with them'.[45] This freedom has three facets for James:

(i) *Attention*. A freedom of what we choose to attend to, and the relative emphasis we give to things.
(ii) *Concepts*. A conceptual freedom of deciding how to carve up the world.
(iii) *Action*. A freedom to contribute new facts to the world.

Attention

James invites us to consider our 'sensations':

> *That* they are is undoubtedly beyond our control; but *which* we attend to, note, and make emphatic in our conclusions depends on our own interests; and according as we lay the emphasis here or there, quite different formulations of truth result.[46]

---

[43] Ibid., 210.
[44] Ibid.
[45] James, 'Pragmatism', 108–109.
[46] Ibid., 108–109.

124 NEGATIVE NATURAL THEOLOGY

For the Englishman, James notes, in a slightly dusty example, 'Waterloo' spells a 'victory', for the 'Frenchman' a 'defeat', or 'for an optimistic philosopher the universe spells victory, for a pessimist, defeat':

> What we say about reality thus depends on the perspective into which we throw it. The *that* of it is its own; the *what* depends on the *which*; and the which depends on *us*.[47]

James writes that both the 'sensational and the relational parts of reality are dumb':

> [T]hey say absolutely nothing about themselves ... A sensation is rather like a client who has given his case to a lawyer and then has passively to listen in the courtroom to whatever account of his affairs, pleasant or unpleasant, the lawyer finds it most expedient to give.[48]

Even 'in the field of sensation', our 'minds exert a certain arbitrary choice':

> By our inclusions and omissions we trace the field's extent; by our emphasis we mark its foreground and its background; by our order we read it in this direction or that. We receive in short the block of marble, but we carve the statue ourselves.[49]

In the room in Greystones, the participants have their eyes shut, attending to their inner sensations and imaginings: the salt spray, the flow of power, the swelling of the ocean.

Concepts

The freedom of where to lay attention and emphasis, according to temperament, preoccupation and interest, leads, for James, to a conceptual freedom also, even at the level of deciding what constitutes 'a thing':

> What shall we call a *thing* anyhow? It seems quite arbitrary, for we carve out everything, just as we carve out constellations, to suit our human purposes.[50]

---

[47] Ibid.
[48] Ibid.
[49] Ibid.
[50] Ibid., 111.

James reflects that for him, the whole audience in front of him is 'one thing, which grows now restless, now attentive', as he has no use 'at present for its individual units', just as when regarding an 'army' or a 'nation', but, that in the eyes of the audience members, being called an 'audience' is an 'accidental way' of being seen:

> The permanently real things for you are your individual persons. To an anatomist, again, those persons are but organisms, and the real things are the organ. Not the organs, so much as their constituted cells, say the histologists; not the cells, but their molecules, say in turn the chemists. We break the flux of sensible reality into things, then, at our will. We create the subjects of our true as well as of our false propositions.[51]

The participants in the Drake ritual name the table with the candle on a mirror 'the stern'. One of their number channels, they say, Elizabeth I, another John Dee.

Action

As well as shaping our world though our choice of attention and emphasis, and through different conceptual choices, there is also the way in which our actions contribute 'new *facts*' to 'the matter of reality'.[52] All of this, taken together, means that 'in our cognitive as well as in our active life we are creative':

> We *add*, both to the subject and the predicate part of reality. The world stands really malleable, waiting to receive its final touches at our hands.[53]

Taken at any particular time in the flux of our lives, we have to consider the immense gathered wave of all the 'mental forms' that have 'already impressed' themselves on all the 'previous truths':

> Every hour brings its new percepts, its own facts of sensation and relation, to be truly taken account of; but the whole of our *past* dealings with such facts is already funded in the previous truths.[54]

The vanishing line of the 'current' experience of reality is thrown up, but is immediately 'squared, assimilated, or in some way adapted, to the humanized mass already there', as we 'can hardly take in an impression at all, in the absence of a

[51] Ibid.
[52] Ibid., 108–109.
[53] Ibid., 112.
[54] Ibid., 108–109.

preconception of what impressions there may possibly be'.[55] And, then, also, we throw out expectations into the future, where we live on 'speculative investments, or on our prospects only':

> But living on things *in posse* is as good as living in the actual, so long as our credit remains good. It is evident that for the most part it is good, and that the universe seldom protests our drafts. In this sense we at every moment can continue to believe in an existing *beyond*. It is only in special cases that our confident rush forward gets rebuked.[56]

'Take my drum to England': in the account Luhrmann provides of the Drake ritual, the *action* of reciting these lines relieves the tension, letting the pent-up power flow out into the wider world.

Humanized truth

To recap: we have the givenness of sensations and experiences, which come with intrinsic conjunctions and relations. We have different elements of freedom in relation to this givenness: of what to attend to, and what to give emphasis to. We also have a freedom of how to name and conceptualize things, and of how to act into the space of experience, and so to shape it. All our experience is shaped by these micro and macrofreedoms, although not all of these involve 'freedoms of choice', or of the will. Any present experience is shaped irreducibly by the past, and by our expectations of the future. This is what it is to live irreducibly in a process, and in transition. All of this James describes as the 'humanizing' of truth. Only the 'smallest and recentest fraction' of reality, James writes, 'comes to us without the human touch', and 'that fraction has immediately to become humanized':[57]

> When we talk of reality 'independent' of human thinking, then, it seems a thing very hard to find. It reduces to the motion of what is just entering into experience and yet to be named, or else to some imagined aboriginal presence in experience, before any belief about the presence had arisen, before any human conception had been applied. It is what is absolutely dumb and evanescent, the merely ideal limit of our minds. We may glimpse it, but we never grasp it; what we grasp is always some substitute for it which previous human thinking as peptonized and cooked for our consumption.[58]

---

[55] Ibid.
[56] James, 'Pure Experience', 334–335.
[57] James, 'Pragmatism', 108–109.
[58] Ibid.

James insists that his position on truth ('the pragmatist view of truth') is not simply an epistemology, or not first and foremost, but rather a view of the whole universe and our place in it.

We can see how the 'whole universe' becomes involved, when we consider how James' denies any hierarchy of experience, which relies on the notion that only some experiences (perceptions, perhaps) *represent* the world, whereas others are 'merely subjective'. James claims not to be able to make 'head nor tail' of the 'notion of a reality calling on us to 'agree with it':

> I try to imagine myself as the sole reality in the world, and then to imagine what more I would 'claim' if I were allowed to. If you suggest the possibility of my claiming that a mind should come into being from out of the void inane and stand and *copy* me, I can indeed imagine what the copying might mean, but I can conjure up no motive. What good it would do me to be copied, or what good it would do that mind to copy me, if further consequences are expressly and in principle ruled out as motives for the claim.[59]

'I cannot fathom', James writes 'but for the honor of the thing, I might as well have remained uncopied'[60]:

> Copying is one genuine mode of knowing [...] but when we get beyond copying, and fall back on unnamed forms of agreeing that are expressly denied to be either copyings or leadings or fittings, or any other processes pragmatically definable, the *what* of the 'agreement' claimed becomes as unintelligible as the why of it.[61]

The sense that some experiences *represent* the world can only itself be based other experiences, or the way in which a certain set of experiences enmesh together. We might say: we experience the world, but we do not experience our experience of the world from a standpoint outside of this experience, which is what we would need to do in order to make judgements about the degree of 'representation'. We are the eye that does not see itself. Certainly, we do not see the relationship—representational or otherwise—between the eye, and what the eye sees.

James returns in a number of places to the claim that 'truth is *made,* just as health, wealth and strength are made, in the course of experience':

> [T]ruths in the plural' 'pay' 'by guiding us into or towards some part of a system that dips at numerous points into sense-percepts, which we may copy mentally or not, but with which at any rate we are now in the kind of commerce vaguely

---

[59] Ibid., 103.
[60] Ibid.
[61] Ibid.

for verification-processes, just as health, wealth, strength, etc., are names for other processes connected with life, and also pursued because it pays to pursue them. Truth is *made,* just as health, wealth and strength are made, in the course of experience.[62]

This makes the concept of truth fluid, dynamic, and, potentially changeable:

> The 'true', to put it very briefly, is only the expedient in the way of our thinking, just as 'the right' is only the expedient in the way of our behaving. Expedient in almost any fashion; and expedient in the long run and on the whole of course; for what meets expediently all the experience in sight won't necessarily meet all farther experiences equally satisfactorily. Experience, as we know, has ways of *boiling over,* and making us correct our present formulas.[63]

We do, indeed, within ourselves, relationships, and communities generate some sense of what the 'objective world' is, in contrast to imaginary worlds or illusions. This arises, for James, because of the way some experiences come together with more momentum than others, and lead us on fruitfully. Experiences that are more densely interconnected and coherent with others are considered 'real' or 'objective'. Experiences that are further away from any such coherent centre are considered more subjective or illusory. But, it is the degree of coherence, interconnectedness, and flow that constitutes these judgements, rather than an *a priori* judgement about 'reality' or 'objectivity' being what licenses us to include such experiences within these interconnecting webs of belief. This licenses a sort of pluralism that is not grounded upon a prior relativism. The pluralism arises just because we accept that there is the plenitude of experiences, where different magnetic centres and constellations arise for different cultures, groups, and people, and within an individual life. There is a fluidity and dynamism in the picture, with little interest in weighing up or calculating the relative merits of very different constellations: if and where experience is very different, then so will be the emerging worldview. Difference is not only tolerated (perhaps as regrettable given our limitations), but expected and celebrated: it is what our fundamental epistemology primes us to accept and be interested in.

One of the tensions or distinctions that has been operative for us throughout the book so far has been the relationship between the subjective and objective perspectives upon ourselves: ourselves seen from inside our sense of our own significance and salience, and ourselves as seen as part of the world, from a third-person perspective. There is a way in which James' 'humanistic' vision of truth softens this distinction, making each perspective more porous to the other: the world that

---

[62] Ibid., 96.
[63] Ibid., 97–98.

presents itself, we know, is suffused with meaning and spirit. With James' denial of a copying type of representation, and his emphasis upon the coherent making of our experienced world, we never encounter a sheer 'other'. There is a type of intimacy and dance between the universe and ourselves, with the universe coming to a type of self-reflexivity and awareness in us. James comments that 'the first great pitfall from which such a radical standing by experience will save us is an artificial conception of the *relations between knower and known*':

> Throughout the history of philosophy the subject and the object have been treated as absolutely discontinuous entities; and thereupon the presence of the latter to the former, or the 'apprehension' by the former of the latter, has assumed a paradoxical character which all sorts of theories had to be invented to overcome. Representative theories simply shoved the subject-object gap a step further, getting it now between object and the representation.[64]

Back to the Drake ritual

We can return now to see whether James' understanding of the 'humanizing' and 'making' of truth help us to make sense of some modern pagan practices. Consider the way in which Tanya Luhrmann describes some of the deep assumptions she sees at work in magical practices. As we saw from the Drake ritual, set out above, there is a florid 'conflation of the self and the world, the collapse of the thin divide which separates subjectivity from an objective world'.[65] The world does not stand 'out there', ready to be copied and represented. It is a co-production, made through perception, action, attention, creativity, and practice. In this way, the world emerges as 'patterned, meaningful and often intentionally compelled'.[66]

This humanized making of the world, Luhrmann comments, leads to an unsettling of the division between the categories of the objective and subjective:

> Their conversational style tends to be what a psychologist might call 'ego-centric', to have difficulty distinguishing between objective reality and subjective experience. They speak as if a change in their own inner perception of events changes (or is) the external reality. This assumption in fact is the lynchpin of magic: that mind and body are linked, so that in special circumstances the imaginative can shift the material. Magicians do not confuse their souls with their tables, nor do they act on the belief that a traffic light has changed if they only wished that it would have done so. However, they do talk about magic in ways that imply

---

[64] James, 'Pure Experience', 319.
[65] Luhrmann, *Persuasions of the Witch's Craft*, 165.
[66] Ibid.

various versions of this sort of assumption. They change their names, their costumes and their bearing as if the adoption of a new identity will produce new abilities and a nominalist fallacy with a potent psychological force.[67]

Even Luhrmann's use of the categories of 'perception' and 'external reality' may impose too representative a scheme on some magical practices and discourse, in ways that James could better understand: there is no outer reality which magical practices may or may not represent or change. Reality is made in the practice. This would account for some of the extraordinary imaginative latitude described by Luhrmann:

> Magicians seem to enjoy interpreting patterned interconnections between events. Performing a ritual allows you to interpret any subsequent event as related to it. You 'work' a ritual to reunite Christian and pagan spiritual currents, and in it use imagery from the stories of Joseph of Arimathea and Bren's voyage to the underworld. All these story elements have associations: Joseph of Arimathea is connected to Glastonbury, famous for its druids and its sacred well; the underworld is a place of darkness, of the unconscious; Christianity is about transcendence, Celtic religion about ancient wisdom. Any event subsequent to the ritual which somehow embodies one of these associations can be seen as related to the rite. A Walt Disney movie about Merlin (a druid, by these accounts), mistletoe hanging in the church (a pagan intrusion into Christianity), a flood of tears (the strong feelings of the unconscious) ending in an embrace (redemption)—all of these *could* be seen as offspring to the rite and presented as evidence that it raised power. Magicians try to avoid saying that some event occurred by chance.[68]

Again, it is striking to see how Luhrmann imposes an 'outer reality/inner experience' model when describing the language of magical practitioners:

> They learn to use a literal language to describe events which have not occurred in reality but have been imagined, and they use a metaphorical language to describe actual events, feelings, and impressions.[69]

A thinker who is really immersed in some aspects of James' worldview might question the legitimacy of this distinction 'occurred in reality', 'have been imagined', and 'actual events'. Everything that occurs in reality, and in imagination, for James, is, to a degree, both imagined and actual, truth made and humanized.

---

[67] Ibid., 165–166.
[68] Ibid., 169.
[69] Ibid., 204.

As well as radicalizing empiricism, we can also see how James here pushes deeper on some Kantian moments. Kant uses the term *Einbildungskraft* (translated as 'imagination') to describe the 'mysterious power', at the deep springs of the self, to recognise, reproduce, and order images, essential as a precondition for even the most basic perception. Kant uses the same term to describe the imagination involved in aesthetic appreciation and the creative arts. A whole tradition of post-Kantian philosophy has variously meditated on the role and limits of finite free imagination, running from basic perception and cognition, to theory building, and in the creative arts.

So, for example, the post-Kantian philosopher Simon Critchley aptly celebrates the philosophical insights from poetry, which offers:

> [A]n experience of the world as mediation, the mind slowing in front of things, the mind pushing back against the pressure of reality though the minimal transfigurations of the imagination.[70]

Critchley is influenced here by the American poet and essayist Wallace Stevens (1879–1955), who writes that 'no fact is a bare fact, no individual fact is a universe in itself',[71] or, more pithily, 'realism is a corruption of reality',[72] if and when 'realism' has consciousness and imagination reductively drained out of it. Or, even more pithily, we could follow Heidegger as he cites Hölderlin: 'poetically, man dwells'.[73] All of this flows through a rich post-Kantian seam, which reflects, as Schelling puts it, that 'the ideal work of art and the real world of objects are *products of one and the same activity*', or Schlegel's 'no poetry, no reality'.[74] The challenge is to find the truth in this thought, without leaping to a grandiose and idealist refusal of a logos-saturated reality that opens up beyond the human mind. If, as Wallace Stevens says, 'poetry is part of the structure of reality', this is not limited to the poetry available on the shelves of any bookshop.

Drawing on the work of Judith Wolfe, we might speak here of the work 'finding and making' that goes on in ordinary perception, in conceptual mediation and interpretation, and in intentional acts of imagination. Wolfe writes that:

> [W]e cannot neatly separate out finding from making, seeing from construing, perceiving from interpreting.[75]

---

[70] Critchley, *Things Merely Are* (New York: Routledge, 2005), 88.

[71] Wallace Stevens, *The Necessary Angel: Essays on Reality and the Imagination* (London: Faber, 1960), 96.

[72] Wallace Stevens, *Opus Posthumous*, ed. Milton J. Bates (London: Faber, 1990), 192; cited by Critchley, *Things Merely Are*, 28.

[73] Cited by Critchley, *Things Merely Are*, 30.

[74] Friedrich Schlegel, *Philosophical Fragments*, trans. Peter Firchow (Minneapolis: University of Minnesota Press, 1991), 70; cited by Critchley, *Things Merely Are*, 24.

[75] Judith Wolfe, *The Theological Imagination*, 12.

132 NEGATIVE NATURAL THEOLOGY

Wallace Stevens was preoccupied with the inextricable binding together of finding and making. He used the image of a 'blue guitar' to evoke the interpretative work done by the mind in receiving the world. When a tune is played upon a blue guitar, the analogy is of the mind interpreting the world. Any tune has a reality independent of a single playing, but what is this reality, until it is played upon a guitar?

> The man bent over his guitar,
> A shearsman of sorts. The day was green.
>
> They said, 'You have a blue guitar,
> You do not play things as they are.'
>
> The man replied, 'Things as they are
> Are changed upon the blue guitar.'
>
> And they said then, 'But play, you must,
> A tune beyond us, yet ourselves.
>
> A tune upon the blue guitar
> Of things exactly as they are.'[76]

It is striking to reflect on the range of thinkers here who dwell on the inextricability of finding and making, and then to consider how the same orientation to this insight can be expressed and manifested in very different worldviews and hopes: from the Christian eschatological hope of the theological imagination (Judith Wolfe), and in the humane turn in philosophy of religion (John Cottingham), as well as in Simon Critchley's atheistic interest in mysticism, or in romanticism (Hölderlin), or in a type of moody nihilism (Heidegger). We may find a similar moment in Coleridge, when he writes:

> Though I should gaze for ever
> On that green light that lingers in the west:
> I may not hope from outward forms to win
> The passion and the life; whose fountains are within.
>
> O Lady! we receive but what we give
> And in our life alone does Nature live.[77]

With William James we have yet another manifestation: pluralistic pantheism, which finds resonances, I have suggested, with some of the practices of modern

---

[76] Wallace Stevens, 'The Man with the Blue Guitar', in *Collected Poems* (London: Faber, 2006), 143.
[77] Coleridge, *Poems,* ed. J. Beer (Dent: London, 1974), 281. Cited by Critchley, *Things Merely Are,* 25.

paganism. It seems that an insight into the significance of finding and making does not determine what the consequence of this insight should be, in terms of a wider metaphysics or worldview. That finding and making is significant is compatible with a wide range of alternative visions of what is found and made.

In itself, this need not be terribly disturbing. Philosophy of religion, and philosophy more generally, is quite familiar with the way in which having a justified belief, and having a true belief, can split apart. You might be rationally justified in your belief, in atheism, or Buddhism, or whatever, given your priors, context, and your experience. This is compatible with me being, at the same time, in a way that you can acknowledge, rationally justified in my belief in Thomism, or absolute idealism, or whatever.

Critical (and not so critical) reflections

This does not mean, of course, that a critical and exploratory conversation stops here, although attempts at direct persuasion from one position to another become more self-reflexive and diaphanous, when we meditate on the range of factors underlying why one person is drawn to one approach, and someone else to a seemingly opposed perspective. Introducing psychological or anthropological dimensions when thinking about 'what is at stake' does not necessarily make things nicer or more accepting, as we will see. I will conclude by briefly surfacing three possible approaches I can envisage being adopted towards pluralistic pantheism and modern paganism, based on the material presented in this paper: a defence, a *reductio* style deflation, and a more hovering, apophatic, and concerned patience.

A defence

James regards pluralistic pantheism as a particularly apt type of spirituality that emerges from the metaphysics and epistemology of finding and making. He draws attention to the 'intimacy' involved in a world where the subjective/objective distinction has been 'humanized'.

James is an agreeable and humane writer, to such an extent that he can tactfully veil his quite stark preferences, sometimes, for some ways of being in the world over others. Although James never puts his case so starkly, I think we can detect three moves that he makes, in defence of pluralistic pantheism. In turn, James claims that pluralistic pantheism:

(i) ... arises from our having correct beliefs about beliefs and experiences—the epistemology and metaphysics of finding and making.

(ii) ... expresses adaptive desires in relation to the world we live in, relative to other options.

(iii) ... is indicative of a more successful and adaptive personality type.

The first claim I have already discussed above. Turning now to the question of having adaptive desires in relation to the world we live in, James locates pantheism between materialism on the one hand, and dualism on the other. The materialist, James finds, will be 'suspicious' of the universe in which she lives: 'cautious, tense, on guard'.[78]

The dualist position, for James, is where 'God and his creation' are perceived as 'entities distinct from each other', where the 'human subject' is left 'outside of the deepest reality in the universe'.[79] James wants intimacy, and there is no more 'intimate a relation' as to be 'substantially fused into it':

> [P]antheistic idealism, making us entitatively one with God, attains this higher reach of intimacy.[80]

With this most intimate type of spirituality, the pantheistic, we can consider our philosophical activity as *itself* 'an intimate part of the universe', which may be a 'part momentous enough to give a different turn to what the other parts signify':

> It may be a supreme reaction of the universe upon itself by which it rises to self-comprehension.[81]

We can begin to see the point I made above being worked out: that introducing psychological considerations, or thoughts about desire, need not make us nicer or more appreciative. For James, not only does the traditional theist have the wrong beliefs about beliefs, but he or she may have the wrong set of desires, in relation to the cosmos: brittleness, wariness, or a type of stand-offish *froidure*.

Things may only get worse when considering James' preferences for personality types. James' radical empiricism, we recall, emphasizes fluidity, fragmentation, occasional and temporary gatherings of coherent experience and worlds, with subsequent redispersals. James finds pluralistic pantheism to be consonant with this, endorsing the 'pluralistic' identification of the 'human substance with the divine substance', which is 'willing to believe that there may ultimately never be' a single all-encompassing and stable vision, which James calls here the 'all-form'[82]:

---

[78] James, 'A Pluralistic Universe', 645.
[79] Ibid., 641.
[80] Ibid.
[81] Ibid., 645.
[82] Ibid.

RADICAL EMPIRICISM AND MODERN PAGANISM   135

[T]hat the substance of reality may never get totally collected, that some of it may remain outside of the largest combination of it ever made, and that a distributive form of reality, the *each*-form, is logically as acceptable and empirically as probable as the all-form commonly acquiesced in as so obviously the self-evident thing.[83]

Not to be a pantheistic pluralist is to show a less than flexible and fluid personality type, the implication seems to be. In the next chapter, I find that James is not fair to the absolute idealist, who he is particularly targeting here.

A reductio-style deflation

An alternative and opposing reaction to the material set out here, is to find the 'Drake ritual', for example, grist to the mill when framing something like the 'Great Pumpkin' objection, often launched against post-foundationalist and coherentist defences of religiously committed traditions that downplay the need for evidence, or chains of reliable inferences going back basically justified beliefs. The objection is: what is there to stop a group believing in the 'Great Pumpkin' as a sort of deity, if a group of people somehow persuade each other to agree with this belief? 'If this is what a finding and making epistemology leads us to', the thought is, 'it shows that there was sometime wrong with the epistemology'.

We have here, I would suggest, an instance of where attending to a concrete anthropological example, rather than an armchair invention ('the Great Pumpkin'), can assist our philosophy. Amongst the participants in the Drake ritual, I doubt you would find a crude brittleness about the beliefs arising from the rite being capital T 'true': the whole scenario is more fluid, ludic, and hard to pin down. Launching the Great Pumpkin objection here seems to be a case of taking a revolver to a Morris Dance: pitching a big 'T' expectation about Truth, when what is in play would need to richer palate of philosophical options. This palate might include types of anti-realism, fictionalism, and acceptance-as-if (as the judge accepts the innocence of the accused, maybe without believing it). All of these textures could be in play, and in a shifting way, where a refusal to be pinned down is also part of the point, based on a mixture of humility, jouissance, and mischievousness.

A hovering, apophatic, and concerned patience

The epistemology of finding and making responds to two perennial magnetic poles of philosophy. On the one hand, there is some sort of givenness in our encounter with the world. There is a friction, a resistance from the world. We cannot simply

---

[83] Ibid.

make up whatever we want. On the other hand, we make what is given intelligible, and a home for us, through the work and layering of concept, imagination, and thought, with all the freedom, choice of attention and play that can involve. And, we cannot find the seam: where the givenness ends, and the making intelligible begins. Even when we identify or announce a seam, this itself partakes in, and is hidden by, the indistinguishable mingling of finding and making.

That does not mean, though, that there cannot be different emphases, and a range of ideas about what responsibility to the given involves. Approaches that engage with finding and making, some of which I identify above, can identify the point of resistance in a number of places. What provides some of the resistance of the given may include the grammar and shape of a tradition, as with Judith Wolfe and Christian Theology, or the discipline of philosophy, as with John Cottingham. One has to wait, sometimes, to discern and feel out where the given, the resistance, mostly comes from, in another person, or movement.

In the process of attending to modern paganism, we note, with Luhrmann, the playful and creative quality of the use of language and ritual. There is another, perhaps, for some, more concerning dimension, also identified by Lurhmann: which is an attraction, in the doing of spells, to a sort of childlike fantasy of omnipotence. That wishing it to be so, and it being so, can be made to run together. Luhrmann is sensitive and delicate, non-judgmental, when making these observations. She writes about the pervasiveness in pagan literature and rituals of facing the 'abyss whose negotiation confers adepthood', where the 'way to personal empowerment and selfhood leads through the valley of dissolution':

> The themes which emerge from this creative amalgam of different myths, stories and symbols are about the nature of power: of the value of losing it to regain it, of the knowledge to control it. Those who become magicians are compelled by these portrayals. They often seem to be people self-sufficient within a withdrawn, subjective fantasy world who are conflicted about their own desire to have impact within the larger social world, and the romantic fantasy constitutes for them some sort of resolution, perhaps as therapy, perhaps as escape. It is as if the magic dramatized the psychodynamic tension of early childhood—the terror of dissolution, the negotiation of the power relations between the powerful other and oneself, the need for autonomy—and characterized its resolution as mature adulthood.[84]

Strikingly, Luhrmann observes that one of the most popular occupations amongst modern pagans is computer programming and science,[85] where reality might be

---

[84] Luhrmann, *Persuasions of the Witch's Craft*, 87.
[85] Luhrmann's own experience was that 'one or two out of every ten magicians I met had something to do with computers' (106). This was confirmed by a questionnaire conducted by Adler in 1985, who found that 16% of respondents were computer programmers, systems analysts and software developers, with an additional 5% working in technical fields. The survey was distributed at pagan festivals to 450 people, with 195 being returned.

amenable, with enough skill and technique, to all manner of desires and fantasy. Without a rush to judgement about what this might mean, we can simply observe, for now, that some of the resistance and friction seems to come here, not from the world, or a tradition, or a discipline, but from personal desire, and a desire to feel some conatus and freedom. There is more making than finding, and the finding, such as it is, comes from the inner world.

Earlier, I cited Wallace Stevens where the poet uses the image of the blue guitar to evoke the making work of the mind, as it receives and plays the music that is somehow given.

Stevens uses another set of images to capture these two moments of finding and making. He talks of the winter thing-in-itself, which is the hard given, the resistance, the friction from the world, and of the summer thing-in-itself, which is the 'poeticized, imaginatively transformed reality', worked upon, made intelligible, stitched into story, myth, meaning.

Modern pagans, we might say, delight in the summer thing-in-itself. Stevens writes:

The world is larger in summer.[86]

This is because, as Simon Critchley puts it, 'the imagination finds what suffices by showing its domination over reality'.[87] We might note the apposite term 'domination' here—spells, the omnipotent and playful child.

Other approaches to finding and making, perhaps, are more prepared to endure harsher seasons than summer:

... dark winter
When the trees glitter with that which despoils them.[88]

One must have a mind of winter
To regard the frost and the boughs
Of the pine-trees crusted with snow;[89]

Other findings and makings have, perhaps, more difficult givens, less amenable to desire, or our playful will to power: the inhuman world, the cross, sin, the difficulty and weight of tradition, the rigour of an argument. Those who carry frostier givens may face a more wintry finding and making, attending, sometimes, in the

---

[86] Wallace Stevens, 'Two Illustrations that the World Is What You Make of It', in *The Palm at the End of the Mind*, ed. Holy Stevens (New York: Vintage, 1967), 376. For citations from this work, I am indebted to Critchley, *Things Merely Are*, 61–66.

[87] Critchley, *Things Merely Are*, 65.

[88] Stevens, 'A Discovery of Thought', in *The Palm*, 366.

[89] Stevens, 'The Snow Man', in *Collected Poems*, 8–9.

due season, to the 'Nothing that is not there and the nothing that is,'[90] and to be willing to enter into the more alienating, dejected, and non-intimate thought, when Stevens attempts to imagine the 'sun without imagination':

> Shine alone, shine nakedly, shine like bronze,
> That reflects neither my face nor any inner part
> of my being, shine like fire,
> that mirrors nothing.[91]

[90] Ibid.
[91] Stevens, 'Nuances of a Theme by Williams', in *The Palm*, 39.

6

Absolute Idealism and Derek Parfit on What Really Matters

William James explicitly articulates and defends his pluralistic pantheism as a contrasting position to Absolute Idealism.

James suggests that where the pluralistic pantheist is comfortable with fluidity, contingency, and change, the absolute idealist desires, above all, peace and stability. For the absolute idealist, everything is either wholly rational or wholly irrational:

> Either the absolute whole is there, or there is absolutely nothing.[1]

It is striking the extent to which James seems to prefer one type of self over the other: clearly, he regards as superior the self that is capable of fluidity and contingency. In this context we can look again at a passage that I cited in the previous chapter:

> It surely is a merit in a philosophy to make the very life we lead seem real and earnest. Pluralism, in exorcizing the absolute, exorcises the great de-realizer of the only life we are at home in, and thus redeems the nature of reality from essential foreignness. Every end, reason, motive, object of desire or aversion, ground of sorrow or joy that we feel is in the world of finite multifariousness, for only in that world does anything really happen, only there do events come to pass.[2]

This psychological profiling of the absolute idealist, I will suggest, is not entirely fair. To show this, I will focus on the 1898–1900 Gifford Lectures given by the Harvard-based absolute idealist, Josiah Royce (1855–1916). I will set out key features of Royce's positions and motivation. We will see why James comes to the judgement that he does, but, also, why this is less than accurate about the whole of Royce's thought. In this connection, I will draw attention to two features of Royce's work here: first of all, the acknowledgement of turmoil and fragmentation, and secondly, the invitation to assume a sort of binocular vision, when we receive the consolations of philosophy. It is important to Royce that his system preserves our sense of our temporality, individuality, and freedom, including our bewilderment

---

[1] James, 'A Pluralistic Universe', 660.
[2] Ibid., 652.

Negative Natural Theology. Christopher J. Insole, Oxford University Press. © Christopher J. Insole 2024.
DOI: 10.1093/9780198933007.003.0007

140 NEGATIVE NATURAL THEOLOGY

and limitations. Royce, I will suggest, recommends a sort of binocular vision, whereby we are able to see our lives as limited by our finite perspective, but also grasp (without seeing) that they are part of a wider symphonic whole. James' account underemphasizes the significance of a sort of pained yearning and acknowledged turmoil that runs through Royce.

We will also see considerable affinities between James and Royce: both deny the idea that our experiences and thoughts somehow 'represent' an independent reality, and both employ the category of divinity as central to their task of overcoming the distinction between subject and object, and between the subjective and objective perspectives upon ourselves.

Josiah Royce: arguing for the Absolute

The movement of thought in Royce's absolute idealism is, briskly speaking, as follows:

1. The world that presents itself to ordinary perception and common sense contains separate and discrete entities in interaction with each other.
2. When examined philosophically, this world is exposed as being rife with antinomies and contradictions.
3. It emerges that the only way to account for the world that presents itself is by understanding it as an aspect of the Absolute, or the All, which is a unified whole.

Royce, for example, considers whether separate substances could be in relation with one another. It transpires, Royce claims, that they cannot: the moment one substance is apparently in relation to another, it effectively has to remain either separate and apart (in which case there is no relation), or it becomes a part of the other. James gives a slightly parodic account of this, riffing on the phrase 'a cat may look at a king',[3] which is worth reproducing here:

First, to know the king, the cat must intend *that* king, must somehow pass over and lay hold of him individually and specifically. The cat's idea, in short, must transcend the cat's own separate mind and somehow include the king, for were the king utterly outside and independent of the cat, the cat's pure other, the beast's mind could touch the king in no wise. This makes the cat much less distinct from the king than we had at first naively supposed. There must be some prior continuity between them, which continuity Royce interprets idealistically as meaning

---

[3] Ibid., 657.

DEREK PARFIT ON WHAT REALLY MATTERS   141

a higher mind that owns them both as objects, and owning them can also own any relation, such that supposed witnessing, that may obtain between them. Taken purely pluralistically, neither of them can own any part of a *between,* because, so taken, each is supposed shut up to itself: the fact of a *between* thus commits us to a higher knower.

But the higher knower that knows the two beings we start with proves to be the same knower that knows everything else.[4]

[Y]ou can deny the whole only in words that implicitly assert it. If you say 'parts', of *what* are they parts? If you call them a 'many', that very word unifies them. If you suppose them unrelated in any particular respect, that 'respect' connects them; and so on. In short you fall into hopeless contradiction. You must stay either at one extreme or the other.[5]

As always, our concern is not so much whether this account is plausible or not, but what implications it might have for the use of the concept of the divine.

James' pithy statement of Royce's argument obscures a striking common concern of both Royce and James. As we saw in the previous chapter, James holds out against the putatively 'representative' nature of experiences, finding that experiences are all on the same plane, without some 'wearing on their sleeves' their superior status as *representing* something beyond the realm of experience. Something like this insight also motivates a main line of thinking in Royce's work. Royce finds that if you separate out a 'World of Fact' and 'World of Idea', one soon becomes 'sunk in an ocean of mysteries'.[6] Although such 'realism' seems like 'common sense', the 'consequences are subject to such remarkable and rapid transformations'.[7]

Speaking briskly, the following is how one line of argument in Royce goes. The premise of all forms of realism is that the external world of fact exists, as it does, 'whether or no' the way in which it is represented in the world of ideas. The world must be 'independent of any knowledge' that claims to refer to 'them from without'.[8] Royce's next move is to point out that the 'external real world' is either made up of Many, or just One.

Either way, Royce argues, there are problems.

Assume, first of all, that the external real world is made of many separate realities. Royce argues that there is an internal problem of making sense of this, and, also, that there is a problem in how we could hope to know anything about these separate realities.

---

[4] Ibid., 658–659.
[5] Ibid., 660.
[6] Josiah Royce, *The World and the Individual: Gifford Lectures. First Series: The Four Historical Conception of Being* (London: MacMillan, 1927), Vol.1, 17.
[7] Ibid., 109.
[8] Ibid., 110.

142 NEGATIVE NATURAL THEOLOGY

We can consider, first of all, the internal problem. What do we mean when we say that two realities are 'independent' or 'separate'? Take an example of two dice, each of which is rolled. Are the dice fully independent of each other? Which is to say, can we give a complete account of one dice roll, which is true and complete 'whether or no' we say anything about the other dice roll. Royce reflects that 'if space and time are thus Wholes of conceptually linked and mathematically interdependent parts':

> [O]f course one has to admit that, in a sense, no two objects, no two events, in space and time can be defined as through and through logically or essentially independent of each other; since in defining each as to its time and space relations, one has to take account of facts which can be recognized only as mathematically linked with the space and time aspects of the other object or event... plainly then, one merely means that while these events are not wholly independent, there is an aspect in which they may be called independent, either because one does not know what the interdependence is, or because knowing, one ignores some aspect of the interdependence as insignificant.[9]

What the realist who believes in the existence of many different things is after, is an account of 'beings such that, as they at first are defined, the existence and the nature of any one of them is essentially indifferent to the presence, or absence, or alternation of any of the others ... no change in that one need correspond to any change in the others'.[10] But, Royce asks, 'when do we actually experience this?':

> Yonder in the ocean there are drops of water. Here on land is my desk. Both are real.[11]

But, when we reflect, we soon find that 'the drop of water in the ocean, evaporated, may enter into the atmospheric circulation, may be carried, as moisture, to my desk, and may there help to warp the world':

> Hence these empirical objects are never known as independent.[12]

This means that 'our human experience ... never shows us how beings would behave if they were mutually independent, in the ideal sense of our exact definition'.[13] When we combine realism with a commitment to the existence of many independent beings, we generate the result that there are 'no possible real linkages

---

[9] Ibid., 114.
[10] Ibid., 123–124.
[11] Ibid., 124.
[12] Ibid., 125–126.
[13] Ibid., 127.

or connections'. Beings are 'moreover wholly sundered, as if in different worlds',[14] with 'no ties, no true relations', 'sundered from one another by absolutely impassable chasms', 'not in the same space nor in the same time, nor in the same natural or spiritual order'.[15] What then happens is that Realism resorts to 'various paradoxical secondary explanations':

> Preestablished harmonies, illusory forms of unreal linkage, or assumptions of intermediating principles, assumptions such as lead the philosopher into a hopeless, because unreasonable, complexity, such are the devices whereby Realism has in such cases sought to join again the sundered fragments of its disintegrated universe, like a careless child tearfully trying to mend a shattered crystal.[16]

That is the 'internal' problem with conceiving of a realistic world with many beings. There is also a problem of how we could know anything about such a world, through ideas that supposedly 'represent' it. Again, the source of the difficulty is the hankering after 'radical independence':

> Realism asserts that existent causal or other linkage between any knower and what he knows is no part of the definition of the object known, or of its real being, or of the essence of the knowing idea if viewed in itself alone as a 'mere idea'.[17]

Consider, then, that we have the following:

> *Object o*
> *Idea o*

For there to be 'radical independence', it must be the case that any amount of change in either can occur without any impact at all on the other:

> [M]ention to me a mere idea, define it as you will, and in a realistic world I have to say that this idea might be all that it now is whether or no any corresponding object exists in the real world.[18]

What, then, could 'representation' be? It must be some sort of third relation, linking the idea and the object. But then impossible things are required of this third relation: it must both 'stick to' the object and the idea, linking them, but not in such a way that the radical independence of the object and idea are compromised. The

[14] Ibid.
[15] Ibid., 131–132.
[16] Ibid., 110–111.
[17] Ibid., 117.
[18] Ibid., 119.

144 NEGATIVE NATURAL THEOLOGY

point seems to be that either the object and idea *are linked,* in which case we do not have the radical independence sought by the realist, or they are *not linked,* in which case, we have not overcome the problem of how our ideas represent independent objects. It makes no difference if the linking occurs through a putative and reified third relation. This, precisely, is the issue set out the King-regarding cat parodied by James, although, as we now see, Royce's position emerges from a similar starting place as James, in terms of challenging the notion of 'representation'.

What if we say that the realist world contains just 'One real being'? We then avoid some of the internal problems in the picture, but we do not overcome the problem of knowledge. All the same problems surface that we encountered in the case of the realist picture with many beings. The 'All' would have to be 'an independent real object, if it were real'[19]:

> [N]o idea, as we know, can refer to any independent reality, since in order for such a reference to be itself real, two irrevocably sundered beings would have to destroy the chasm whose presence is determined by their own very essence.[20]

In brief, then, Royce finds that 'the realm of a consistent Realism is not the realm of One nor yet the realm of Many, it is the realm of absolutely Nothing':

> This judgement is not due to us. The consistent realist merely happens to remember that his ideas too are, by his own hypothesis, existences; that also, by his own hypothesis, the objects of his ideas are other existences independent of his ideas; that this independence is a mutual relation; and, finally, that two beings once defined, in his way, as independent, are wholly without inner links, and can never afterwards be linked by any external ties. The consistent realist remembers all this. And then he at once observes that if this be true, his own theory, being an idea, and at the same time an independent entity, has no relation to any other entity, and so no relation to any real world of the sort that the theory itself defines. He observes then that his whole theory has defined precisely a realm of absolute void. Nothing can be real merely in his sense.[21]

What emerges then, is that reality is full of linkages. The whole of everything that there is, the All, is such that everything within it is dependent upon, connected with, everything else—all, in that sense, is one. Furthermore, the All is not separate from us, something to be represented in our experiences and ideas: we are part of the All. And we can know some core features of the All. The All is conscious, because we are, and we are part of the All, and something that is true of a part, is true of the whole of which it is a part, because there is nowhere any radical separateness

---

[19] Ibid., 136.
[20] Ibid., 136–137.
[21] Ibid., 137.

or independence. The logic at work here goes as follows: the Absolute is the whole, and the whole cannot be *less* its parts. Consequently, the All cannot know or be conscious of less than we are:

> [U]nless the Absolute knows what we know when we endure and wait, when we love and struggle, when we long and suffer, the Absolute in so far is less and not more than we are.[22]

As William James puts it, because we, as conscious and thoughtful beings, are elements of 'one great all-inclusive fact', 'the absolute makes us by thinking us', 'just as we make objects in a dream by dreaming them'[23]:

> To *be,* on this scheme, is, on the part of a finite thing, to be an object for the absolute; and on the part of the absolute it is to be the thinker of that assemblage of objects. If we use the word 'content' here, we see that the absolute and the world have an identical content. The absolute is nothing but the knowledge of these objects; the objects are nothing but what the absolute knows. The world and the all-thinker thus compenetrate and soak each other up without residuum. They are but two names from the same identical material, considered now from the subjective, and not from the objective point of view.[24]

If 'we ourselves are enlightened enough to be believers in the absolute':

> [O]ne may then say that our philosophizing is one of the ways in which the absolute is conscious of itself. This is the full pantheistic scheme, the *identitätsphilosophie,* the immanence of God in his creation, a conception sublime from its tremendous unity.[25]

Royce uncovers the truth about 'this world of our daily experience, with precisely its stars and milky ways, with its human life and its linkages':

> For now we already begin to see, as from afar, the realm of truth that is not independent of, but the very heart and life of this fragmentary finite experience of ours. We begin to see what later we shall view nearer by, the realm of truth where indeed nothing, not the least idea, not the most transient event, is absolutely independent of the knowledge that relates to it, or of any other fact in the entire universe. In this realm it does, then, in the long run, make a difference to all objects, divine or material, whether they are known or not, by any being. That a

---

[22] Ibid., 364.
[23] James, 'A Pluralistic Universe', 646–647.
[24] Ibid., 646—647.
[25] Ibid., 647.

relative independence, and that both individuality and freedom have their concrete meaning in this truer realm, we shall indeed in due season learn.[26]

The realist's world of 'absolutely independent beings, beings that could change or vanish without any result whatever for their fellows' is exposed as a 'hopeless contradiction.'[27] The world delivered by absolute idealism, is one where 'no fact, however slight, transient, fleeting, is absolutely independent of any of its fellow facts':

> [T]his is the realm where when one member suffers others suffer also, where no sparrow falls to the ground without the insight of One who knows, and where the vine and the branches eternally flourish in a sacred unity. That is the city which hath foundations, and thither our argument already, amidst these very storms of negation, is carrying us over the waves of doubt.[28]

All of this has a dramatic consequence, in relation to regarding our lives from the internal and external perspectives. What is revealed by philosophy is that the external perspective (Royce calls it the 'external meaning') is 'genuinely continuous with the internal meaning, and is inwardly involved in the latter':

> [W]hen we learn the true relations, we may come to see the genuine and final unity of internal and external meaning.[29]

'Subject and Object' first of all seem to 'meet as foreign powers,'[30] constituting the 'world-knot.'[31] In the end, though, this 'problem' receives its answer when we 'get behind the appearances', and realize that 'at bottom, the external meaning is only apparently external':

> [A]nd in very truth, is but an aspect of the completely developed internal meaning.[32]

There is a striking feature of absolute idealism, which can be drawn out by an analogy. Imagine I am standing in a room with table and chairs. I am a Lockean realist, let us say, and I am in the room with a Berkeleain idealist. If asked 'what is in the room?', do we agree with each other? In a sense, yes. In a sense, no. Yes, in that we

---

[26] Royce, *The World and the Individual*, 137–138.
[27] Ibid., 138.
[28] Ibid.
[29] Ibid., 33–34.
[30] Ibid., 35.
[31] Ibid.
[32] Ibid., 36.

agree that there are ten chairs around an oval table. No, in that we have a fundamentally different account of what fundamentally constitutes this reality. But this disagreement will be limited, at least for immediate practical purposes. We will agree on how much weight the chairs can take, how to mend the chairs, how to stack them, and on whether placing hot coffee mugs on the table will damage the varnish. There is a sense in which *nothing is added to the picture* by virtue of being a Berkeleian idealist: we are presented with the same reality, it is just that we have given a different account of its fundamental constitution. It seems to me plausible to say something similar of the absolute idealist: nothing extra is added to this reality (a 'God'), it is just that a 'correct' account of the fundamental constitution of this reality is given which arrives at the notion of the Absolute, of the All, which, in some cases, with some thinkers, is amenable to leaning into the concept of the divine.

In this connection, Royce underscores that it is more important to know '*What* God is', than to know '*that* God is',[33] where a proper analysis of Being itself will unearth 'unexpected connections' with 'the concrete interests of religion'.[34]

Just as 'the most frivolous or scandalous gossip really manifests an intense, if rude concern, for the primal questions of moral philosophy', so also many mundane conversations and assumptions are really about 'ontology':

> Yet once face the true connection of abstract theory and daily life, and then one easily sees that life means theory, and that you deal constantly, and decisively, with the problems of the Theory of Being whenever you utter a serious word. This then is the reason why our ontological studies will bear directly upon the daily concerns of religion.[35]

We might sum this up by saying that 'nothing is added'; but, at the same time, we can also say that 'nothing is lost', because anything that is experienced by any finite being, is a part of the All, and is preserved in the All:

> For all these states of ours mean something ... [N]othing that is known to the finite is lost to the Absolute; and finitude is a condition for the attainment of perfection, in precisely the sense in which the temporal is a condition for the consciousness of the eternal, or [...] precisely as the successive chords of the music are a condition of the beauty of the whole succession when it is viewed *as* a whole.[36]

---

[33] Ibid., 12–13.
[34] Ibid., 13.
[35] Ibid., 13–14.
[36] Josiah Royce, *The World and the Individual: Gifford Lectures. Second series: Nature, Man, and the Moral Order* (London: MacMillan, 1929), 364.

148 NEGATIVE NATURAL THEOLOGY

This means that our individuality, our temporality, and our freedom, are real facts 'for the Absolute as for us':

> The difference between the human view and the Absolute's view of the temporal order is simply that, for men, only very brief series of successive events can be viewed *totum simul,* while for the Absolute, *all* events are thus viewed, while all events remain, for such an inclusive view, non the less successive as they are for us.[37]

The Absolute is the All, omnipresent to all temporal moments. Therefore, 'the Absolute *possesses a perfect knowledge at one glance of the whole of the temporal order, present, past, and future*':

> [H]is knowledge is ill-called foreknowledge. It is eternal knowledge. And as there is an eternal knowledge of all individuality, and of all freedom, free acts are known as occurring like the chords in the musical succession, precisely when and how they actually occur.[38]

> In God you possess your individuality.[39]

James suggests that a driving desire behind this spirituality, is a yearning for peace, a sense that:

> [H]owever disturbed the surface may be, at bottom all is well with the cosmos— central peace abiding at the heard of endless agitation. This conception is rational in many ways, beautifully aesthetically, beautiful intellectually (could we only follow it into detail), and beautiful morally, if the enjoyment of security can be accounted moral.[40]

Yearning for a deep peace

This type of conception is so in demand, James writes, that to 'the end of time there will be absolutists', people 'who choose belief in a static eternal, rather than admit that the finite world of change and striving, even with a God as one of the strivers, is itself eternal'.[41] James finds two sorts of problem with this purported 'deep peace'. First of all, how does it help *us,* in our finite individuality, if there is a perspective

---

[37] Ibid., 344.
[38] Ibid., 374.
[39] Ibid., 417.
[40] James, 'A Pluralistic Universe', 681.
[41] Ibid.

such as that adopted by the Absolute? There is such a 'radical discrepancy between the absolute and the relative points of view' that there is 'almost as great a bar to intimacy between the divine and human breaks out in pantheism as that which we found in monarchical theism'[42]:

> When we speak of the absolute we *take* the one universal known material collectively or integrally; when we speak of its objects, of our finite selves, etc., we *take* that same identical material distributively and separately. But what is the use of a thing's *being* only once if it can be *taken* twice over, and if being taken in different ways makes different things true of it? ... Ignorance breeds mistake, curiosity, misfortune, pain, for me; I suffer those consequences. The absolute knows of those things, of course, for it knows me and my suffering, but it doesn't itself suffer. It can't be ignorance, for simultaneous with its knowledge of each question goes its knowledge of each answer. It can't be patient, for it has to wait for nothing, having everything at once in its possession. It can't be surprised; it can't be guilty.[43]

James mocks the motto of absolutism, 'Let us imitate the All':

> As if we could, either in thought or conduct! We are invincibly parts, let us talk as we will, and must always apprehend the absolute as if it were a foreign being.[44]

As well as this problem of perspective, there is also a version of the problem of evil, as the absolute 'introduced all the tremendous irrationalities into the universe which a frankly pluralistic theism escapes':

> It introduces a 'problem of evil' namely, and leaves us wondering why the perfection of the absolute should require just such particular hideous forms of life as darken the day for our human imaginations.[45]

The problem of perspective, and the problem of evil, can be seen to combine, as 'does not our very failure to perceive the perfection of the universe destroy it?':

> In so far as we do not see the perfection of the universe, we are not perfect ourselves. And as we are parts of the universe, that cannot be perfect.[46]

---

[42] Ibid., 648.
[43] Ibid., 647–648.
[44] Ibid., 648.
[45] Ibid., 682–683.
[46] Ibid., 684–685.

150   NEGATIVE NATURAL THEOLOGY

Even if 'the absolute' gives us 'absolute safety', it is, at the same time 'compatible with every relative danger'[47]:

> You cannot enter the phenomenal world with the notion of it in your grasp, and name beforehand any detail which you are likely to meet there. Whatever the details of experience may prove to be, *after the fact of them* the absolute will adopt them.[48]

In a way James is offering the thought that even if we concede the frame of reference of the Absolute, there might be an element of choice whether or not to regard the Absolute as divine. This is what we have found at other points in the book, where there seems to be some freedom (in the sense of movement of the whole personality) as to whether we call the Absolute divine, or not, and as before, it has something to do with what sort of attitude or disposition we feel encouraged to take with respect to it. As before, 'freedom' need not be read in narrow terms, concerned only with 'freedom of the will' or 'freedom of choice', but can include the whole movement of a personality. James' shows his psychological interests here, diagnosing a split between personality types who are drawn to his pluralistic pantheism, and absolute monism. With some—one suspects insincere—self-deprecation, James writes that 'the pluralistic empiricism' which he professes offers 'but a sorry appearance':

> It is a turbid, muddled, gothic sort of an affair, without a sweeping outline and with little pictorial nobility.[49]

At this point, we can return to the opening criticism of absolute idealism made by James: that it embodies a fantasy about total peace and safety, with an implied inability to engage with our temporal limitations and bewilderment. I commented that James' account underemphasizes the significance of a sort of pained yearning and acknowledged turmoil that runs through Royce.

Royce talks of the 'Self' yearning 'the Absolute as that Other which it seeks to know as the Real', and seeking 'to win union with that Absolute', whilst being, as 'this present finite Self' conscious of its '*contrast* with that world which it views as beyond its present range of experience'.[50] Nor is there any deep individual consolation, in the sense of there being some eschatological promise, or movement towards perfection and peace:

> We have long since ceased, indeed, to suppose that this theory means to view God's perfection, or his self-consciousness, as the temporal result of any process of evolution, or as an event occurring at the end of time, or at the end of any

---

[47] Ibid., 687.
[48] Ibid.
[49] Ibid., 650.
[50] Royce, *The World and the Individual: Second Series,* 348.

one process, however extended, that occurs in time. The melody does not come into existence contemporaneously with its own last note. Nor does the symphony come into full existence only when its last chord sounds. On the contrary, the melody is the whole, whereof the notes are but abstracted fragments; the symphony is the totality, to which the last chord contributes no more than does the first bar. And precisely so it is, as we have seen, with the relation between the temporal and the eternal order. God in his totality as the Absolute Being is conscious, not *in* time, but *of* time, and of all that infinite time contains. In time there follows, in their sequence, the chords of his endless symphony. For him is this whole symphony of life at once.[51]

This is what I mean by talking about Royce as embodying a sort of binocular vision, whereby we are able to see our lives as limited by our finite perspective, but also grasp (without seeing) that they are part of this wider symphonic whole. Although, it would have to be said, if there is consolation, it is not necessarily very personal: it is a bracing sort of spirituality.

With absolute idealism, as with other movements of thought we have considered, we have found a freedom of whether or not to regard the same metaphysical picture as divine or not. F.H. Bradley makes some similar moves to Royce: he goes from antinomies and contradictions in the notion of a 'realistic' and represented world of finite things in relation, to affirm the fundamental reality of an all-inclusive All, the Absolute. But Bradley is clear that 'the Absolute is not God'.[52] The reason Bradley gives resonates with our thought that one will only call a dimension of reality, or reality as a whole, 'God' if one, in some sense wants to engage with it, and Bradley sees no value in, or possibility of, engaging with the Absolute: the Absolute is simply *there*, as the only satisfactory framing account of all the appearances that present themselves. So, Bradley affirms, that 'God for me has no meaning outside of religious consciousness, and that essentially is practical':

> The Absolute for me cannot be God, because in the end the Absolute is related to nothing, and there cannot be a practical relation between it and the finite will. When you begin to worship the Absolute or the Universe, and make it the object of religion, you in that moment have transformed it. It has become something forthwith which is less than the Universe.[53]

Bradley sees a dilemma here. Either God is conceived of as being perfect, or we have an imperfect God. To conceive of the Absolute as God is to render God perfect, as the Absolute is perfection. But anything that is perfect will have no engagement

---

[51] Ibid., 419.
[52] F.H. Bradley, 'On God and the Absolute', in *Essays on Truth and Reality* (Cambridge: Cambridge University Press, 2011), 428–459, 428.
[53] Ibid., 428.

with our finite and imperfect will, for 'if religion is practical, then it is certain that my will must count'.[54] Bradley identifies a 'fundamental inconsistency in religion':

> For, in any but an imperfect religion, God must be perfect. God must be at once the complete satisfaction of all finite aspiration, and yet on the other side must stand in relation with my will. Religion (at least in my view) is practical, and on the other hand in the highest religion its object is supreme goodness and power.[55]

If one seizes the other horn of the dilemma and affirms an imperfect God, we undercut a central purpose of religion, as we 'follow our Leader blindly and, for all we know, to a common and overwhelming defeat'.[56]

It is Royce's determination to engage with the Absolute, in a way that brings us a bracing type of consolation, that makes it appropriate to call it God. Bradley does not engage with the Absolute in this way. As James pithily puts it, the Absolute, at most, permits a Professor to think that he, or she, may as well as not go on a type of 'moral holiday'. Although the Absolute may have some 'holiday-giving value', James does not find it worth the metaphysical trouble, dealing with the intellectual acrobatics:

> I just *take* my moral holidays; or else as a professional philosopher, I try to justify them by some other principle.[57]

James calls the Absolute a 'metaphysical monster':

> [A]ll that we are permitted to say of it being that whatever it is, it is at any rate *worth* more (worth more to itself, that is) than if any eulogistic adjectives of ours applied to it. It is us, and all other appearances, not one of us *as such*, for in it we are all 'transmuted', and its own as-suchness is of another denomination altogether.[58]

James is interesting on the comparison between Bradley and Royce writing that for Bradley, if there is any consolation about from the reality of the absolute, it belongs secretly to the absolute, and not to us:

> [T]he absolute must already have got the relief in secret ways of its own, impossible for us to guess at. *We* of course get no relief, so Bradley's is a rather ascetic doctrine.... Royce ... tried to bring the absolute's secret forms of relief more sympathetically home to our imagination.[59]

---

[54] Ibid., 432.
[55] Ibid., 428.
[56] Ibid., 430.
[57] James, 'Pragmatism', 39.
[58] James, 'A Pluralistic Universe', 650.
[59] Ibid., 725.

Parfit's non-metaphysical realism

On just one fairly narrow front, a recent position in moral philosophy has some interesting parallels with absolute idealism: this is Derek Parfit's defence of a non-naturalistic but non-metaphysical notion of the normative. For Parfit, a proper and correct account of everything that there is reveals not an extra metaphysical dimension beyond and behind reality, but, rather a notion of the normative, of the good, which is an irreducible part of what is. In a sense, 'nothing has been added', but a correct account frames our whole understanding of reality in these terms, such that, in moral terms, 'nothing is lost'.

Parfit chooses not to call this notion of the good, of 'what really matters', divine, but the conceptual space he leans into would seem to share some divine features. Parfit, is, similarly to Nagel, in principle atheistic. He never indulges in categories that he understands to be religious or theological. But he does hold out for a conception of the normative—of moral rightness—that cannot be reduced to, nor identified at all with naturalistic facts, even if expansively conceived. When we think of the whole 'world', as it were, of non-naturalistic normative properties, in combination with each other, it is hard to resist trying to get a grasp on what *sort of thing* these properties, and this world, *could be*. It is this difficulty, presumably, that keeps the majority of secular philosophers on the side of naturalism, albeit, some of them, hoping for a better and bigger naturalism.

Let us think about this a little. I will call this whole world of non-naturalistic normative properties, the 'good'. We can get quite far in simply 'negative' terms, by reflecting on what sort of properties the good must have *if* it cannot be identified with naturalistic facts, or properties. First of all, the good will not be made up of matter. The good will be the constitutive source of moral rightness, and moral laws. The good will be unchanging, and not limited to a particular time and place, although it might be able to support particular laws that apply in closely specifiable types of time and place. The good will exist/apply, insofar as it exists/applies, everywhere. The good will be unchanging, although it will be able to apply to circumstances that are themselves changing. This list mirrors, more or less stage by stage, questions 3 to 10 of the first part of Thomas Aquinas' *Summa Theologiae,* where Thomas is setting out the properties that belong to God. It also mirrors what Royce or Bradley might say about the Absolute: in other words, Royce, Bradley, and Parfit can all be construed as 'paired' down classical theists, selecting some, but not all, features of the divine life and being.

This does not mean, of course, that Parfit, therefore, 'believes in God'. But it does, I think, mean this: that when regarding the properties of the 'good', for someone like Parfit, who thinks we must go beyond the naturalistic, a theologian can say, to paraphrase what Aquinas says about Aristotelian reflections on the concept of the first cause, 'and that we call God'. What Aquinas precisely says, of course, is 'and this is what everybody understands by God' (*ST,* Ia. 2,3). This can no longer be said, if it ever could. But we can offer the more toned-down reflection that a dimension of reality that is the source of goodness, and which is unchanging, and limitless, and which exists everywhere, is part (and not the whole) of what (some) people who believe in God mean, and have meant by, God. Or, as Aquinas puts it, 'the one common good, which is God' (*ad unum bonum commune, quod est Deus*) (*ST* 2a2ae.25.1). Imagine the whole stretch of the concept of God, everything that this concept might mean: well, if you believe in non-naturalistic normativity, you believe in some stretch of this God concept.

One might consider here ways in which Parfit's comments about the normative parallel both Platonic and Christian conceptions of deity. Parfit writes that 'instead of saying that what we are interested in is therefore good', Parfit wants to say that 'the goodness is in the object, and we ought therefore to be interested in it'.[60] Such goodness, Parfit affirms, using a nice Platonic image, would give us reasons in the way the sun gives light: 'because it's out there, shining down'.[61] Parfit is clear that such 'irreducibly normative facts' could be considered to be causally efficacious:

> Nor should we assume that all causes of natural facts must be natural . . . We can also understand, I believe, how certain irreducibly normative facts might be, or might have been, part of the cause of many natural facts . . . If the actual Universe had been the best possible Universe, in the sense that reality was as good as it could be, this fact might not have been a mere coincidence. Reality might have been this way *because* this way was the best . . . On this *Axiarchic View*, facts about goodness would explain many natural facts. But this fact could not be usefully taken to imply that goodness was a natural property.[62]

Fundamental normative facts are not 'contingent, empirically discoverable facts about the actual world'. They are in a 'separate, distinctive category, which cannot be stated in non-normative terms'[63]:

> If, as I believe, reason-involving normative facts are in a separate distinctive category, there is no close analogy for their irreducibility to natural facts. These normative facts are in some ways like certain other kinds of necessary truths. One example are mathematical truths, such as the fact that $7 \times 8 = 56$ . . . normative and natural facts differ too deeply for any form of Normative Naturalism to succeed.[64]

---

[60] All quotes from Parfit are from his trilogy, *On What Matters*, vols. I–III (Oxford: Oxford University Press, 2011). References are given to volume number and page, I:46.

[61] Ibid.

[62] Ibid., II: 306–307.

[63] Ibid., II: 307.

[64] Ibid., II: 326.

Parfit explicitly draws parallels between the way in which he, and theologians, may be involved in a tragic waste of time:

It *would* be a tragedy if there was no *single true morality*.[65]

If there were no such reason-involving normative truths, I and some other people would have wasted much of our lives, since we have spent many years trying to answer questions about what we mistakenly believed to be such truths.[66]

It is clear that we waste our time when we look for something that we know doesn't exist. Many theologians could plausibly believe that, if God doesn't exist, they would have wasted some of the years that they have spent thinking about this non-existent being. I can plausibly believe that, if there were no irreducible normative truths, I would have wasted some of the years that I have spent thinking about these non-existent truths.[67]

The only consolation is the rather wry thought that 'it wouldn't matter that we had waisted much of our lives, since we would have learnt that nothing matters'.[68]

In my drawing out some parallels between Parfit's idea of the good, and the absolute idealist's notion of God, I expect to be accused of pulling some sort of trick. In the course of discussing something else, Parfit himself perhaps puts his finger on the sort of linguistic stunt I might be suspected of attempting. Parfit imagines someone saying, 'God is love', and seeming to say something controversial, implying the existence of God. But then our interlocutor adds, 'love is God', and 'there is love', and so, therefore, 'there is God'. But all our interlocutor has done is changed the meaning of the term God, to mean something far less ambitious and bizarre, which can be easily found in the world: from 'God is good', to 'good is God', leading to 'there is good', and 'there is God'.

I would push back that I am not changing the meaning of the concept of God, but, rather, accusing Parfit, and others, of having an over-restrictive, unhistorical, and untextured understanding of what the concept of God can mean, and has meant, for vast swathes of the tradition of philosophical reflection upon God. A more apposite analogy might be the situation parodied by another philosopher, Bernard Williams, where Oxford philosophers in the early part of the twentieth century prepared translations of Aristotle. Williams describes one philosopher insisting on translating a Greek term, entirely anachronistically, as 'moral obligation', and then, proceeding to write articles complaining about Aristotle's 'inadequate theory

---

[65] Ibid., II: 154.
[66] Ibid., III: 44.
[67] Ibid., III: 45.
[68] Ibid., 45.

of moral obligation'.[69] Secular philosophers have accepted, I am suggesting, inadequate translations of the concept of God: 'God is *this*', they say, where what is pointed out ranges from a childish wish fulfilment fantasy, to an intelligent designer, an interventionist watchmaker, or a voluntaristic commander of divine laws. And then, obviously enough, they say 'I do not see how anyone could believe in this God'. But the problem is more with how the concept of God has been translated and mediated, than with the concept itself. It must be to some degree significant that the Stoics, the Epicureans, and Thomas Aquinas—and I would add, Descartes, Leibniz, Spinoza and Kant, and Heidegger—all talk, in different ways, about the concept of God and the divine in ways that do not fit this simple translation.

There is another sort of accusation that might be made: that we are engaging with a sort of 'Enlightenment' gap-filling natural theology. Consider: it can look as if we have identified an explanatory gap, when it comes to explaining or justifying our language of normativity, or of objective value ('what sort of thing could this possibly *be?*'). We then suggest that 'God' might provide the requisite justification. It is precisely against such a move that we can understand some common ground between Nagel and Parfit, in relation to 'moral and evaluative realism'. Both Nagel and Parfit recommend a normative realism that is, as they both put it, 'non-metaphysical'. So, Nagel writes that 'realism is not a metaphysical theory of the ground of moral and evaluative truth', and that it is 'metaphysical only if the denial of a metaphysical position like naturalism itself counts as a metaphysical position':

> But value realism does not maintain that value judgments are made true or false by anything else, natural or supernatural.[70]

It is, of course, the case that some 'natural facts are what make some value judgments true, in the sense that they are the facts that provide reasons for and against action'.[71] So, 'the fact that you will run over a dog if you don't step on the brakes makes it the case that you should step on the brakes'. Nonetheless:

> The general moral truth that licenses this inference—namely that it counts in favor of doing something that it will avoid grievous harm to a sentient creature—is not made true by any fact of any other kind. It is nothing but itself.[72]

In this way, the 'dispute between realism and subjectivism is not about the contents of the universe':

---

[69] Bernard Williams, 'Philosophy as a Humanistic Discipline', in *Philosophy as a Humanistic Discipline,* 180–199, 181.

[70] Nagel, *Mind and Cosmos,* 101.

[71] Ibid., 102.

[72] Ibid.

It is a dispute about the order of normative explanation. Realists believe that moral and other evaluative judgments can often be explained by more general or basic evaluative truths, together with the facts that bring them into play (the fact about the dog). But they do not believe that the evaluative element in such a judgement can be explained by anything else. That there is a reason to do what will avoid grievous harm to a sentient creature is, in a realist view, one of the kinds of things that can be true in itself, and not because something of a different kind is true. In this it resembles physical truths, psychological truths, and arithmetical and geometrical truths.[73]

My suggestion that Parfit's 'world of the good' (the collection of normative statements about what really matters) is, to a degree, what 'we would call God', might seem to fall immediately foul of Nagel's warning against looking for something 'behind' the set of truths that 'makes them true'. Indeed, it is unclear what sort of thing could be 'behind the truths' (they are 'nothing but themselves', to paraphrase Nagel), or how the conceptual 'plumbing' could work such that one kind of thing could operate in order to make another kind of thing (the moral truths) hold.

This line of response misunderstands what is being suggested. We are not suggesting that God must be 'behind' moral truths, by virtue of being their cause, justification, or creator. Rather, we are suggesting that when contemplating the whole set of moral truths (in themselves, with nothing behind them), that there are such moral truths is simply what has been called (in part) 'God'. That there are such truths, that such truths stretch out into the universe, is what some people 'call God'. It is not that God is invoked to *explain* a spooky dimension of hidden forms, or truths, or that God thinking, or willing, the truths makes them true. It is simply: their being true is (part of what is called) God. This might be contested. Quite so: but, then, *this* is the claim that should be investigated, and reflected upon, and not the different claim that God grounds or explains the realist truth of moral statements. The claim is insistent, but gentle: not that the philosopher *must believe in God,* but that when the philosopher talks about the normative, after exhausting the naturalistic, this is what the theological tradition 'would call God'. This is not the same as forcing the philosophers to call it God, but nor can the believer or theologian really be barred from finding that such normativity or cosmic salience has 'divine' features.

[73] Ibid.

7

Becoming Divine

Kant and Jung

I began Chapter 5 by setting out the distinction between Nagel's fourth and fifth responses to the cosmic question:

IV   The question has an 'outside-in' answer, in terms of our place in a wider reality or purpose, although we do not need to go beyond a sufficiently rich understanding of immanent reality, of the world.

We have distinguished this from the fifth type of response:

V   The question has an 'outside-in' answer that appeals to a dimension beyond the world, a transcendent realm or reality.

I admitted to not being always clear where the border between IV and V lies, because of the stretch of things that might be meant by a 'sufficiently rich understanding of immanent reality, of the world'. In this chapter, we push to the edge of this issue. I will set out parallel work done by the concept of the divine in the work of Kant, and in the work of a self-declared Kantian (of sorts), the psychologist Carl Gustav Jung. To assist in this discussion, I will also draw on the work of the theologian David Burrell, and (more briefly) the philosopher and psychoanalyst Jonathan Lear, and the poet Elizabeth Bishop. I will suggest that on a (correct) interpretation of Kant, there clearly is *both* a transformed understanding of the world (with a type of immanent transcendence), and a transcendence beyond the world, in the shape of God. With Jung, the matter remains richly ambivalent: there is certainly an immanent transcendence within the world (the true self, the collective unconscious), where God is a symbol of the whole and entire self, which symbol needs to remain open to not being exhausted by this symbolic meaning. With Kant, the access to this divinity comes through the concept and value of autonomy, which is where I begin this discussion.

When reflecting upon the concept of autonomy, we might distinguish between two sorts of 'Kantian' thought, which I will call the metaphysical and the grammatical. I will set out, first of all, the main shape of the 'metaphysical Kant', as I've come to understand it. 'Autonomy' within Kant's thought-world, so interpreted, expresses a type of religious hope: it involves a self-transcending participation in reason as such, which is identical, fundamentally, in a way that never appears to us, to freedom,

Negative Natural Theology. Christopher J. Insole, Oxford University Press. © Christopher J. Insole 2024.
DOI: 10.1093/9780198933007.003.0008

and to happiness. I will then sketch an account of a 'grammatical' Kantian approach to 'autonomy': this involves perceiving certain analytical relationships between the concepts of reason, freedom, individuality, and the universal and communal.

The task will be to reflect on what the relationship might be between these, and whether drawing on the metaphysical Kant can help our constructive grammatical thoughts about autonomy, in relation to the concept of God.

The metaphysical Kant

This is not the place to attempt a defence of the sweeping interpretative picture ('the metaphysical Kant') I am about to draw. This I have attempted in various publications.[1] But it might be helpful, here, to locate my claims in the wider realm of 'Kant studies': I associate myself with a recently resurgent 'metaphysical' reading of Kant, which understands Kant as having more substantive commitments—ethical, ontological and theological—than more deflationary commentators thought possible or proper for Kant.[2] Within this movement, I have a particular interest in Kant's theological commitments, especially with respect to human freedom as it relates to divine action. A number of recent commentators have also been interested in Kant's theological convictions. My most distinctive claim, perhaps, is to affirm that although Kant believes in God and in a meaningful conception of transcendence, he consciously diverges from Christianity as he would have received it. My grounds for saying this have been that Kant avoids the categories of revelation, tradition, and authority, as well as denying that God can be the final or efficient cause of human action. Kant also rejects the traditional claim that loving and knowing God is our highest good. I have found this to be a more productive lens for appreciating Kant than approaches which judge Kant to be a more or less lousy Christian of some stripe (with different emphases on Lutheranism or a more Platonically infused theological rationalism).[3]

---

[1] Christopher J. Insole, *Kant and the Divine* (Oxford: Oxford University Press, 2020); *The Intolerable God* (Grand Rapids, Michigan: William B. Eerdman's Publishing Company, 2016); and *Kant and the Creation of Freedom* (Oxford: Oxford University Press, 2013). For articles, see the following: 'A Kantian Response to the Problem of Evil: Living in the Moral World', *Religions* 14/2 (2023), Article 227, https://doi.org/10.3390/rel14020227; 'Free Belief: the Medieval Heritage in Kant's Moral Faith', *Journal of the History of Philosophy*, 57/3 (2019), 501–528; 'Kant, Divinity, and Autonomy', *Studies in Christian Ethics*, 32/4 (2019), 470–484; 'Kant on Christianity, Religion, and Politics: Three Hopes, Three Limits', *Studies in Christian Ethics*, 29/1 (2016), pp. 14–33; 'A Thomistic Reading of Kant's 'Groundwork of the Metaphysics of Morals: Searching for the Unconditioned', *Modern Theology*, 31/2 (2015), 284–311; 'Kant's Transcendental Idealism and Newton's Divine Sensorium', *Journal of the History of Ideas*, 72/3 (2011), 413–436; and 'Intellectualism, Relational Properties and the Divine Mind in Kant's Pre-Critical Philosophy', *Kantian Review*, 16/3 (2011), 399–428.

[2] Influential 'metaphysical' readers of Kant include Karl Ameriks, Rae Langton, Desmond Hogan, and Andrew Chignell. More deflationary commentators include figures such as Henry Allison and Andrews Reath. A previous generation of commentators, represented by Peter Strawson, tended to read Kant as having metaphysical commitments, but in a way that was thoroughly disreputable and contrary to the deepest principles of his thought.

[3] Commentators who read Kant as attempting, but often failing, to express a philosophical Lutheranism, combining elements of Platonic theological rationalism, include Palmquist, Pasternack, Wood, Kain, Marina, and Kanterian.

160 NEGATIVE NATURAL THEOLOGY

Having marked out the terrain a little, I will now move at a bracing pace through my main interpretative headlines. The aim is to get quite quickly to Kant's concept of autonomy, and the notion of the divine that comes downstream of this, but coming at the issue from quite a long way off (a sort of Google-Earth sweep downwards) does help, I think, to understand Kant's deep motivation for his position. Simply to jump immediately to the conclusion—'autonomy occurs beyond and behind space and time'—often does not achieve much beyond a baffled stare: 'really?', 'how does that help?', 'why say *that*?'.

For all the undoubted difficulty of Kant's texts, a firm grasp of four principles serves to illuminate the fundamental contours of his 'critical' thinking (broadly speaking, Kant's thought after 1770):

(i)   The 'inner value' of the world is freedom, *and nothing else.* Freedom means: setting ends for yourself, without being impacted upon by anything external to you. Other things may be admirable, or impressive, but they lack this value.

(ii) Reason is a larger category than knowledge. There is far more that we can have rational beliefs about, than we can know about. This means that Kant would not recognize the ultimate validity of a debate between 'faith and reason': because faith, religious belief (*Glaube*), is entirely within the stretch of reason, even though it goes beyond the bounds of knowledge.

(iii) Thinking about the 'conditions of possibility' of something can expand your knowledge, and your set of rational beliefs. Consider: if you know something, or have a rational belief about something, you can then ask, 'what else must be the case, or, what else do I need to believe, in order to make this possible?'. You then have warrant for affirming, for 'holding-for-true', whatever comes out of this conceptual investigation. You might not *know* it, but, as we have seen, from the second principle, knowledge is not everything. There is a caveat here: anything you come up with must not contradict something that you know. But that is a fairly minimal test, precisely because we do not know very much.

(iv) Kant thinks in a way that is big and binary. His philosophy tends to lead us to a crossroads, where he finds that *everything* (created and uncreated) is either *this way* or *that way*, where what is offered is an entire package, a whole and encompassing worldview. In relation to the question of morality and freedom the options are these: we either live in a 'moral world' where freedom is possible, or, we live in a world of mechanistic determinism, where freedom and morality are impossible. The former world has value, the latter world is a 'mere desert', entirely without value. Kant finds that we can, indeed, must rationally believe that the entire and whole world is undergirded by freedom, and not mechanism, and so, that it is a world with value.

Kant's 'transcendental idealism' arises from Kant's ability to affirm such a world undergirded by freedom. Putting it briskly, the idea is this: if space and time are features of the world in itself, and directly created by God, they go 'all the way down' into reality, and we are contained within them. This is bad news for freedom, because, Kant believes, space and time are through and through deterministic in ways described by Newtonian mechanism. If, then, space and time are features of our reception of the world, and not in the world in itself, this is good news for the possibility of freedom. It enables us to believe in freedom and morality. There is a conceptual space for fundamental reality to be quite other than it appears to be. Here we can recall the third principle: something providing the 'conditions of possibility' of something is itself permitted to provide warrant for a belief, if it does not contradict what we know, because, reason is a larger category than knowledge (the second principle).

For Kant, the 'noumenal realm' is the ground of the world of appearances ('phenomena'— 'that which appears'), whereby 'noumenal objects' affect us. These noumenal objects bring about our experience, which experience is always mediated through our forms of intuition, space and time. Although we understand that all our experience is always on this side of this mediation, coming downstream of how we receive the world, we also understand that it is dependent upon the world as it is in itself, even though we cannot know anything substantial about this world, except that it does indeed ground our experience. This interpretation of transcendental idealism is known in the literature as the 'noumenal affection' account.

'Transcendental idealism', on this interpretation, has three dimensions. First of all, it sets the limits to knowledge (which, as we have seen, is a more constrained category than reason). Secondly, within those limits, knowledge is made secure. Thirdly, it opens up possibilities for rational thinking beyond the limits of knowledge. That is to say, transcendental idealism retains epistemic humility about what we can know, whilst opening up the possibility that the way things are is fundamentally different from the way things appear to be. Things appear to be determined, but this is just an appearance. We can believe in freedom without epistemic irresponsibility, precisely because belief in freedom is a 'condition of possibility' of morality.

Once we are properly equipped with such an interpretation of transcendental idealism and noumenal freedom, we are ready to understand the type of transcendence that is really at work in Kant's philosophical religiosity. The history of human actions, as with everything that appears, is the appearance of that which is fundamentally non-spatial and non-temporal, where there is no sense in which we move towards or further away from the noumenal dimension wherein morality and freedom resides. For this reason, Kant emphasizes the invisibility of moral action, stating, for example in the *Groundwork,* we can never recognise whether an

162 NEGATIVE NATURAL THEOLOGY

action is actually grounded on conformity with the moral law, rather than happening to coincide with it.

This position can be understood as delivered by a combination of the four principles set out above. Kant asks, 'what sort of *entire world* is the condition of possibility of the freedom that is the inner value of the world?' (principle four). Transcendental idealism is part of Kant's answer. Because it does not contradict what we know, but only goes beyond it, it is rational to believe it (principle two). Because, Kant thinks, it is the *only entire world,* the only way the world can be, that can sustain such an ambitious conception of freedom (principle one), we should believe in it (principle three). Furthermore, it is not rational to believe more than is required, in order to sustain the possibility of the freedom that is the inner value of the world. In these two constraints ('we should believe' and 'believe no more than is required') lie Kant's epistemic discipline and humility.

With this in place, we are able to understand Kant's conception of autonomy. Autonomy never appears, for Kant, in space and time. Autonomy is only possible if there is a realm of noumenal freedom, where rational will is able to will itself, in its activity of end setting. We note, then, that the possibility of autonomy is *itself* the great philosophical and religious hope of Kant's whole system. Only if there is a dimension of reality beyond mechanism, is the setting of ends, and so autonomy possible. The alternative to a moral world with freedom, is a universe without end setting, and without freedom, which Kant tells us repeatedly, would be a sort of 'desert' with no 'inner value'. Believing in the possibility of autonomy already, and in itself, leans into what we might call religious hope: the hope that things are not as they seem, and that there is a dimension to reality which is saturated with reason, wherein we find our 'proper selves'. The result of a fully autonomous Kingdom of Ends, where everyone acts harmoniously and universally, would be the 'happiness' of the highest good, where 'everything goes according to the wish and will' of every 'rational being in the [moral] world' (*CPrR,* 5: 124).[4]

---

[4] References to Kant refer to the *Akademie* edition, *Kants gesammelte Schriften,* edited by the Royal Prussian (later German) Academy of Sciences (Berlin: Georg Reimer, later Walter de Gruyter & Co., 1900). These references are cited by volume: page number, and are prefaced by an abbreviation of the title of the work, as set out below.

CPrR   Critique of Practical Reason in *Immanuel Kant: Practical Philosophy* (Cambridge: Cambridge University Press, 2008), trans. and ed. by Mary J. Gregor, 5: 3–309.

GW   *Groundwork of the Metaphysics of Morals,* in *Practical Philosophy,* 4: 385–463.

OPA   *The Only Possible Argument in support of a Demonstration of the Existence of God,* in *Immanuel Kant: Theoretical Philosophy, 1755–1770,* trans. and ed. by David Walford and Ralf Meerbote (Cambridge: Cambridge University Press, 1992), 2: 63–163.

Rel   *Religion within the Boundaries of Mere Reason,* in *Immanuel Kant: Religion and Rational Theology,* trans. and ed. by Allen W. Wood and George di Giovanni (Cambridge: Cambridge University Press, 1996), 6: 3–202.

TP   On the Common Saying: That May be Correct in Theory, but it is of no Use in Practice (1793), in *Practical Philosophy,* 8: 275–312.

The grammatical Kantian approach

So much, then, for the metaphysical Kant. The transition to setting out the 'grammatical' Kantian thought is hardly seamless: indeed, it is marked by a rather visible seam. That, in a way, is the point: to present apparently incommensurate styles of thinking and reflection, so as to dramatize the question of what sort of relationship there might be between them. Forget, for now, the metaphysical Kant. In the next section, I will return to the question of how the metaphysical Kant might relate to the grammatical Kantian claims, especially in relationship to Kant's understanding of God. The grammatical Kantian thought moves from reason to freedom, to the individual, to the universal and collective, finding that all of this is furled into a proper understanding of autonomy. It does all of this without any substantive or strange metaphysics (or with the most minimal possible).

First of all: consider the relationship between reason and freedom. To be rational is to employ concepts. In the very act of conceptualizing the world, we manifest freedom and imagination, because, to have a concept of the way a world is, is at the same time, to have a concept of how it might be otherwise. As the philosopher John McDowell puts it, when we 'conceptualize the world', we must have the ability to 'conceptualize the thinker's own place in the world', which immediately means that the imagination can 'roam over other possibilities'.[5] This is precisely because rationality allows the mind to roam over alternative ways the world might have been, or yet be. To name something as an injustice, we need imagination to see a different world beyond the injustice, and imagination needs the freedom from sheer contingencies and events that only conceptualizing reason brings.

The relationship between reason and freedom brings us to the link between reason and individualism. Akeel Bilgrami draws this out effectively:

> I had a parent, a mother (and others in the family as well) who would often say, 'Bilgramis don't do this. So, stop doing it. It's just not what Bilgramis do.' And, there came a point when I thought, and actually said aloud, 'Look, I've now come into reason. I'm not a kid and just by the fact of the realization of my possession of reason, I must ask, I'm obliged to ask, "*Should* I be doing what the Bilgramis are doing?"'[6]

Bilgrami generalizes from this experience:

> Everybody grows up in a social setting, whether it's a family, or a caste, or a wider form of kinship. Everybody is brought up in a group, with the group's mentality

---

[5] John McDowell, 'Two Sorts of Naturalism', in *Mind, Value and Reality* (Cambridge, MA and London: Harvard University Press, 2002), 167–197, 170.

[6] Akeel Bilgrami, 'Autonomy, Value, and the Unalienated Life: An Interview with Akeel Bilgrami', in *Redeeming Autonomy,* ed. Benjamin DeSpain and Christopher Insole (forthcoming).

164 NEGATIVE NATURAL THEOLOGY

and behaviour shaping them. Coming into reason makes it possible for individuals in the group to ask, 'should I be thinking and doing this?'. If this is so, then the very concept of reason in a way intrinsically generates an individualism. This is a ubiquitous rite of passage that everyone undergoes. So, individualism in the matter of autonomy is, *prima facie*, built into the very idea of reason. All of our philosophizing has to first acknowledge and then grapple with this basic intrinsic link between reason and an individualistic conception of autonomy, and see whether one can, *having acknowledged it, transcend it.*

This final thought, of 'transcending' the individualism, takes us to the next analytical link: between individual reason and the transcending of the individual, into the universal and communal. This link can be obscured, because of the assumption that the individual will only be concerned with self-interest, which seems to be opposed to a type of universal and communal thinking. But, insofar as it is *reason* giving birth to the individual, there is, I would maintain, something radically *impersonal* involved. Consider the question, 'should I do what the Bilgramis do?'. This is not, in its primary and usual form, a question about self-interest, but is rather an enquiry into whether there is *good reason* to do what the Bilgramis do. This is because, as Bilgrami puts it, reason is the 'sort of thing that makes one capable of *detaching oneself* from *anything,* any ongoing tendency we are enmeshed in (whether the group's or anything else)':

> [T]herefore, it may even require one to ask, 'Should I be so self-interested?', if one's ongoing tendencies are to think and behave self-interestedly. Reason brings about a movement of *general* detachment, from anything ongoing.

A similar point is put in a more dramatic form by the twentieth-century philosopher Pierre Hadot, commenting on Plato's Socratic dialogues, especially the *Phaedo,* where Socrates reflects upon the relationship between reason and death, in the shadow of his imminent execution. The point Hadot makes is this: that when we enter the space of reasons, there is a sort of death to the self, because we move from saying 'this because I want it', to 'this because it is good', where what is good may not be what I want, or, at least, my wanting it is not what makes it good. With reason we can detach ourselves even from ourselves, and see ourselves from the third-person perspective.

Hadot suggests that this is the less obvious meaning behind Socrates insistence that philosophy is an exercise in preparing for death: because every movement into the space of reasons is a type of mini death, a turning away from selfishness and self-obsession. Socrates tells his friends:

> Other people are likely not to be aware that those who pursue philosophy aright study nothing but dying and being dead. Now if this is true, it would be absurd

to be eager for nothing but this all their lives, and then to be troubled when that came for which they had all along been eagerly practising.[7]

A number of French thinkers in the mid twentieth century gave pithy expression to this link between reason and death, with Rene Schaerer writing that 'corporeal individuality ceases to exist the moment it is externalized in the *logos*',[8] and Brice Parain observing that 'language develops only upon the death of individuals'.[9]

So, we have, I am suggesting, an analytical arc, which connects freedom with reason (the ability to frame a concept entails the ability to imagine things being other than they are), and reason with individuality, and individuality with a capability for self-detachment, which opens up to the universal and communal. When thinking along these grammatical Kantian lines, we might think of the concept of 'autonomy' as pointing to the appropriate attitude, or set of attitudes, to this set of relationships between freedom, reason, individuality, universality, and community. This is, so far, just to point to a conceptual task, rather than to have completed the task: but this is, in itself, some sort of an achievement. Just to have identified the relevant aspiration, what it is we are looking for, is something. We will only know if we have found an answer, if we know what we are looking for. All of this can be achieved, it seems, without the weight, or potential embarrassment, of the metaphysical Kant.

Jungian reflections: The relationship between the metaphysical and the grammatical Kant

I am mindful that there is plenty that is controversial and contestable within both presentations above, the metaphysical and the grammatical. Nonetheless, my focus here is on the question of the relationship between these two approaches.

There is quite a lot that one might say in terms of biography, genealogy, and intellectual history: perhaps, studying the metaphysical Kant was essential in my own intellectual story, without which I would not have been 'ready' to see the grammatical links, or, less personally, perhaps the history of philosophy unfurled in a certain way, such that without the 'metaphysical Kant', the Kant-of-history, we would not have received the Kant-event, the grammatical Kant. I am going to ignore all such explorations here, because, even if true, they all share a common feature: which is to dispense with the metaphysical Kant in a sort of history of

---

[7] Plato, *Phaedo,* 64A. Cited by Pierre Hadot, *What is Ancient Philosophy?,* trans Michael Chase (Cambridge, MA and London: Harvard University Press, 2004), 31–32.

[8] Rene Schaerer, *La question platonicienne* (Neuchâtel and Paris: Vrin, 1938), 41. Cited by Hadot, *What is Ancient Philosophy?,* 68.

[9] Brice Parain, *Le Langage et l'existence,* in the collection *L'Existence* (Paris: Gallimard, 1945), 173. Cited by Hadot, *What is Ancient Philosophy?,* 68.

166 NEGATIVE NATURAL THEOLOGY

progress towards the more urbane and breezy grammatical Kant. I want to know, rather, if there is anything of abiding interest and significance in attempting to relate the metaphysical and grammatical Kantian pictures.

In fact, I consider that the metaphysical Kant may offer an essential corrective to the grammatical approach. At the heart of the matter, is the following: for (the metaphysical) Kant, everything that occurs in our empirical biography, including our interior lives (which would feature dreaming and imagination) is an unfurling, in space and time, of something that lies beyond it. 'As a human being', Kant writes, a person is 'only the appearance of himself'.[10] For the metaphysical Kant, our empirical selves are not unrelated to our noumenal selves: they are the appearance in space and time, the moving image of eternity, of our true selves outside of space and time. Kant's 'proper self'[11] is the locus and source of true freedom: this self never directly and fully appears, yet is the generative source of everything that does appear across the stretch of our psychic lives, including the conceptual relationships mapped out by the grammatical Kantian approach.

This is hugely significant. We might recall Iris Murdoch's provocative comparison of the ideal Kantian subject with the figure of Lucifer in Milton's *Paradise Lost*:

> ... free, independent, lonely, powerful, rational, responsible, brave, the hero of so many novels and books of moral philosophy ... the offspring of the age of science, confidently rational and yet increasingly aware of his alienation from the material universe which his discoveries reveal.[12]

Now think about what Kant is actually saying, if his 'metaphysical dimension' is taken seriously, and not brushed aside, or read in a deflationary way as offering an 'as if' thought experiment. Kant is telling us that the 'autos' in 'autonomy' is never our empirical self, or the self of our empirical ego biographies. It is not a striving and conscious heroic individual. It is the whole, entire, true, proper self, which remains unknown to us, but is the source of what we know of as 'us'.

A similar thought is found in Jung's treatment of the 'whole self'.[13] The whole self never directly and entirely appears, yet, everything that occurs psychically, is a

---

[10] Kant, *GW*, 4: 437.

[11] Ibid.

[12] Iris Murdoch, *The Sovereignty of Good* (London and New York: Routledge, 1989), 80.

[13] For a discussion of Kant's influence on Jung, to which I am indebted here, see Philip Kime, 'Regulating the Psyche: The Essential Contribution of Kant', *International Journal of Jungian Studies*, 5/1 (2013), 44–63. The following system is used for Jung references: *Memories, Dreams and Reflections* (London: Fontana Press, 1995), are referred to as *Memories*. Other references are to Jung's *Collected Works* (volume number: page number) published by Routledge and Kegan Paul. Volume 9 is bound in two volumes, referred to as 9.1 and 9.2. The volumes cited here include *Freud and Psychoanalysis*, Vol.4; *Psychological Types*, Vol. 6; *The Structure and Dynamics of the Psyche*, Vol. 8; *The Archetypes and the Unconscious*, Vol. 9.1; *Aion*, Vol. 9.2; *Psychology and Religion: West and East*, Vol.11; *Alchemical Studies*, Vol. 13.

manifestation of the whole self. The 'unconscious', Jung writes, 'is the matrix out of which the whole psychic future grows'[14]:

> Under these circumstances the unconscious seems like a great X, concerning which the only thing indisputably known is that important effects proceed from it.[15]

The 'psyche', the 'whole self', Jung writes, is 'unknowable', except through its effects:

> [A]ll we know is that effects come to us from the dark sphere of the psyche which somehow or other must be assimilated into consciousness if devastating disturbances of other functions are to be avoided ... [These effects] have as many meanings and facets as the unconscious itself.[16]

The deep Kantian principle that undergirds Jung's approach here is the often suppressed entailment of transcendental idealism: which is that although things-in-themselves, including our proper selves, never directly appear in space and time, nonetheless, *everything that appears in space and time is nothing other than an appearance of this underlying and generative reality.* The common Kantian and Jungian insight is that the whole self is far larger, deeper, and stranger than the conscious self.

Jung himself understood his reflections on the unconscious as a faithful Kantian reflection, writing in 1961:

> We are therefore obliged to assume, whether we like it or not, the existence of a non-conscious psychic sphere, even if only as a 'negative borderline concept' like Kant's *Ding an sich*.[17]

'What Kant demonstrated in respect of logical thinking', Jung writes, 'is true of the whole range of the psyche'.[18] In his early reading, Jung found that only Kant and Schopenhauer addressed the whole 'psyche', revealing what Jung called 'the grandeur of "God's world"'.[19]

Looked at through a Jungian lens, the metaphysical Kant takes on a different and more fascinating salience, which offers a helpful corrective to a certain breeziness in the grammatical Kant. The grammatical Kant is concerned with our ability

---

[14] Jung, 8: 367.
[15] Jung, 8: 368.
[16] Jung, 8: 367.
[17] Jung, 4: 317.
[18] Jung, 5; 6: 512.
[19] Jung, *Memories*, 122, 95.

168 NEGATIVE NATURAL THEOLOGY

to detach ourselves from, and then, perhaps to reattach ourselves to, various external factors, or, at least, factors beyond ourselves: from our own contingent impulses and desires, from kinship groups and communities that are both nurturing and controlling, from sheer selfishness, self-interest, and the pressure of other contingent interest groups, towards the universal. But, the missing thing in the frame is this: the need to detach ourselves from the interior hindrances and obstacles to our own freedom, to our becoming who we are. These obstacles can take a number of forms: unconscious complexes (constellations of 'feeling-toned' memories and beliefs), core fantasies ('I am the unloved one'), and developmentally out of date ego strategies and avoidances ('seek approval', 'hide your anger', 'fear confrontation'). We are maimed, damaged, and controlled in ways that are not immediately apparent. As the philosopher and psychoanalyst Jonathan Lear puts it, such fantasies and techniques can be 'effective in organizing and unifying the psyche, in ways that often bypass—and sometimes distort—rational, self-conscious thought'.[20]

This indicates that if we only have the grammatical Kant, we may find it difficult, even if we want to, to pull away from rather thin liberal notions of autonomy. The metaphysical Kant underscores that our deeper and entire selves are not under our conscious control, and that many of the most generative and destructive obstacles to conscious freedom sit deeply within ourselves, and that the task of engaging with these obstacles involves a difficult engagement, a process, and a journey. The metaphysical Kant provides an ecstatic and transcendent dimension to our thinking about the self; the grammatical Kant reminds us that our purpose here is the practical task of growing into our freedom and autonomy. The two approaches are incomplete without each other.

On the one hand, we remain interested in the analytical arc unfurled in the grammatical Kantian approach, where we connect freedom with reason, and reason with individuality, and individuality with a capability for self-detachment, which opens up to the universal and communal. On the other hand, this task is set against the understanding that the conscious ego is not the whole self, and that, as Jung himself puts it:

We are a psychic process which we do not control, or only partly direct.[21]

The task of being autonomous must reckon also with the way our conscious ego is embedded in an entire self, which only reveals itself partially, step by step, with shifting complexions: why would this not be the constant framing of the invitation to become more autonomous, more integrated, more whole, rather than a sign that the task of attaining autonomy is misguided? The *autos* in autonomy should stand

---

[20] Jonathan Lear, *Freud* (London and New York: Routledge, 2005). I am indebted to Lear for the example of the core fantasy 'I am the unloved one', 7.
[21] Jung, *Memories*, 14.

for the entire self, the whole self, and not just the conscious ego. Then it becomes highly relevant for autonomy that, as David Burrell puts it, 'conscious thinking is embedded in the unconscious much like an organism subsists in an environment', such that:

> If *ego* is the me that I have a hand in making, self is what I am invited to discover. The *self* functions as a lure; it represents what I am called to become and holds the power which, released, will bring me there. The self, then, always outreaches my actual self now, yet contains the materials which intimate what I will be.[22]

The 'process of becoming one's self", Burrell observes is 'never so expansive as that neutral idiom suggests':

> It is more like negotiating precipitous slopes and narrow defiles, or like a hand-to-hand struggle in spiritual conflict.[23]

To recognize all this is the 'rational' thing to do, in the full sense of rationality, of that which displays a proper *ratio* to the reality that presents itself. The point of undertaking this journey is not to become dispersed, or possessed, or inflated, but, in fact, to achieve a fuller freedom, a fuller and more integrated autonomy, which needs less anxious and tensive attempts to stay 'in control', without becoming dangerously lost.

We saw, in both the metaphysical and grammatical Kant, the significance of a type of impersonality: a self-transcending participation in reason as such, in the metaphysical Kant, and a movement from the individual to the universal and communal, in the case of the grammatical Kant. This movement towards the impersonal is also found in Jung. 'The self', Jung writes, 'which can only be perceived subjectively as a most intimate and unique thing, requires universality as a background'.[24] As David Burrell puts it, what talking about the 'whole self' provides is a 'background of universality' wherein someone 'can discern a pattern rich enough to make a story of his own life by affording it a plot':

> One becomes a person only through incorporating something impersonal.[25]

Where the grammatical Kant opens us up into the impersonal universality of reason, the metaphysical Kant—with the never fully appearing whole self—may

---

[22] David Burrell, 'Jung: A Language for Soul', in *Exercises in Religious Understanding* (Eugene, Oregan: Wipf and Stock, 1974), 182–237, 211, 217.
[23] Ibid., 222. See Jung, 11: 196.
[24] Jung, 11: 190.
[25] Burrell, 'Jung', 220–221.

open the door to other psychic elements which do not lie on the surface. Jung takes up this invitation, and seeks the 'common humanity'[26] that emerges when we explore the 'uncharted part of our self that we name *the unconscious*'.[27] Jung and Kant (and Plato) suffer from interpretations that tend to reify as 'queer objects' things-in-themselves, archetypes, or forms, where these science-fiction entities somehow interact with us. This is a distorted construal. We do not have two worlds, two types of object, but one reality, with textures and depths, and with limited degrees of disclosure to our conscious experience and reason, according to our limited and finite capacities. The noumenal, like Jung's unconscious, is a negative limit, that which lies beyond and behind conscious thought. It is that which is in principle unknowable and ungraspable, but which is also the generative source of that which does appear.

I perceive here a connection with Jonathan Lear's repeated emphasis that psychoanalytical approaches are not about the analyst discovering hidden secrets, laid down in the past, in a reified and mysterious realm ('the unconscious').[28] Rather, psychoanalysis is about consciousness and the future: how to grow in awareness, freedom, autonomy, and vitality, taking this into the future, into a fuller way of living. Something similar needs to be said, I am convinced, about the Platonic realm of ideas, and the Kantian noumenal: our task is not to hunt down 'hidden realities' (ideas, things-in-themselves); rather, it is about orienting towards a transcendent, because ungraspable, horizon towards which we move, growing, as we do, in autonomy, freedom, and consciousness.

In 1967 Jung again draws the direct parallel between the thing-in-itself and the unconscious, a 'merely negative borderline concept'.[29] About the archetypes, Jung writes that we know of them only through their impacts upon us, and the way they shape a psychic life, our experience and behaviour. Jung claims that the contents of the collective unconscious are 'similar' to the 'Kantian categories'[30], although Kant 'reduced the archetypes to a limited number of categories of understanding'.[31]

Translated into metaphysical Kantian terms, the contents of the unconscious constitute the deep structures of the unknown x, the thing-in-itself, the whole self. Elements of this whole self appear, partially and mediated, in consciousness. There is no position outside of our experience, beyond our finite and limited cognitive relationship to the proper self/psyche, to see and map the plumbing that makes us ourselves. We cannot offer a reductive and comprehensive explanation, but are

---

[26] Jung, 9.2, 169.
[27] Burrell, 'Jung', 195.
[28] See, for example, 'Wisdom Won from Illness', in *Wisdom Won from Illness* (Cambridge, MA: Harvard University Press, 2017), 11–29.
[29] Jung, 13: 82.
[30] Jung, 8: 14.
[31] Jung, 8: 276.

headlong in the midst of life, and must do what we can to discern our way into a new future, given our limitations. This will involve a process of difficult, always veiled, discernment.

At several points, Burrell comments elliptically on Jung's respect for the 'critical factor demanded of anyone who wants to deal with such issues after Kant', and of how Jung profits from 'Kant's radical critique'.[32] These comments look strange on certain interpretations of Kant, or against the framework of the grammatical Kant. I am unclear precisely what Burrell means, but I find that these remarks, placed alongside the metaphysical Kant, make good sense: the point of Kant's 'epistemic discipline' is not to have as reductive a worldview as possible. This is not epistemic discipline: this is its own type of excess and ideology, expressing a desire for ego control and total transparency. Epistemic discipline means: having as rich a worldview as you need to, in order to deal with *experience as it fully unfurls for us*, without at the same time, and by enthusiasm or association, bringing in magical thinking or superstition, or futile speculations.

Jung can be understood to offer a further (disciplined) expansion of the category of 'experience', so that we consider not only perceptual states ('I see a red patch', 'I see x causing y') and moral commitments, but the whole range of psychic phenomena which constitutes our lives. Jung writes that the 'unconscious is not this thing or that':

[I]t is the Unknown as it immediately affects us.[33]

As Burrell puts it:

[T]he *unconscious* reveals its reality in the unwelcome ordeals it concocts and in the power which one can feel being released as he negotiates them.[34]

Burrell affirms Jung's insight that 'we can neither overlook nor minimize the influence of this unconscious dimension on our actions':

And if it really affects our lives, we cannot very well deny its reality. Jung can even show how it takes its revenge if we do.[35]

In a nice phrase, Burrell writes that it was 'as an empiricist that [Jung] encountered the transempirical'.[36] Jung's unwillingness to suppress or deny this encounter

---

[32] Burrell, 'Jung', 211, 213.
[33] Jung, 8: 68.
[34] Ibid., 198.
[35] Ibid., 197–198.
[36] Ibid., 210.

forced him to reach for a new scientific paradigm—'one closer to *interpretation* than to *explanation*'.[37]

Jung, of course, develops strategies for engaging with the unconscious in ways that are more productive, imaginative, and concrete than Kant, reflecting upon distinct tasks of the self across a lifetime, engaging with a depth of fantasy, and with symbolism that emerges through dreams and the active free play of imagination. I would offer here a parallel thought to that set out by Jonathan Lear, in relation to Plato and Aristotle. Lear draws attention to Aristotle's nonrational soul, and Plato's tripartite and 'psychodynamic' account of the self—rational, spirited, and appetitive—imaged through the metaphorical figures of the human, the lion, and the many-headed hydra. Lear comments that these classical philosophers have an 'unfinished' intimation of the need for an integration of the unconscious.[38] Just so, Kant makes no systematic exploration of the unconscious and psychodynamic relations within the self, although these territories are not entirely untouched by Kant. We might consider here Kant's musings on Schwedenborg in *Dreams of a Spirit Seer,* and Jung's appreciative words about this text, which he read as a medical student. 'Kant's *Dreams of a Spirit Seer* came just at the right moment', Jung reports: 'the world gained depth and background'.[39] Kant has his own developmental theory that human beings achieve moral maturity ('becoming ourselves') in their forties, and he has some interest in the free play of the imagination, as it enjoys intimations (which are not knowledge) of the deeper structure of an unalienated relationship between freedom and nature, or, of ourselves as we appear, and of ourselves as we deeply are. Jung offers a faithful extrapolation, I would maintain, from the lessons of the metaphysical Kant, which lessons the grammatical Kant could never deliver.

I find it nicely ironic that a benefit arising from attending to the 'metaphysical Kant' may be to put a dampener on our pretensions to know and experience our entire self, within our conscious lives. The metaphysical Kant, read in a Jungian way, may be what takes us beyond Kantian constructivism.

Lear writes that his own philosophical interest in Freud 'goes against the grain of our times', at least in terms of the academic humanities.[40] Something even stronger would have to be said in relation to Jung, who, I sense, is so intellectually unfashionable as to be barely studied at all in many mainstream university settings. Notably, Lear himself only references Jung once, in a neutral but peripheral fashion, across two books on philosophy and psychoanalysis. At the same time, and insightfully, Lear laments that psychoanalysis has an 'impoverished' insight into 'religious experience', derived in part from Freud's own 'brittle' reductions

---

[37] Ibid.
[38] See, for example, Jonathan Lear, *Wisdom Won from Illness*, 34, and *Freud.*
[39] Jung, *Memories*, 123.
[40] Ibid., 5.

(religion as 'infantile wish fulfilment', and so on). Lear wishes it to be otherwise, writing that 'if psychoanalysis is to live up to its promise of being a moral psychology', in relation to religious belief, 'it must find ways to mourn Freud's legacy and move on'.[41] The wide neglect of Jung, I suspect, is a lost opportunity, not least when thinking religiously and theologically about autonomy, freedom, and reason. As is well known, Jung has a far more expansive and generous appreciation of religion and theology than Freud's 'brittle' genealogical account. Both Kant and Jung lead us to meditations on limits, but both have more expansive aspirations than Freud, when thinking about the relationship between divinity, interiority, and the whole self.[42]

Autonomy and the divine

This brings me to a second area where a Jungian gaze on the metaphysical Kant, especially in relation to the concept of the divine, makes me question a way of speaking that had become almost habitual for me. In previous published work I have tended to emphasize respects in which Kant is not straightforwardly Christian. In particular, I have emphasized that Kant's ambitions for human freedom are in tension with a traditional 'concurrence' notion of divine and human action, which amounts to saying that God can act immediately and directly in each creature's actions, without destroying the freedom of that creature. The motivating impulse towards a concurrence account is not the conviction that it provides an intuitive and elegant account of causation, but the desire to respect two demands on thought, which do not seem to be easily commensurate: that we have as 'large' a view of God as possible, with God acting *ex nihilo* upon and throughout creation, and that the human being is indeed genuinely free.

One way in which Kant's rejection of concurrence expresses itself is in his insistence that when, in freedom, we set ends, becoming members of the Kingdom of Ends, we must have no 'external *object*', whether that is conceived of as an efficient cause pushing us, or a final cause pulling us. In my work on Kant, I have asked the question: what *sort of desire* has no external object? The immediate answer, readily available to Kant, is *divine desire*. God's own self-enjoyment, on a classical account, does not depend upon an external object, or anything outside of God. Throughout his life, in his early and late philosophy, Kant writes about this divine desire. Talking about the divine ideas, which are the storehouse of all possibility,

---

[41] Ibid., 203–204.

[42] As with any thinker, when working with Jung, there will need to be reflection and critical distance, with a careful handling of issues, such as Jung's fascination with Gnosticism, or his interest in aspects of occultism, or the seepage between an (eternal) 'archetype' and a (contingent and constructed) 'stereotype'.

174 NEGATIVE NATURAL THEOLOGY

Kant writes that 'the possibilities of things themselves, which are given through the divine nature, harmonize with *God's great desire*', and that 'goodness and perfection' themselves 'consist in this harmony'.[43] God has 'the highest desire' for the 'unity, harmony and order' 'found in the possibilities of things'.[44] In the 1780s Kant describes the creation as a diffusion of divine self-delight. God's 'well-pleasedness with himself', he writes, is such that God 'cannot be thought to shut himself up within himself'. Rather, God produces 'the highest good beyond himself just by his consciousness of his all-sufficiency'.[45]

What emerges, then, is that the sort of happiness we enjoy in the Kingdom of Ends is *itself* a type of divine happiness. With Aquinas, we participate in divine desire, by loving and knowing God in the beatific vision. With Kant, the participation in divinity is not through loving and knowing an external object, but through an immanent and free imitation and enactment of the divine: through a participation in the harmonious and plenitudinous setting of ends, and through membership in a community of rational end setting, a 'systematic union', as Kant describes it. Deep happiness and delight is the necessary consequence of being in this state.

Typically, the direction my thought then takes is to acknowledge that whatever we might say about God, a notion of desire without receptivity and vulnerability, at least for *human beings,* has something unsettling about it. At its worst, it may mark a disturbing transition from thinking about desire as love, to desire as power. I usually then try to make the situation look less grave for Kant ('he's not that bad'), perhaps pointing out, for example, how annihilating to our freedom Kant considers all of spatio-temporal reality to be, suggesting perhaps that he is more of an Atlas figure than Prometheus: trying to hold things together in the face of an abysmal mechanistic cataclysm.

All of this, possibly, misses or obscures a significant point, which only emerges when we attend to the deeper and shadowy layers of the metaphysical Kant. This point is that the self who has no external object is never our empirical and conscious self: it is the whole self, unknowable, and constantly and partially disclosed to us. I frequently stressed that with Kant there is a sort of identification of our proper selves with the divine, in that we participate in self-transcending reason as such, but I didn't attend enough, I now think, to the fact that it is our *proper (never visible) selves* who are so identified. In this connection, I'm struck by Jung's thought that the idea of God is a symbol of the whole self, of an entirely integrated whole (harmonizing ego and unconscious). Kant also reaches for notions of wholeness and integration, in relation to the concept of God. God, and God alone, has a

---

[43] Kant, *OPA,* 2: 91.
[44] Kant, *OPA,* 2: 91–92.
[45] Kant, *TP,* 8: 280n.

will, Kant writes, that 'necessarily harmonizes with the laws of autonomy'.[46] For Kant, God is primarily and paradigmatically the *ens realissimum,* the all-of-reality, wherein all compossible actualities are fully and entirely realized, providing, I have suggested, a parallel for the Kingdom of Ends, our divinization, wherein all compossible ends are desired, which state is one of happiness.[47] There is a burgeoning and technical literature which worries that Kant's concept of God ('the all-of-reality') contains too many incommensurable realities and actualities, that cannot be internally held together.[48] From both a traditional theological and a Jungian perspective, the sense of incommensurability may be entirely apt. As David Burrell points out, for Nicholas of Cusa, God is a—for us—paradoxical and ungraspable coincidence of opposites, which is a more dramatic underscoring of Aquinas' insistence that the goodness of God is far removed from the assessments we might make of it.[49] The *'complexio oppositorium'* of the God-image', Jung writes, enters into us 'not as a unity, but as conflict'.[50]

It may be important to note that Jung himself was resistant to the suggestion that he was 'reducing' the theological concept of God to a psychological category. Rather, within the disciplined limits of his concerns—healing and integrating the psyche—Jung was interested in the therapeutic meaning of the concept. As Burrell comments, in relation to Jung:

> Transcendence, that is being called beyond one's present self, is simply a fact of Jung's personal and therapeutic experience.[51]

We might note that there are Augustinian strands of reflection which push into our deepest interiority, to find God at the other side of this inside. Where Jung seems inclined to find that 'metaphysical notions' leave no 'remainder' after their therapeutic usefulness, this is not so with 'theological symbols', because, here, the 'remainder itself' appears 'to have therapeutic worth':

> [T]he fact that revelation is *from* God enhances its value immeasurably.[52]

The identification of the symbol of God with the idea of the whole self should not lend itself to an inflation of the self, but, more, to a diminution of, and challenge to, the ego. The 'point of God-language', in this connection, Burrell reflects 'lies in

---

[46] Kant, *GW,* 1: 139.
[47] See *Kant and the Divine,* chs.17–18.
[48] See, for example, Andrew Chignell, 'Kant and the "Monstrous Ground of Possibility"', *Kantian Review,* 19/1 (2014), 53–69.
[49] Burrell, 'Jung', 208–209.
[50] Jung, *Memories,* 334, cited by Burrell, 'Jung', 222.
[51] Ibid., 218.
[52] Ibid., 231.

176 NEGATIVE NATURAL THEOLOGY

affirming that one does not create himself', which challenges the ambitions of the 'runaway *ego*' and of relentless 'planning and control'[53]:

> There is something more to reality, an other, unconscious dimension. The complete reality which *self* symbolizes can be attained only by respecting this other dimension. Attained, not achieved; and respect accounts for the difference.[54]

On this, Burrell finds Jung 'properly religious'.[55] Whenever we feel 'more "together", more "at one", and are able to call upon the new power which this releases', Jung comments that this, 'is felt as grace'.[56] Such growth and grace usually involves a sort of death to the pretensions of the conscious ego. Burrell writes about the 'contours of a Judeo-Christian anthropology' in Jung's individuation process:

> [T]he measure of attainment comes only gradually, as successive images for self are shattered by failure—and yet we realize that it is not all over. The process of attaining oneself is not one of achievement; the images appropriate to it are never so linear as progress. Rather the pattern is one the Gospels invoke for Jesus' death and resurrection: the seed must be buried in the ground (and 'die') for the plant to emerge. 'Death' amounts to exposing a particular self-image as an ego-projection and hence an idol.[57]

I feel a sense of embarrassment that I did not see this in the picture set forward by the metaphysical Kant: I would praise and celebrate the picture for its beauty, coherence and vision, but not for the more shadowy elements that undoubtedly accompany Kant's emphasis on all that we do not know, and cannot access. Kant talks about the process of coming to greater integration—entering the universality and harmony of the moral law—as a type of death of the old self, the 'death of the old man', the 'crucifying of the flesh'.[58] He describes the free movement towards the fullness of universality and harmony as a type of supersensible grace, a 'surplus' which is 'imputed to us *by grace*', although Kant distinguishes this from a type or 'supernatural' action.[59] Kant even speaks, and precisely in this connection, about the 'archetype' of the Son of God, as the figure of perfection, whose death prefigures, and facilitates, the transformative death we each need to undergo.

Previously, when considering such passages, I could only see the reductive translation of Christian doctrine (atonement, grace) into the terms of 'practical reason'.

---

[53] Ibid., 220, 199.
[54] Ibid., 199.
[55] Ibid.
[56] Ibid., 335, cited by Burrell, 'Jung', 199.
[57] Ibid., 189. See Jung 9.1: 84.
[58] Kant, *Rel,* 6: 75.
[59] Ibid.

But I did not dwell enough on the strangeness of the metaphysical Kant, and what this means for how we think of the textures and limitations of such 'reason'. Such reason is concerned with the unknowable proper self, the whole self, beyond yet behind all that appears. This self is addressed only by reflection on what underlies that which appears in the realm of our moral, and perceptual, experiences and commitments. Kant chose to write on this, and to employ the categories of death, crucifixion, grace, archetype and revelation, when talking about our free turning towards that which is universal and harmonious. I find that there is something chastening about this: that in a generative 'modern' source for how we think of autonomy, there was something like a dark night of the soul, and an awareness for our capacity for illusion, where we think 'we have arrived the moment we have spied the goal'.[60]

Although she is not writing, at all, about Kant, I find that some words of the twentieth-century American poet and essayist Elizabeth Bishop somehow precisely evoke for me the type of Kantian/Jungian wisdom I sense is worth exploring. Bishop writes:

Perhaps we shall never know the companion in ourselves who is with us all our lives, the nearness of our minds at all times to the rare person whose heart quickens when a bird climbs high and alone in the clear air.

I find this a striking evocation of something like the Kant's 'proper self', and Jung's 'whole self': the free, whole, entire and originary source of all our thoughts and actions, disclosed but veiled in each moment of our empirical biographies, which pass for us like the moving images of our own eternity, which eternity happens not somewhere else, remote from us, but in an inaccessible nearness. As Bishop puts it, within a never known 'companion in ourselves who is with us all our lives', where in a 'quiet hour', the 'mind finds its Sea, the wide, quiet plane with different lights in the sky and different, more secret sounds'.[61]

---

[60] Jung, *Memories*, 202. See Jung 16: 294–295.
[61] Elizabeth Bishop, 'On Being Alone', in *Poems, Prose, and Letters,* ed. Robert Giroux and Lloyd Schwartz (New York: The Library of America, 2008), 323.

Epilogue

The Varieties of Philosophical Experience

Unearthing some of the work done by the concept of the divine, in the different contexts explored in the chapters of this book, does not, in itself, determine what judgements we might make about such uses.

This, in a way, is one of the claims of the book: that reason must reckon with a humility in the face of the concept of God, and that, consequently, there is a degree of non-coercive freedom, when it comes to speaking about God, or not speaking about God.

We saw this, in Chapter 3, with respect to the question of whether to name our shared human predicament a state of mystery, or absurdity. The humanist, as we saw in Chapter 4, turns their face away from the sense of tension that generates both a sense of mystery and absurdity, and doing so requires a degree of striving and determination. The different ways in which the concept of divinity arises for the modern pagan (Chapter 5), and the absolute idealist (Chapter 6), may, in part, arise because of some deep and unconscious springs of action and desire: in the former case, a draw towards fluidity, flexibility, imagination, and vitality, in the latter case, a yearning for peace, order, and harmony. To some extent, in Chapter 7, we might see both of these facets, these 'personality types', come together, with a yearning, on the one hand, for consciousness, and harmony, and, on the other, for vitality and the integration of unconscious life, embodied respectively in Kant, and in the post-Kantian thinker—as I construe him to be—Carl Gustav Jung.

The determined atheist, and a certain sort of traditional theologian, can remain undisturbed by all of this. The atheist can agree that some of the conceptual space reached for by secular philosophers was once part of what was intended, when thinkers reached for the idea of God. But, so what? With richer philosophical vocabularies, we can retain this conceptual space, without the spookiness of divinity. The traditioned theologian, of a certain stripe, might agree with the atheist that yearnings for non-alienated life, for feeling at home in the universe, in themselves have nothing much to do with the God who reveals Godself in scripture, offering redemption from our fallen condition.

With the freedom and humility of reason in relation to the material presented, I cannot block either perspective on whatever it is that I have uncovered.

I cannot myself accept either the reductive atheist, or the dismissive theological perspective on the material. I would prefer to reach for an alternative theological

Negative Natural Theology. Christopher J. Insole, Oxford University Press. © Christopher J. Insole 2024.
DOI: 10.1093/9780198933007.003.0009

approach, which is neither reductive nor dismissive. It would be possible, for example, to entertain high theological grounds for being interested in, tolerant of, and patient in front of what might be called non-standard and alternative uses of the concept of the divine. I will not present, here, an argument *for* this high theological position. Rather, I will offer a thought experiment.

The experiment is simple enough: what might we expect if we combine a huge God—simple and triune, omnipotent, omniscient, all loving, and the creator of everything *ex nihilo*—with our finite and limited capacities to know and apprehend such a God? Well, we might expect to receive the vastness of such a living God in fragments, shards, half-lights, both unveiling, and distorting. And, if God is all loving, we might hope that God can make God known to us in ways that are appropriate to our capacities, gifts, and limitations.

In 1902 the philosopher and psychologist William James[1] addressed the question of the variety of types of religious experience and commitment. James asks the following:

[I]s the existence of so many religious types and sects and creeds regrettable?

The answer that James gives is one that I would associate myself with:

I answer 'No' emphatically. And my reason is that I do not see how it is possible that creatures in such different positions and with such different powers as human individuals are, should have exactly the same functions and the same duties. No two of us have identical difficulties, nor should we be expected to work out identical solutions. Each, from his peculiar angle of observation, takes in a certain sphere of fact and trouble, which each must deal with in a unique manner.[2]

When we think about it, and the people we know and cherish, as well as the people we find intolerable, isn't this sort of obvious? Although, as with many things, it can be forgotten in the heat of arguing for something we deeply care about.

When thinking about God, it is simply not possible to hope for knowledge, or certainty, or anything even remotely approaching certainty, such as high probability. Nor, I would submit, will knowledge, or certainty, or anything remotely approaching certainty ever be possible.

That we hit a limit to what reason and investigation can do in this area is not an accident. We have two types of reason for expecting to fail: one more *a priori* and theological, the other more *a posteriori* and inductive.[3] The theological grounds

---

[1] William James, 'The Varieties of Religious Experience: A Study in Human Nature' in *William James: Writings 1902–1910* (New York: Library of America, 1987), 3–477.

[2] Ibid., 436.

[3] For this insightful distinction, I am indebted to the D.Phil. thesis of Joel Gutteridge, 'Philosophical Theology and the Limits of Explanation', presented at the University of Oxford in January 2024.

arise from the type of God that we speak of: simple, infinite, transcendent, eternal and outside of time, yet equally present to each moment in time, the creator *ex nihilo*. We should not expect to be able fully to fathom such an ineffable God. The *a posteriori* and inductive grounds come to light when we think of all of the time spent arguing about God, over all the centuries, and the failure to arrive at agreement or certainty: all the disputation and disagreement, some of it peaceful and intellectual, some of it violent and primitive.

Think of your own case: how amenable are *you,* really, to a powerful argument or piece of evidence unsettling and changing your own belief or non-belief, or your long held agnosticism?

So, when thinking and talking about God—that is, those of us who cannot help ourselves, and who cannot stop ourselves doing this—what are we going to do next?

Bibliography

Thomas Aquinas, *Summa Contra Gentiles,* ed. and trans. Vernon Bourke (Notre Dame, IN: University of Notre Dame Press, 1975).

Aristotle, *Posterior Analytics. Topica,* trans. Hugh Tredennick and E. S. Forster, Loeb Classical Library 391 (Cambridge, MA: Harvard University Press, 1960).

Augustine, *Confessions,* trans. F.J. Sheed (London: Sheed and Ward, 1944).

A.J. Ayer, *Language, Truth and Logic* (Harmondsworth: Penguin Books, 1971).

Akeel Bilgrami, 'Autonomy, Value, and the Unalienated Life: An Interview with Akeel Bilgrami', in *Redeeming Autonomy: Theological and Secular Crossings,* ed. Benjamin DeSpain and Christopher Insole (London and New York: Bloomsbury, 2025).

Akeel Bilgrami, 'The Wider Significance of Naturalism: A Genealogical Essay', in *Naturalism and Normativity,* ed. Mario de Caro and David Macarthur (New York: Coloumbia University Press, 2010), 23–54.

Elizabeth Bishop, 'On Being Alone', in *Poems, Prose, and Letters,* eds. Robert Giroux and Lloyd Schwartz (New York: The Library of America, 2008), 323.

Laurence Bonjour, 'Against Naturalized Epistemology', *Midwest Studies in Philosophy* XIX (1994), 283–300.

David Bourget and David J. Chalmers, 'What do Philosophers Believe?', *Philosophical Studies* 170/3 (2014), 465–500.

F.H. Bradley, 'On God and the Absolute', in *Essays on Truth and Reality* (Cambridge: Cambridge University Press, 2011), 428–459.

David Burrell, 'Jung: A Language for Soul', in *Exercises in Religious Understanding* (Eugene, Oregan: Wipf and Stock, 1974), 182–237.

Albert Camus, 'Caligula', in *Caligula and Other Plays,* trans. Stuart Gilbert (London and New York: Penguin Books, 2013), 1–62.

Albert Camus, *The Fall,* trans. Robin Buss (London: Penguin Random House UK, 2013).

Albert Camus, 'Letters to a German Friend: Fourth Letter', in *Resistance, Rebellion, and Death,* trans. Justin O'Brien (New York: Random House, 1960), 3–25.

Albert Camus, *L'Homme Révolté* (Paris: N.R.F. Gallimard, 1951).

Albert Camus, *Lyrical and Critical Essays,* ed. Philip Thody, trans. Ellen Conroy Kennedy (Random House, New York: Vintage Books, 1970).

Albert Camus, *The Myth of Sisyphus,* trans. Justin O'Brien (London: Penguin Books, 2000).

Albert Camus, *The Outsider,* trans. Stuart Gilbert (London: Hamish Hamilton, 1965).

Albert Camus, *The Plague* (London: Penguin Books, 1984).

Albert Camus, 'La Remarque sur la Révolte', in *Existence* (Paris: Gallimard, 1945), 12–27.

Clare Carlisle, 'Spinoza and Autonomy', in *Redeeming Autonomy,* ed. Benjamin DeSpain and Christopher J. Insole (London and New York: Bloomsbury, 2025).

Clare Carlisle, 'Spiritual Desire and Religious Practice', *Religious Studies* 55/3 (2019), 429–446.

David Carroll, 'Rethinking the Absurd: *Le Mythe de Sisyphe*', in *The Cambridge Companion to Camus,* ed. Edward J. Hughes (Cambridge: Cambridge University Press, 2007), 53–66.

Andrew Chignell, 'Kant and the "Monstrous Ground of Possibility"', *Kantian Review* 19/1 (2014), 53–69.

Samuel Taylor Coleridge, *Poems,* ed. J. Beer (Dent: London, 1974).

David Copp, 'Normative Naturalism and Normative Nihilism', in *Reading Parfit on What Matters,* ed. Simon Kirchin (London and New York: Routledge, 2017), 28–53.

Simon Critchley, *Continental Philosophy: A Very Short Introduction* (Oxford: Oxford University Press, 2001).

182 BIBLIOGRAPHY

Simon Critchley, *Things Merely Are* (New York: Routledge, 2005).

Richard Dawkins, *The Magic of Reality: How We Know What's Really True* (London: Black Swan, 2021).

Mario De Caro and David Macarthur (eds.), *Naturalism and Normativity* (New York: Columbia University Press, 2010).

Helen De Cruz, 'Religious Disagreement: An Empirical Study Among Academic Philosophers', *Episteme* 14/1, 2017, 71–87.

Benjamin DeSpain, 'All Too Human', *The Varieties of Philosophical Experience: Negative Natural Theology* (forthcoming).

Fyodor Dostoevsky, *A Writer's Diary, Volume 1: 1873–1876,* trans. Kenneth Lantz (London: Quartet Books, 1994).

J.L. Dowell and David Sobel, 'Advice for Non-Analytical Naturalists', in *Reading Parfit on What Matters,* ed. Simon Kirchin (London and New York: Routledge, 2017), 153–171.

Fiona Ellis, *God, Value, and Nature* (Oxford: Oxford University Press, 2016).

Fiona Ellis, 'Is Liberal Naturalism Possible', in *Naturalism and Normativity,* ed. Mario De Caro and David Macarthur (New York: Columbia University Press, 2010), 69–88.

Matthew Engelke, "The Coffin Question: Death and Materiality in Humanist Funerals', *Material Religion* 11/1 (2015), 26–49.

Matthew Engelke, '"Good without God": Happiness and Pleasure Among the Humanists', in *Values of Happiness: Towards an Anthropology of Purpose in Life,* ed. Iza Kavedzija and Harry Walker (London: Hau Books, 2017), 144–161.

Jamie Ferreira, 'Review of Janet M. Soskice: "Metaphor and Religious Language"', *The Thomist* 51/4 (1987), 719–725.

Philip Goff, *Consciousness and Fundamental Reality* (Oxford: Oxford University Press, 2017).

John Gray, 'An Illusion with a Future', *Daedelus* 133/3 (2004), 428–459.

Joel Gutteridge, 'Philosophical Theology and the Limits of Explanation', D.Phil. thesis presented at the University of Oxford in January 2024.

Pierre Hadot, *Philosophy as a Way of Life: Spiritual Exercises from Socrates to Foucault* (Oxford: Blackwell, 1995).

Pierre Hadot, *What Is Ancient Philosophy?* (Cambridge, MA: Harvard University Press, 2004).

Thomas L. Hanna, 'Albert Camus and the Christian Faith', *The Journal of Religion* 36/4 (1956), 224–233.

Stanley Hauerwas, *The Hauerwas Reader* (Durham, North Carolina: Duke University Press, 2001).

Martin Heidegger, 'Letter on Humanism', in *Basic Writings,* ed. David Farrell Krell (London and New York: Routledge, 2008), 141–182.

Simon Hewitt, *Negative Theology and Philosophical Analysis* (London: Palgrave, 2020).

Jeremy Hooker, *Diary of a Stroke* (London: Shearsman Books, 2016).

Ronald Hutton, *The Triumph of the Moon: A History of Modern Pagan Witchcraft* (Oxford: Oxford University Press, 1999).

Sean Illing, 'Between Nihilism and Transcendence: Camus's Dialogue with Dostoevsky', *The Review of Politics* 77/2 (2015), 217–242.

Christopher J. Insole, 'Free Belief: The Medieval Heritage in Kant's Moral Faith', *Journal of the History of Philosophy* 57/3 (2019), 501–528.

Christopher J. Insole, 'Intellectualism, Relational Properties and the Divine Mind in Kant's Pre-Critical Philosophy', *Kantian Review* 16/3 (2011), 399–428.

Christopher J. Insole, *The Intolerable God: Kant's Theological Journey* (Grand Rapids, Michigan: William B. Eerdman's Publishing Company, 2016).

Christopher J. Insole, *Kant and the Divine: From Contemplation to the Moral Law* (Oxford: Oxford University Press, 2020).

Christopher J. Insole, *Kant and the Creation of Freedom: A Theological Problem* (Oxford: Oxford University Press, 2013).

Christopher J. Insole, 'Kant, Divinity, and Autonomy', *Studies in Christian Ethics* 32/4 (2019), 470–484.

BIBLIOGRAPHY   183

Christopher J. Insole, 'Kant on Christianity, Religion, and Politics: Three Hopes, Three Limits', *Studies in Christian Ethics* 29/1 (2016), 14–33.

Christopher J. Insole, 'Kant's Transcendental Idealism and Newton's Divine *Sensorium*', *Journal of the History of Ideas* 72/3 (2011), 413–436.

Christopher J. Insole, 'A Kantian Response to the Problem of Evil: Living in the Moral World', *Religions* 14/2 (2023), Article 227. https://doi.org/10.3390/rel14020227.

Christopher J. Insole, 'A Thomistic Reading of Kant's *Groundwork of the Metaphysics of Morals*: Searching for the Unconditioned', *Modern Theology* 31/2 (2015), 284–311.

William James, 'Is Radical Empiricism Solipsistic?' (1905), in *Pragmatism and Other Writings*, 337–340.

William James, 'A Pluralistic Universe: Hibbert Lectures at Manchester College on the Present Situation in Philosophy', in *William James: Writings 1902–1910* (New York: Library of America, 1987), 627–819.

William James, 'Pragmatism' (1907), in *Pragmatism and Other Writings*, 1–132.

William James, 'Varieties of Religious Experience', in *Writings 1902–1910,* (New York: The Library of America, 1987), 1–478.

William James, 'A World of Pure Experience' (1904), in *Pragmatism and Other Writings*, ed. Giles Gunn (London: Penguin, 2000), 314–336.

Max Jammer, *Einstein and Religion* (Princeton, New Jersey: Princeton University Press, 1999).

Robinson Jeffers, *The Wild God of the World: An Anthology of Robinson Jeffers,* selected with an introduction by Albert Gelpi (Stanford: Stanford University Press, 2003).

Byron R. Johnson, and Jeff Levin 'Religion Is Dying? Don't Believe It', *Wall Street Journal,* (28 July 2022).

Carl Gustav Jung, *Collected Works,* trans. R.F.C. Hull, ed. Herbert Read, Michael Fordham, Gerhard Adler (London: Routledge and Kegan Paul, 1957-1990).

Carl Gustav Jung, *Memories, Dreams and Reflections* (London: Fontana Press, 1995).

Immanuel Kant, 'Critique of Practical Reason' in *Immanuel Kant: Practical Philosophy*, trans. and ed. Mary J. Gregor (Cambridge: Cambridge University Press, 2008), 5: 3–309.

Immanuel Kant, 'Groundwork of the Metaphysics of Morals' in *Immanuel Kant: Practical Philosophy,* trans. and ed. Mary J. Gregor (Cambridge: Cambridge University Press, 2008), 4: 385–463.

Immanuel Kant, *Kants Gesammelte Schriften*, ed. Royal Prussian (later German) Academy of Sciences (Berlin: Georg Reimer, later Walter de Gruyter & Co., 1900-).

Immanuel Kant, 'On the Common Saying: That May be Correct in Theory, but it is of No Use in Practice (1793)', in *Practical Philosophy* 8: 275–312.

Immanuel Kant, 'The Only Possible Argument in Support of a Demonstration of the Existence of God', in *Immanuel Kant: Theoretical Philosophy, 1755–1770,* trans. and ed. David Walford and Ralf Meerbote (Cambridge: Cambridge University Press, 1992), 2: 63–163.

Immanuel Kant, 'Religion within the Boundaries of Mere Reason', in *Immanuel Kant: Religion and Rational Theology*, trans. and ed. Allen W. Wood and George di Giovanni (Cambridge: Cambridge University Press, 1996), 6: 3–202.

Karen Kilby, *God, Evil and the Limits of Theology* (London: Bloomsbury, 2020).

Karen Kilby, *Karl Rahner: Theology and Philosophy* (London and New York: Routledge, 2004).

Brian Kim and Matthew McGrath (eds.), *Pragmatic Encroachment in Epistemology* (London: Routledge, 2019).

Philip Kime, 'Regulating the Psyche: The Essential Contribution of Kant', *International Journal of Jungian Studies* 5/1 (2013), 44–63.

David E. Klemm and William Schweiker, *Religion and the Human Future: An Essay on Theological Humanism* (Oxford: Wiley-Blackwell, 2008).

Hilary Kornblith, 'In Defense of a Naturalized Epistemology', *The Blackwell Guide to Epistemology*, ed. John Greco and Ernest Sosa (Malden, MA: Blackwell, 1999), 158–169.

Hilary Kornblith, 'Naturalistic Epistemology and Its Critics', *Philosophical Topics* 23/1 (1995), 237–255.

Saul Kripke, *Naming and Necessity* (Oxford: Blackwell Publishing, 1972).

184   BIBLIOGRAPHY

William Lane Craig and J.P. Moreland (eds.), *The Blackwell Companion to Natural Theology* (London: Wiley-Blackwell, 2009).

Stephen Law, *Humanism: A Very Short Introduction* (Oxford: Oxford University Press, 2011).

Jonathan Lear, *Freud* (London and New York: Routledge, 2005).

Jonathan Lear, *Wisdom Won from Illness: Essays in Philosophy and Psychoanalysis* (Cambridge, MA: Harvard University Press, 2017).

Brian Leftow, 'Naturalistic Pantheism', in *Alternative Concepts of God: Essays on the Metaphysics of the Divine,* ed. Andrew A. Buckareff and Yujin Nagasawa (Oxford: Oxford University Press, 2016), 64–90.

James Lenman, 'Naturalism without Tears', in *Essays on Derek Parfit's on What Matters*, ed. Jussi Suikkanen and John Cottingham (Oxford: Wiley-Blackwell, 2009), 21–38.

King-Ho Leung, 'Hart and Sartre on God and Consciousness', *International Journal of Philosophy and Theology* 82/1 (2021), 34–50.

John Loose, 'The Christian as Camus's Absurd Man', *The Journal of Religion* 42/3 (1962), 203–214.

T.M. Luhrmann, *Persuasions of the Witch's Craft: Ritual Magic in Contemporary England* (Cambridge, MA: Harvard University Press, 1989).

Michael Luntley, *Contemporary Philosophy of Thought: Truth, World, Content* (Oxford: Blackwell Publishers, 1999).

Clare MacCumhaill and Rachael Wiseman, *Metaphysical Animals: How Four Women Brought Philosophy Back to Life* (London: Penguin, 2023).

Alisdair MacIntyre, *After Virtue: A Study in Moral Theory* (London and New York: Bloomsbury, 2011).

M.M. Madison, 'Albert Camus: Philosopher of Limits', *Modern Fiction Studies* 10/3 (1964), 223–231.

John McDowell, *Mind and World* (Cambridge Mass: Harvard University Press, 1996).

John McDowell, 'Two Sorts of Naturalism', in *Mind, Value and Reality* (Cambridge Mass. and London: Harvard University Press, 2002), 167–197.

J.M.E. McTaggert, *Some Dogmas of Religion* (London: Edward Arnold Press, 1916).

Mary Midgley, *The Owl of Minerva: A Memoir* (London: Routledge, 2006), 120.

Charles Moeller, 'Albert Camus: The Question of Hope', *Cross Currents* 8/2 (1958), 172–184.

Joseph G. Mueller, 'Forgetting as a Principle of Continuity in Tradition', *Theological Studies* 70 (2009), 751–781.

Stephen Mulhall, *The Great Riddle: Wittgenstein, Nonsense, Theology and Philosophy* (Oxford: Oxford University Press, 2018).

Iris Murdoch, *The Sovereignty of Good* (London and New York: Routledge, 1989).

Jennifer Nagel, 'Intuitions and Experiments: A Defense of the Case Method in Epistemology', *Philosophy and Phenomenological Research* 85/3 (2012), 495–527.

Thomas Nagel, 'The Absurd', in *Mortal Questions* (Cambridge: Cambridge University Press, 1991), 11–23.

Thomas Nagel, *The Last Word* (Oxford: Oxford University Press, 1997).

Thomas Nagel, *Mind and Cosmos* (Oxford: Oxford University Press, 2012).

Thomas Nagel, 'Secular Philosophy and the Religious Temperament', in *Secular Philosophy and the Religious Temperament: Essays 2002–2008,* (Oxford: Oxford University Press, 2009), 3–17.

Thomas Nagel, *The View from Nowhere* (Oxford: Oxford University Press, 1989).

David Newheiser, *Hope in a Secular Age: Deconstruction, Negative Theology and the Future of Faith* (Cambridge: Cambridge University Press, 2019).

Friedrich Nietzsche, 'On Truth and Lies in a Nonmoral Sense', in *Philosophy and Truth: Selections from Nietzsche's Notebooks of the Early 1870s,* trans. and ed. Daniel Breazale (Brighton: Harvester Press, 1979), 79–100.

Martha Nussbaum, 'Non-relative Virtues: An Aristotelian Account', in *The Quality of Life*, ed. Martha Nussbaum and Amartya Sen (Oxford: Oxford University Press, 1993), 242–269.

Brice Parain, *L'Existence* (Paris: Gallimard, 1945).

Derek Parfit, *On What Matters,* vols. I–III (Oxford: Oxford University Press, 2011).

BIBLIOGRAPHY   185

Henri Peyre, 'Albert Camus: An Anti-Christian Moralist', *Proceedings of the American Philosophical Society* 102/5 (1958), 477–482.

Henri Peyre, 'Camus the Pagan', *Yale French Studies* 25 (1960), 20–25.

Josef Pieper, *Happiness and Contemplation,* trans. Richard and Clara Winston (South Bend, IN: St Augustine's Press, 1979).

Karl Rahner, *Foundations of Christian Faith: An Introduction to the Idea of Christianity,* trans. William V. Dych (New York: Crossroad, 2016).

Russell Re Manning (ed.), *The Oxford Handbook of Natural Theology* (Oxford: Oxford University Press, 2013).

Philipp W. Rosemann, *Charred Root of Meaning: Continuity, Transgression, and the Other in Christian Tradition* (Grand Rapids, Michigan: William B. Eerdman's Publishing Company, 2017).

Josiah Royce, *The World and the Individual: Gifford Lectures. Second Series: Nature, Man, and the Moral Order* (London: MacMillan, 1929).

Josiah Royce, *The World and the Individual: Gifford Lectures. First Series: The Four Historical Conception of Being* (London: MacMillan, 1927).

Bede Rundle, *Wittgenstein and Contemporary Philosophy of Language* (Oxford: Wiley-Blackwell, 1990).

Bertrand Russell, *The Conquest of Happiness* (London: Allen & Unwin, 1930).

Gillian Russell and Delia Graff Fara (eds.), *The Routledge Companion to Philosophy of Language* (New York: Routledge, 2012).

Jean-Paul Sartre, *Being and Nothingness: An Essay in Phenomenological Ontology,* trans. S. Richmond (London: Routledge, 2020).

Jean-Paul Sartre, *Existentialism and Humanism,* trans. Philip Mairet (York: Methuen, 2017).

Rene Schaerer, *La Question Platonicienne: Études sur les Rapports de la Penseé et de l'expression dans les Dialogues* (Neuchâtel and Paris: Vrin, 1938).

Friedrich Schlegel, *Philosophical Fragments,* trans. Peter Firchow (Minneapolis: University of Minnesota Press, 1991).

Nathan A. Scott, 'The Modest Optimism of Albert Camus', *The Christian Scholar* 42/4 (1959), 251–274.

Thomas Sheehan, 'Rahner's Transcendental Project', in *The Cambridge Companion to Karl Rahner,* ed. Declan Marmion and Mary E.Hines (Cambridge: Cambridge University Press, 2005), 29–42.

Scott Soames *Beyond Rigidity: The Unfinished Semantic Agenda of Naming and Necessity* (Oxford: Oxford University Press, 2002).

Janet Martin Soskice, *Metaphor and Religious Language* (Oxford: Oxford University Press, 1985).

T.L.S. Sprigge, 'What I Believe', in *The Importance of Subjectivity: Selected Essays in Metaphysics and Ethics,* ed. Leemon B. McHenry (Oxford: Oxford University Press, 2010), 4–14.

Olga Stavrova, Detlef Fetchenhauer, and Thomas Schlösser, 'Why are Religious People Happy? The Effect of the Social Norm of Religiosity across Countries', *Social Science Research* 42 (2013), 90–105.

Wallace Stevens, *Collected Poems* (London: Faber, 2006).

Wallace Stevens, *The Necessary Angel: Essays on Reality and the Imagination* (London: Faber, 1960).

Wallace Stevens, *Opus Posthumous,* ed. Milton J. Bates (London: Faber, 1990).

Wallace Stevens, *The Palm at the End of the Mind,* ed. Holy Stevens (New York: Vintage, 1967).

Brendan Sweetman, 'Introduction' in *A Gabriel Marcel Reader* (South Bend, Indiana: St Augustine's Press, 2011), 1–15.

Charles Taylor, *A Secular Age* (Cambridge, MA: Harvard University Press, 2007).

David Tracey, *Fragments: The Existential Situation of Our Time: Selected Essays* (Chicago: University of Chicago Press, 2019).

Denys Turner, *God, Mystery, and Mystification* (Notre Dame, Indiana: University of Notre Dame Press, 2019).

Graham Ward, 'Metaphor in Bone', *Modern Theology* 31/4 (2015), 618–624.

BIBLIOGRAPHY

Amy C. Wilkins, '"Happier than non-Christians": Collective Emotions and Symbolic Boundaries among Evangelical Christians', *Social Psychology Quarterly* 71/3 (2008), 281–301.
Rowan Williams, *The Edge of Words: God and the Habits of Language* (London: Bloomsbury, 2014).
Bernard Williams, 'The Human Prejudice' in *Philosophy as a Humanistic Discipline* (Princeton and Oxford: Princeton University Press, 2006), 135–152.
Judith Wolfe, *The Hulsean Lectures 2022: The Theological Imagination* (Cambridge: Cambridge University Press, 2024).
William Wood, 'Analytic Theology as a Way of Life', *Journal of Analytic Theology* 2 (2014), 43–60.

Index

For the benefit of digital users, indexed terms that span two pages (e.g., 52–53) may, on occasion, appear on only one of those pages.

absolute idealism
  conclusions 178
  cosmic question 19, 25
  and Derek Parfit 153, 155
  divine trace 6
  idea of 113–14
  and Josiah Royce 150–51
  understanding 139–42
  and *What Really Matters* (Parfit) 144–45, 146–48
  and William James 148–49, 150, 152
absurdity 57–59, 57–58n.1, 60–61, 63, 64, 66–67, 68, 74, 80
After Virtue (MacIntyre) 103–4
American Humanist Association 110
Anselm 40–41
apophaticism 30–31
Aquinas *see* Thomas Aquinas
Aristotle 9, 48–49, 153–54, 155–56, 172
atheism
  belief in God 52–53, 178–79
  commitment to 35
  false notion of God 78
  and humanism 85, 91
  introduction 6–7, 8, 10
  philosophers 30
  sceptical 25
  types of belief in God 30–31
Augustine 8–9, 175
autonomy 158–59, 160, 162, 163–64, 165, 166, 168–69, 173
Ayer, A. J. 40, 113–14

Barth, Karl 9, 26
Berkeley, George 146–47
Bilgrami, Akeel 15–16, 17–18, 62, 104, 163–64
Bishop, Elizabeth 158, 177
borderlands 29
Bradley, F. H. 25, 151–52, 153
British Humanist Association (BHA) 32, 87–89, 88n.19, 95–96, 98
Burrell, David 158, 168–69, 171–72, 174–76

Caligula 58–59, 64–65, 73, 75
Camus, Albert
  and the 'average European' 97–98
  and completeness 66
  cosmic question 23, 25, 26
  and divinity 73–74
  and Dostoyevsky 63
  and holy mystery 72
  and inhumanism 106–7
  and Kierkegaard 72
  language of transcendence 61–62
  logic of suicide 63, 64, 65, 74–77
  meridian of thought 69–70
  and the National Socialists 65
  nature and the world 67
  and negation of human reason 72
  Neo-Stoic overtones 58–59, 59n.2
  and objective truth 83
  problem of the absurd 16–17, 57–59, 57–58n.1, 60, 61–62, 63, 68, 70, 71
  relationship between philosophy and Christianity 79–80, 81
  state of rebellion 57–58, 60n.5, 60, 66, 68, 71, 79
  subjective/objective perspectives 104–5
  supernatural being denial 78
  and transcendence 67
Carlisle, Clare 20, 88
'Carmel Point' (Jeffers) 108
Christianity
  classical 29
  and the cosmos 83
  and Einstein 52–53
  and God 51
  and humanism 87, 91, 92, 105
  introduction 8, 9, 10
  and Kant 159, 173
  religious experience 42
  theology/philosophy 79
  see also divine/divinity; God
'Cicero' 46
Clamence, Jean-Baptiste 68

188 INDEX

Clement of Alexandria 9
Cocteau, Jean 86
Coleridge, Samuel Taylor 132
Confessions (Augustine) 8
cosmic question 11–12, 23–24, 57, 82, 94,
    114, 158
Cottingham, John 132, 136
Critchley, Simon 131, 132, 137

Dawkins, Richard 10, 88–89, 98–99, 101–2, 105
death 13, 63, 74–75, 87, 164, 165, 176–77
DeSpain, Benjamin 33
divine/divinity
    accounts of nature of 51
    and Albert Camus 73–74
    and autonomy 173
    and belief in God 52–53
    borderlands 29–30
    concept of, 23, 31, 32, 35–36, 41, 43–44, 45,
        50, 51, 52, 178
    conceptual roles played by 50–51
    darker side to 73
    freedom 32
    impoverishment of theology 10
    introduction 1, 2–3, 5, 25, 26
    and Kant 160, 173–74
    language of God 53–55
    leaping towards 73
    present in otherness and distance 78
    resisting the concept of 57
    trace 6
    see also Christianity; God
Dostoevsky, Fyodor 63
Drake ritual 121, 129, 135
Dreams of a Spirit Seer (Kant) 172

Einstein, Albert 23–24, 44–45, 52–53
Engelke, Matthew
    credit 25, 32, 82, 87–88
    and Enlightenment 100–1
    and humanism 88–90, 91–92, 93, 98, 102–3,
        111, 112
Enlightenment 90–91, 95–96, 100–1, 156
'enskyment' 110
Epicureanism 60
Euclid 60, 75–76, 94
eudaimonia 93
evil 92–93, 121, 149

faith/life 79
The Fall 58–59
Ferdowsi, Rostam 8
flags 30
fortitude 48

freedom
    and the Absolute 148
    of choice/will 100–26
    conceptual 124
    explanation 32
    and Kant 160–61, 162, 165, 173
    and Karl Rahner 77
    of naming 58
    non-coerced 75–76
    of practical reason 94–95, 99
    and reason 163
    self, nature/world 59
Freud, Sigmund 172–73, 173n.42
Fry, Stephen 90
funerals 111

Gelpi, Albert 108–9
genes 39, 41, 45
Gifford Lectures (1898–1900) 139–40
God
    the Absolute 43–45
    belief in 52–53
    Bradley's view 151–52
    'cause and source of all that is' 45–46
    concept of 23–24, 39–43, 50, 52, 178, 179
    conceptual roles played by 50–51
    conscious Absolute Being 150–51
    cosmic question 11, 12, 13, 16–17
    and creation 134
    and Derek Parfit's view 153–54, 155–56, 157
    distinctions 27, 28, 29
    divine trace 6
    existence of 35–37, 76–77, 178
    existence of word 35
    experience of 78
    explicit language about 69–71
    flags 30–31
    freedom 33, 34
    and holy mystery 77
    and humanism 85–86, 89, 91, 92, 105
    and Jung 175
    and Kant 159, 161, 163, 173–75, 176
    knowing in the beatific vision 174
    language of 53, 54–56, 175–76
    metaphysical ontology about 70, 71
    name for our transcendence 71
    and negation of human reason 72
    philosophy impoverishment 6, 7–8
    possessing your individuality 148
    pre-conceptual/unthematic experience
        of 79–80
    prologue 1–5
    resisting the concept of 57
    role of 37–38

INDEX 189

shared predicament 5
subjective/objective 17, 21, 22
talking/thinking about 49, 179–80
theology impoverishment 8, 9, 10
transcendence in the shape of 158
who/what is 147
the word 36, 44–45, 54–55, 56, 69–70
see also Christianity; divine/divinity
Gray, John 82, 86, 105
Grayling, A. C. 98
Great Pumpkin objection 135
grey areas 52
Groundwork of the Metaphysics of Morals
(Kant) 161–62
guilt 19–20, 63, 92

Hadot, Pierre 11–12, 60, 95, 164
happiness
as an ideological commitment 91, 92
centrality of 88
divine 174–75
and humanism/inhumanism 92, 106
and Kant 162
linked to evidence 93–94, 100, 104, 105
no God/no religion 88
the only good 90–91
reasons for 90
search for 82–83
Thomistic central focus on 92
Heidegger, Martin 85, 131, 132
Hölderlin, Friedrich 131, 132
Holy Mystery 57–58, 59–60, 77, 81
Holy Spirit 102
Hooker, Jeremy 21
humanism
belief in progress 105
contemporary 23, 26
and divine trace 6
explanation 82–83
happiness 88
and inhumanism 106, 107, 110, 111
and refusal 54
source of happiness 90
truth 105
Humanists UK 82, 87–88, 89
human prejudice 97–99
humility 31, 32, 33
Husserl, Edmund 73
Hutton, Ronald 25, 52, 115, 116, 117–18, 120

Illing, Sean 63
individualism 64, 117, 163–64
Ingersoll, Richard 90
Inhumanism 106–7, 110, 111

irreconcilable completeness 66
Islam 43

James, William
and Absolute Idealism 139–40, 141, 143–44,
145, 149–50, 152
concept of God 23–24
conceptual freedom 124–25
Drake ritual 121
humanizing of truth 126–29
and humility 32
magical practices 130
pluralistic pantheism 115, 132–34
radical empiricism 23, 25, 113–14, 118–20,
123–24, 134–35
and Thomas Nagel 84
variety of religious experience 179
yearning for peace 148–49
Jeffers, Robinson 107–11
Judaism 43
Jung, Carl
concept of the divine 158, 173, 174–75,
176, 177
a faithful Kantian 32
and family relationships 20
integration of unconscious life 178
metaphysical/grammatical Kant 165
just temperament 1–2

Kant, Immanuel
concept of the divine 158–59, 173–75,
176, 177
cosmic question 11–12
grammatical approach 163
and humanism 89, 101–2, 101n.63
and 'imagination' 131
integration of unconscious life 178
and Jung 32, 165
limits of reason 81
metaphysical 159, 176–77
priority of practical reason 95–96
prologue 5, 9
reflexive and critical philosophy 79
subjective/objective perspectives 18
and truth 101
Kierkegaard, Søren 72, 73
Kilby, Karen 25, 80
Kingdom-of-Ends 173–75
Kripke, Saul
natural kinds, rigid designation 36, 38, 39–
40, 42–43
theories of reference 45–46, 47, 48

Law, Stephen 95–96

190 INDEX

Lear, Jonathan 158, 167–68, 170, 172–73
le Carré, John 122
Leftow, Brian 37
Leibniz, Gottfried 101
'Letter to a German Friend' (Camus) 65
Lewis, C. S. 14–15, 22, 121, 122
Locke, John 146–47
Luhrmann, Tanya
  Drake ritual 121, 122–23
  magical practices 129–30
  and paganism 25, 115–16, 117–18, 136–37,
    136n.85
  and witchcraft, 32, 52, 120–21
Luntley, Michael 46–47
Lutheranism 2–3

McDowell, John 163
MacIntyre, Alisdair 103–4
McTaggart, J. M. E. 23–24
Madison, M. M. 64, 66–67
Manicheanism 8
Marcel, Gabriel 32–33
Metaphor and Religious Language
  (Soskice) 36, 40
Midgley, Mary 113–14
monotheism 38, 44
moral realism 6, 7
Mueller, Joseph 33
Murdoch, Iris 166
mystery 32–33, 59, 77, 79, 80
mysticism 132
The Myth of Sisyphus 58–59, 63, 67, 74

Nagel, Thomas
  concept of God 23–24
  the cosmic question 114, 158
  and Derek Parfit 153, 156, 157
  flying the atheist flag 30–31
  harmony with the universe 57, 82
  and humanism 82, 84–85, 87, 101
  not a traditional Christian theologian 26
  perspectives on life 11–12, 12n.7,
    12n.9, 13–14
  prologue 2, 10
  rethinking subjective/objective
    perspectives 17–18, 19
  subjective/objective perspectives 14–15,
    16, 104
naming 72
Naming and Necessity (Kripke) 36, 46
naturalism 12, 12n.8, 27–28, 96–97, 113, 153
Nicholas of Cusa 174–75
Nietzsche, Friedrich 2–3, 12, 13, 76
normative non-naturalism 25

normative notion 153, 154, 155, 156, 157
noumenal realms 161–62, 169–70
Nussbaum, Martha 25, 48–49

objectivity 93
'Orual' (Lewis) 22
Other 150

paganism
  introduction 19, 25, 26
  and irreconcilable completeness 67
  modern 114, 115–17, 118, 123, 132–33, 136,
    137, 178
pan–consciousness 43–44
panpsychism 19, 24, 43–44, 67
pantheism 25, 30–31, 44, 67, 114, 115
Paradise Lost (Milton) 166
Parain, Brice 165
Parfit, Derek 10, 25, 96–97, 153
personal/impersonal 29
Phaedo (Plato) 164
philosophy
  and humanism 83, 85
  impoverishment of 6, 8
  unsatisfying but satisfactory 79
The Plague (Camus) 106
Plato 164, 169–70, 172
Platonism 8, 9
positive theology 5
Power, Sister Mary James 107
pragmatic encroachment 95–96
proposal 49
Proslogion 41

radical empiricism 113–14, 115
'radical orthodoxy' movements 4
Rahner, Karl
  and anonymous Christians 80–81
  existence of word God 35
  experience of God 78
  and holy mystery 72
  introduction 23, 25, 26
  metaphysical ontology about God 70, 71
  notion of transcendence 62
  pre-apprehension of holy mystery 57–58, 59,
    61, 63, 66, 68
  relationship, philosophy/Christianity 79–
    80, 81
  and suicide 65–66
  and transcendental experience 67, 69
  the word 'God' 36, 44–45, 54–55, 56, 69–70
  and worship 71, 77
Ramsey, Frank 13
Realism 142–45, 156–57

INDEX

reason 163, 165
reductionism 2
reductio–style deflation 135
reference 45–46, 47–48
refusal 54
reticence 53
  rigid designation 36, 38–42, 45
ritual magic 32
Road Runner 103–4
romanticism 132
Rosemann, Philipp 33
Round the World in 80 Days (Cocteau) 86
Royce, Josiah
  and Absolute Idealism 139–42, 143–44, 150–
    51, 152, 153
  concept of the divine 23–24
  daily experience, truth 145–46
  introduction 23, 25, 26
  what God is 147
Rundle, Bede 49–50
Russell, Bertrand 13, 101–2

Sartre, Jean-Paul 24, 82, 85–86, 99
Schaerer, Rene 165
Schelling, Friedrich 131
Schlegel, Friedrich 131
Schopenhauer, Arthur 167
Scott, Nathan 64–65, 75
'scriptural reasoning' movement 4
A Secular Age (Taylor) 117
secularism 6–7, 11
Shestov, Lev 72
Socrates 11–12, 15–16, 26, 75–76, 79, 164–65
solipsism 13
Soskice, Janet Martin
  Anselm's formula 41
  God through religious experience 42–43
  introduction 25
  a 'natural kind' term 36, 40–41
  notion of the divine 51
  rigidly designated terms 45–46
  talking about God 49
Spinoza, Baruch 23–24, 44

Sprigge, Timothy 43–45
state of rebellion 59–60, 66, 68
Stevens, Wallace 114, 131, 132, 137–38
stoicism 8
The Stranger 58–59, 74–75
subjective/objective perspectives 14, 104
subjectivism 156
suicide 63, 64–65, 74, 75–76
Summa Theologiae (Aquinas) 153

Taylor, Charles 5, 5n.10, 117
temperament 1–2
theism 30–31, 41–42, 78, 134
Thomas Aquinas, 9, 24, 26, 40–41, 153–
    54, 174–75
Thomism 19–20, 53, 92
Thus Spoke Zarathustra (Nietzsche) 13
Till we Have Faces (Lewis) 22
transcendental idealism 161–62, 167
truth
  daily experience 145–46
  expectation about 135
  humanized 123, 126
  objective 82–83, 85, 93, 98–99, 100, 105
  and the universe 101, 104
Tuchman, Barbara 38
twice-appearing freedom 69

virtue 48–49

West, Andrew 90, 92
'Western Mysteries' 115
Wicca 115, 120
  see also witchcraft
Williams, Bernard 83, 92–93, 97, 98–
    99, 155–56
Williams, Rowan 3–4, 3n.7
witchcraft 32, 52, 120–21
Wittgenstein, Ludwig 12, 49–50, 54, 71, 75,
    88, 97–98
Wolfe, Judith 21–22, 131, 132, 136

Yale school 4